Routledge Revivals

Private Members' Bills in the British Parliament

Originally published in 1956, P. A. Bromhead, with this book, filled a gap in the literature on the British Parliament by examining the role which Private Members' Bills had to play in the modern political system at the time. He describes in detail the procedure through which Private Members' Bills had to pass, and indicates the pitfalls which had to be negotiated. He examines the proceedings on such bills during the previous fifty years, with particular attention to the period since 1945, and observes the changes which had taken place in the habits of Parliament with regard to the types of bills introduced and the character of the debates on the bills. The author pays particular attention to the role of the Government and of the parties in this field, and suggests that a significant evolution was taking place, so that Parliament was coming to assign a special place of positive value to these measures in a fairly distinct field of legislative activity. Today it can be read in its historical context.

Private Members' Bills in the British Parliament

P. A. Bromhead

First published in 1956
by Routledge & Kegan Paul Ltd

This edition first published in 2025 by Routledge
4 Park Square, Milton Park, Abingdon, Oxon, OX14 4RN

and by Routledge
605 Third Avenue, New York, NY 10017

Routledge is an imprint of the Taylor & Francis Group, an informa business

© 1956 P. A. Bromhead

All rights reserved. No part of this book may be reprinted or reproduced or utilised in any form or by any electronic, mechanical, or other means, now known or hereafter invented, including photocopying and recording, or in any information storage or retrieval system, without permission in writing from the publishers.

Publisher's Note
The publisher has gone to great lengths to ensure the quality of this reprint but points out that some imperfections in the original copies may be apparent.

Disclaimer
The publisher has made every effort to trace copyright holders and welcomes correspondence from those they have been unable to contact.

A Library of Congress record exists under LCCN: 56004258

ISBN: 978-1-032-89801-8 (hbk)
ISBN: 978-1-003-54470-8 (ebk)
ISBN: 978-1-032-89813-1 (pbk)

Book DOI 10.4324/9781003544708

PRIVATE MEMBERS' BILLS
IN THE BRITISH
PARLIAMENT

by

P. A. BROMHEAD

Lecturer in Political Theory and Institutions,
the Durham Colleges

ROUTLEDGE & KEGAN PAUL
London

*First published 1956
by Routledge & Kegan Paul Ltd.
Broadway House, Carter Lane, E.C.4
Printed in Great Britain
by Butler & Tanner Ltd.
Frome and London*

ACKNOWLEDGEMENTS

I SHOULD like to express my very deep gratitude to the Rt. Hon. Lord Percy of Newcastle, to Mr. R. A. W. Dent, C.B., Clerk Public Bills at the House of Commons, and to Mr. C. A. James and Mr. Eric Taylor, of the Clerk's Office at the House of Commons; to Mr. Wilfred Harrison, of the Queen's College, Oxford; to Professor W. J. M. Mackenzie, Professor of Government at the University of Manchester, for reading the manuscript, pointing out errors, and giving without stint a great deal of advice and encouragement of inestimable value.

For advice on particular points, and for general friendly encouragement, I should like to record my debt to the Rt. Hon. Lord Strathclyde, Minister of State for Scotland, to the Hon. T. G. D. Galbraith, M.P., to Sir Stephen King-Hall, to Professor F. C. Hood, of the University of Durham, and to my wife. I should like also to acknowledge the assistance of the Durham Colleges Research Fund.

Part of chapter VII appeared, in a slightly different version, in the autumn number of Parliamentary Affairs for 1955 (vol. VIII, pp. 492–502). I am grateful to the hon. Editor for permission to reproduce this material.

I must of course add that for all the statements and views expressed in the course of this book I myself take complete responsibility.

P. A. B.

Durham, 1955.

CONTENTS

Acknowledgements v
Introduction 1

Chapter I. The Organization of Private Members' Time

1. HISTORY 9
   A. *The Total Time Allocated*
      (i) *Limitation of Private Members' Time before 1902* 9
      (ii) *The Scheme of 1902* 10
      (iii) *Further Incursions by Sessional Orders* 11
      (iv) *The New Scheme of 1948–9* 11
   B. *Distribution of the Time* 12

2. PRESENT PRACTICE: METHODS OTHER THAN THE BALLOT 13
   A. *Indirect Legislative Proposals: Amendments to Government Bills, Private Members' Motions and other occasions* 13
   B. *Bills*
      (i) *General Rules for the Introduction of Bills* 15
      (ii) *The Different Methods of Introducing Private Members' Bills* 17
         (a) *Unballoted Bills without Preliminary Proceedings* 17
         (b) *The Ten Minutes Rule* 19

3. BALLOTED BILLS 20
   A. *The Ballot* 20
   B. *The Choice of a Day* 21
   C. *The Choice of a Bill: Pressures on Members* 23
   D. *The Task of Drafting* 26

CONTENTS

4. PRIVATE MEMBERS' BILLS BEFORE PARLIAMENT AND THE DIFFICULTIES IN THEIR WAY 26

   A. *Obstacles at Second Reading*
   (i) *The Problem of Keeping a House* 26
   (ii) *The Problem of Getting a Decision: the use of obstruction as a means of defeating bills; the Speaker's practice with regard to accepting a motion for the closure* 27

   B. *Obstacles after Second Reading*
   (i) *Financial Resolution* 32
   (ii) *The Committee Stage*
   (a) *General Rules regarding Standing Committee* 32
   (b) *The Choice between Standing Committee and a Committee of the Whole House* 34
   (c) *The Composition of the Standing Committee* 36
   (d) *Quorum in Standing Committee* 36
   (e) *The Committee Proceedings* 37
   (f) *Obstruction in Standing Committee* 37
   (g) *The Power of a Committee to Destroy a Bill* 38
   (iii) *The Later Stages*
   (a) *Report and Third Reading: the Question of Finding Time* 40
   (b) *The House of Lords* 41

5. SOME POSSIBLE REFORMS OF PROCEDURE ON PRIVATE MEMBERS' BILLS 42

   A. *The Device of a Steering Committee* 42
   B. *Priority according to Volume of Support* 43
   C. *General Considerations* 44

Chapter II. A Historical Survey of Private Members' Bills since 1900

1. GENERAL TRENDS: TOWARDS A CONCEPTION OF A DISTINCTIVE FUNCTION 46

2. TYPES OF BILL BEFORE 1914 48

CONTENTS

3. TRENDS AND INFLUENCES AT WORK IN 1918–39   50
   A. *The Labour Members and their Party Bills*   50
   B. *Major Bills brought in by non-Labour Members*   52
   C. *Summary*   53
4. PRIVATE MEMBERS' BILLS SINCE 1948   55
   A. *Examination of the Bills in Detail*   56
   B. *Conclusions*   73

Chapter III. The Interest Shown in the Debate

1. THE INCIDENCE OF ALL-DAY DEBATES   75
2. THE INCIDENCE OF DIVISIONS   76
3. THE FREQUENCY WITH WHICH THE HOUSE HAS BEEN COUNTED OUT ON PRIVATE MEMBERS' BILLS   81
4. THE DIFFERENCE BETWEEN LABOUR MEMBERS' BILLS AND OTHER BILLS WITH RESPECT TO ALL-DAY DEBATES AND DIVISIONS, 1920–39   81

Chapter IV. The Government and Private Members' Bills

1. GENERAL PRINCIPLES GUIDING THE GOVERNMENT'S ATTITUDE   86
   A. *Ministers do not propose Bills as Private Members*   87
   B. *The Rôle of Ministers in the Debates*
      (i) *The Duty of Participation*   88
      (ii) *The Timing of the Minister's Intervention*   88
      (iii) *The Duty of Attendance by a Departmental Representative*   88
      (iv) *Which Minister should Speak?*
         (a) *General*   89
         (b) *The Modern Tendency for Junior Ministers to Speak in Private Members' Debates*   90
      (v) *The Character of the Minister's Intervention*   91
      (vi) *Should a Second Minister Contribute?*
         (a) *Officially*   94
         (b) *Unofficially*   94

CONTENTS

 C. *Unanimity of Ministers in Divisions*   96
 D. *How the Government Forms its Opinions*   98

2. THE AMOUNT OF PARTICIPATION BY MINISTERS IN DIVISIONS   100

3. THE GOVERNMENT'S USE OF ITS POWERS   102

 A. *Weapons for use against Unacceptable Bills*   102
 B. *The Government's Positive Contribution on Matters of Detail*
  (i) *General Considerations*   107
  (ii) *The Government in Standing Committee*   109
 C. *Conclusion*   111

4. THE RÔLE OF THE OPPOSITION LEADERS   112

Chapter V. The Rôle of Associations and of Royal Commissions

1. ASSOCIATIONS IN THE COMMUNITY   117
2. ASSOCIATIONS AND MEMBERS OF PARLIAMENT—ELECTORAL PRESSURE—CIRCULAR LETTERS—PETITIONS   118
3. THE IMPORTANCE OF CONSULTATION WITH ASSOCIATIONS   122
4. ROYAL COMMISSIONS   123

Chapter VI. The Criteria of Suitability for Treatment in Private Members' Bills

1. THE PRESENT POSITION: GENERAL   126
2. SOME FACTORS MAKING FOR UNSUITABILITY   126
 A. *Proposals for Constitutional Change*   127
 B. *Subjects requiring Special Negotiations*   129
3. SUBJECTS WHICH APPEAR TO BE SUITABLE   131
 A. *Proposals for Moral and Social Betterment: Drink—the Sabbath—Gambling—Censorship of Publications—Protection of Animals—Rational Reforms—Minor Amendments of Acts*   132
 B. *Legal Reforms*   144
 C. *Regulation of Professions*   147

CONTENTS

Chapter VII. Alternative Methods of Proposing Legislation

1. NON-BALLOTED BILLS BROUGHT IN WITHOUT PRELIMINARIES — 150
2. BILLS UNDER THE TEN MINUTES RULE — 155
3. PRIVATE MEMBERS' MOTIONS — 161
4. INCIDENTAL OPPORTUNITIES FOR ADVOCATING LEGISLATION — 164

Chapter VIII. Conclusion — 166

APPENDIX A. *The Standing Orders relating to Private Members' Time* — 178
APPENDIX B. *The Hairdressers' Registration Bill and the Hunting and Coursing Bill of 1949* — 181
APPENDIX C. *Table of Bills introduced and of Bills passed, 1902–54* — 190
APPENDIX D. *A List of the Private Members' Bills enacted in 1948–53, with indication of the scope of each Bill* — 191
APPENDIX E. *Table showing the parliamentary stages of the Private Members' Bills which received the Royal Assent in 1948–54* — 198
APPENDIX F. *Table of balloted Bills introduced but not passed, 1948–54* — 206

Bibliography — 211
Index — 212

INTRODUCTION

Private Members' bills and their place in our system of government deserve special study for several reasons, both theoretical and practical. In the first place, debate and decision on the legislative proposals of the people's representatives seem, by definition, to be among the most important functions of a body which is called a democratic legislature. Most modern parliaments, including the American and the French and most of those of Western Europe, do in fact devote much of their time to such proposals. In the British House of Commons, on the other hand, nearly all the time spent in debate is allocated among the various topics of the day by a process of informal discussion and agreement between officers of the Government and Opposition Parties. Only a small amount of time (mainly on Fridays) is kept free in each annual session for the treatment of private Members' proposals, and the distribution of this time is left to the chances of a ballot. Even these few days are not guaranteed; in some sessions the Government decides that it needs all the time for its own business, and without much difficulty persuades the House of Commons to give up the few days that would normally be reserved for private Members' debates.

The extent of the contribution of private Members' bills to our legislation in recent times can be indicated, albeit rather crudely, by some statistics. In the post-war period, up to the end of 1953, there were four sessions in which time was provided for private Members' bills. In all four sessions the time was left intact. Thirty-six private Members' bills were enacted, occupying between them some 130 pages of the Statute Book. In the same four sessions 317 Government bills were enacted, occupying together rather more than 5000 pages of the Statute Book. Not a single one of the private Members' bills enacted was controversial enough to be made the subject of a division on either second or third reading in either House; eighteen of the thirty-six were so extraordinarily uncontroversial that they were allowed to pass through their second reading, or most important, stage in the House of Commons without debate and without a word, even of explanation, being said on their behalf.

The remarkable thing about our Parliament is that it has come to assign to private Members' bills a very restricted place, and yet has incurred no serious charge of being 'undemocratic' for doing so. An attempt to explain this somewhat paradoxical development should contribute something towards an understanding of British institutions. In this connection we must notice the example of the Australian Commonwealth Parliament, where private Members' bills appear to have ceased to have any place at all. This is significant for us, because the Australian system, having been modelled on our own, has come to exhibit many features which seem to be the logical conclusion of tendencies which we observe in our own system.

In the second place, there have been significant changes in the practice of Parliament with regard to private Members' bills during the past fifty years. Formally and superficially the debates and the processes of decision have remained substantially unchanged, but within this unchanging framework the objectives of the initiators of bills and the atmosphere and purpose of the debates on private Members' bills have been largely transformed. A study of the process of transformation should contribute something towards our understanding of the British system of government in general. The series of changes, sometimes deliberate, sometimes fortuitous, often unperceived at the time, usually piecemeal, which have been undergone by every part of the British constitution, must be recognized as inseparable from the very nature and essence both of that part and of the whole to which it belongs.

In the third place, the system of private Members' bills has in the past generation been more often attacked than defended, and if its continued existence is to be justified it seems necessary to enquire just what purposes the system really does serve. In the course of our examination of the system of private Members' bills we must be concerned with the need to pass judgment on it, and to examine the various arguments which have been put forward for and against the system. On one side it is claimed that

INTRODUCTION

the domination of the Government in all things is injuring the character of our Parliament, and that the decline in the status of private Members' bills is to be deplored, because it increases the power in the hands of the Government. On the other side it is suggested that the small amount of time that Parliament spends on private Members' bills is generally wasted, and should be reduced still further or even abolished. It is sometimes said that the only really substantial Acts of Parliament initiated by private Members in the present century have been Mr. (now Sir) Alan Herbert's Matrimonial Causes Act and perhaps Mr. Lever's Defamation Act of 1952; these two measures received much help from the Government. Our whole approach to the subject must reflect the necessity for taking these arguments into account, and for deciding how far we should agree with either of these points of view.

The arguments against the worthwhileness of private Members' time take two main forms, one fundamental, claiming that it is intrinsically bad that private Members should introduce bills, the other incidental, being related to the mechanical difficulties. The two forms overlap at some points, and they meet at the point at which it is complained that on private Members' Fridays the House is reduced to the level of a debating society.

The fundamental argument is related to the modern conception of governmental responsibility. We have moved so far, in Britain at any rate, from the principle of the separation of the legislative and executive powers, that there is a widely-held supposition—not, perhaps, explicitly stated, but clearly recognizable—that the Government of the day, because it will be responsible for administering any new Act of Parliament, ought not to be expected to have to take responsibility for administering any new Act that it had not itself decided to introduce. The obverse side of this argument is that it is wrong for individual Members of Parliament, as individuals, to introduce measures for the administration of which they will themselves have no responsibility. It may be suggested that the legislative work of Parliament in any one session should be regarded as a single whole, and that the allocation of priorities among different proposals ought to be decided entirely by the Government, whose responsibility for the whole of the legislative programme should be undivided.

Along the same lines it may be argued that private Members

cannot have the authority which is necessary for piloting bills through Parliament. In the words of Harold Laski, 'In general, if a matter is important enough to be embodied in a bill, it is desirable that the responsibility for its passage should rest with the Government.' Laski, writing in 1938, refers to the success of Mr. A. P. Herbert in securing, 'by his zeal and energy, a small measure of divorce law reform', but he does not accept the widely-held opinion that this was a really substantial contribution to legislation. In Laski's words: 'Because his bill was not a Government bill, he was compelled to accept drastic amendments which narrowed its scope in high degree; and the truncated measure which resulted will probably prevent the serious rationalization of the marriage laws for many years to come. If anything, Mr. Herbert's experience shows plainly that when any big theme requires legislative action, only the Government has the requisite authority to deal with it on an ample scale.'[1] Laski apparently chose the Matrimonial Causes Bill to illustrate his point because it was fresh in the public mind, and was then regarded (as it still is) as an outstanding example of the great results that could be achieved by skill and assiduity.

Again, it may be said, Ministers and their staffs ought to be concerned with administration, with the preparation of their own legislative proposals, and with the explaining and defending of their own policies before Parliament, whose proper function is to check and criticize the Government's work, in small things as well as great. Thus both Ministers and Parliament waste their time and energies in considering and deciding upon proposals thrust upon them through the whims of non-responsible people who cannot see the needs of the nation as a whole.

People who argue against the value of private Members' bills think that the use of the term 'Private Members' Rights' in connection with the right to introduce bills confuses the real issues. They would consider, quite rightly in a way, that all the time of Parliament is private Members' time, except perhaps for the time spent by front-bench speakers in the opening and closing speeches of debates. They point out that if there are ten Fridays spent on private Members' bills, the private Members have to sacrifice an equivalent amount of time which would otherwise have been

[1] H. J. Laski, *Parliamentary Government in England* (Allen & Unwin, 1938), p. 166.

INTRODUCTION

available to them for the performance of their more essential functions of contributing to debates on Government bills and of calling the Government to account for its administrative activities. The validity of this argument will be generally conceded. Indeed it was while arguing (from the Opposition benches) for an extension of private Members' rights that Mr. Pickthorn in a recent debate admitted: 'Private Members' Rights, with capital letters, are less important to unofficial members than their opportunities of speaking in main debates.'[1]

The incidental arguments are concerned with the practical difficulties which seem to limit the real usefulness of the time which private Members have for their bills. Just because the time is limited, it is difficult to ensure that it is used to the best advantage.

Some attempt to deal with the incidental arguments can be made in the course of a discussion of the organization of private Members' time, but the fundamental arguments can be adequately discussed only in the light of the fuller survey of the rôle of private Members' bills which it is proposed to undertake in the main body of the present study.

Chapter I is largely descriptive, and deals with the procedure for introducing and debating private Members' bills, indicating the difficulties which confront Members who introduce bills. The chapter ends with a brief examination of some possible reforms of the procedure.

Chapters II and III trace in outline the history of private Members' bills in the past fifty years. In the section dealing with the period up to 1939 little more is attempted than an indication of general trends and changes of attitude with regard to the uses of such bills. For the period since the restoration of private Members' time in 1948–9, the bills introduced year by year are examined in rather more detail. Chapter III is statistical, and is based on tables dealing with such matters as the length of debates on particular bills, the frequency of divisions, and the number of Members voting in the divisions. The figures seem to confirm the general impression that private Members' bills are coming more and more to perform a distinctive function and to avoid really controversial subjects.

Chapter IV discusses the attitude of the Government towards

[1] H.C. Debs., 8th November 1950, vol. 480, col. 958.

INTRODUCTION

private Members' bills, the type of contribution that the Government has to make, the degree of freedom which Ministers permit to themselves in relation to those matters which are technically outside the field of governmental responsibility, and in general the amount of interest which Ministers show with regard to private Members' bills. The argument proceeds, principally, by the method of illustration from actual experience.

Chapter V is concerned with the activities of Associations and Societies of various kinds, and with the importance of these activities in relation to the work of Parliament. There is also some reference to the rôle of Royal Commissions.

Chapter VI attempts to define the fields within which, at present, it seems that private Members' bills have a special contribution to make to the general legislative work of Parliament. Having suggested certain grounds for unsuitability, it arranges the appropriate types of subjects in a number of classes, and illustrates the general principles by means of examples of bills brought forward.

Chapter VII describes the means by which a Member may advocate legislation in the House of Commons if he fails to get an opportunity of doing so under the ballot. It deals principally with bills brought in not under the ballot, either without preliminary proceedings or under the Ten Minutes Rule, and then treats of the ways of advocating legislation indirectly by making use of opportunities which present themselves at various stages of the parliamentary session.

Chapter VIII suggests some broad conclusions about the part which private Members' bills have to play in the general operation of the British system of government, and attempts some assessment of their usefulness in the context of the requirements of the modern state.

The appendices supply some supplementary information. Appendix A reproduces that part of the Standing Orders of the House of Commons which is concerned with private Members' bills and the provision of time for debate on them. It should be made clear that the provisions of these Standing Orders have not in fact been complied with since 1939, and that there seems little prospect that actual practice will ever again conform to the present Standing Orders. There is included therefore a reproduction of the sessional order passed for the session of 1954-5, which describes the pattern that has in fact been followed lately.

INTRODUCTION

Appendix B gives a detailed description of the parliamentary process in connection with some recent bills, for the sake of a broader illustration of the general points which have been made in the main text. Appendix C gives the statistics of bills introduced and of bills passed during the past fifty years.

Appendices D, E and F give, in tabular form, detailed information relating to the private Members' bills of 1948-54. Appendix D gives a list of the bills which received the Royal Assent in this period, indicating the general scope of each bill. Appendix E tabulates the parliamentary stages of these bills, indicating the length of the debates on the successive stages and the order in which the bills were taken, from their first introduction under the ballot or otherwise, down to their final stages. Appendix F supplies similar information regarding the balloted bills which were introduced but not passed during the same period.

Chapter I

THE ORGANIZATION OF PRIVATE MEMBERS' TIME

1. HISTORY

AN evaluation of the place of private Members' bills in our present governmental system must take some account of the developments of the past century and a half in the procedure for dealing with them. In one sense, these developments seem to have taken us further and further towards the domination of the Government over Parliament; the Government has progressively taken more and more of the time of the House for its own business. Yet it would be an over-simplification to suggest that there has been merely a process of attrition in which the importance of private Members' bills has been whittled away through the constant encroachments of the Government. It would be fairer to say that there has been a process of change, in which adaptations of the parliamentary process with regard to private Members' bills have corresponded in a fascinating way with changes in the character of government in the modern world.

A. *The Total Time Allocated*

(i) *Limitation of Private Members' Time before 1902.* If we go back to the unreformed Parliament before 1832, we find that its legislative work, though abundant, was mainly concerned with the regulation of questions of local and limited interest.[1] There was little difference in character between Government business and private Members' business, and therefore no need for rules for the allocation of time as between these two types of business. Well before 1832, however, in the words of Redlich, 'by courtesy of the House, it was understood that, on two days a week (Monday and Friday), the Government should have precedence for their business, but not on other days'.[2] After 1832 the Government introduced more bills on its own account, and by 1837 it was finding itself seriously embarrassed at being deprived of some of its time through occasional obstruction.[3] A Select Committee on Procedure was appointed to enquire how the organization of the time of the House might be improved. On the Committee's advice the House adopted a Standing Order which effectively guaranteed precedence for Government business on two days a week. A further reform, brought in in 1852, gave the Government three days a week.[4] Meanwhile more and more of the legislative work of Parliament was concerned with Government bills, and by the end of the nineteenth century almost all the major legislation passed by Parliament was founded on bills initiated by the Government.

During the present century private Members' time has been subjected to further restrictions, first under a revision of the Standing Orders in 1902[5] and then by sessional orders each valid for the current session only. There was also a revision of the Standing Orders in 1927, but this only rearranged the time without restricting it.

(ii) *The Scheme of 1902*. Mr Balfour's scheme of 1902, popularly known as the 'parliamentary railway time-table', gave precedence to Government business on all days except the latter part of some Tuesday and Wednesday sittings and the whole of certain Fridays. The half-days on Tuesdays and Wednesdays were used for private Members' motions, and the Fridays, in practice about fourteen or fifteen each session, for private Members' bills.

[1] Redlich, *The Procedure of the House of Commons* (London, 1908), vol. I, p. 121.   [2] Ibid., p. 78.
[3] Cf. Sir Gilbert Campion, *Introduction to the Procedure of the House of Commons*, 2nd ed. (Macmillan, 1947), p. 38.
[4] C.J. (1852), p. 353.   [5] C.J. (1902), p. 501.

HISTORY

(iii) *Further Incursions by Sessional Orders.* Even this reduced time was not guaranteed to private Members. There was nothing to stop the Government of the day from coming to the House at any time with a proposal that for the remainder of the current session Government business should have precedence at every sitting.[1] Long before this time party discipline had become so firmly established that any Government with a working majority could be fairly sure of getting a favourable vote for such a motion. There was already ample precedent from the period before 1902 for the partial restriction of private Members' time in particular sessions, although it was hoped that the reduced 'Rights' under the new Standing Orders, being clearly defined, would be respected.

For the first few years after 1902 private Members' time was left intact, but in 1910 and 1911 Mr. Asquith secured acceptance of motions taking the greater part of it for Government business.[2] During the war of 1914-18 the only private Members' time allowed was a few days for motions in 1915; in the remaining war years there was no private Members' time at all. Between the wars the Government took some of the time in several sessions, and all the time in 1928-9, in 1931-2, and in 1934-5.[3] In each of these sessions there was a special reason for the Government's action. There was no private Members' time in the war of 1939-45, or in the first three post-war sessions. In 1945-8 the plea was merely that the Government had a heavy legislative programme, which left no time for private Members' proposals. By taking all private Members' time for three consecutive peace-time sessions the Government made an important innovation.

(iv) *The New Scheme of 1948-9.* All this time the old Standing Orders, as modified in 1927, remained in force.[4] The House had

[1] In 1887, for example, the Government took all the time up to Easter. (Cf. Parl. Debs., 17th February and 18th March 1887.)
[2] C.J. (1910), p. 24; (1911) pp. 32 f., and 18th April (1911) p. 150. H.C. Debs., 5th series, vol. 14, col. 658; vol. 20, col. 161; and vol. 21, col. 1398.
[3] H.C. Debs., 7th November 1928, vol. 222, cols, 51-78, and C.J. (1928-9), p. 10; H.C. Debs., 3rd February 1932, vol. 261, cols. 137-92; C.J. (1931-2), p. 62; H.C. Debs., 21st November 1934, vol. 295, cols. 87-154; C.J. (1934-5), p. 7
[4] The revision of 1927 did not reduce the total time, but made some changes in its distribution. It gave the whole of each of certain Wednesdays, instead of the latter half of certain Tuesdays and Wednesdays, to private

THE ORGANIZATION OF PRIVATE MEMBERS' TIME

become so accustomed to the passing of sessional orders temporarily replacing the Standing Orders, that when the Government decided to allow private Members' time to be restored in 1948-9, under a severely modified time-table, no revision of the Standing Orders was made. Instead, a sessional order was passed, valid for that session only, giving ten Fridays for bills.[1] No time was provided for motions. In the short session of 1950 five Fridays were provided for motions, but none for bills.[2] For the session of 1950-1 twenty Fridays were given to private Members, ten for motions and ten for bills.[3] In each session since then, a similar sessional order has been passed,[4] so that by now the scheme, which follows the recommendations of the Procedure Committee of 1945-6, seems to have become a regular institution. The Standing Orders have not been revised, however, and still remain in a form which has no relation to actual practice.[5] The twenty Fridays are equivalent to about fifteen normal days, because a Friday sitting provides only five hours for the main business, as compared with the six to six and a half hours, subject to extension, of an ordinary sitting.

B. *Distribution of the Time*

Important changes in the distribution of the private Members' days were made in 1927 (by a revision of the Standing Orders) and in 1950 (by the adoption of a new practice.) If private Members' bills are to have any hope of passing into law in private Members' time, some of the days must be given to the

Members' motions, and made changes in the arrangement of the Fridays for bills. (Cf. below, pp. 12 f.). It also provided that the Friday sittings should be from 11 a.m. to 4 p.m., instead of from noon until 5 p.m. as hitherto (C.J. (1927), p. 391).
[1] C.J. (1948-9), p. 76.
[2] C.J. (1950), p. 63.
[3] C.J. (1950-1), p. 14. Strictly, this Order provided that on the days given to private Members' bills, private Members' bills and motions should have precedence, in that order, and on the other days, private Members' motions and bills, in that order. Theoretically, bills could be taken during the last part of the sitting on a motion day, if all the motions down were disposed of before 4 o'clock.
[4] C.J. (1951-2), p. 46; (1952-3), p. 7, etc.
[5] The relevant Standing Orders, together with a recent sessional order, are reproduced below, in Appendix A.

later stages, instead of to the second readings, of bills. Before 1927 two Fridays late in the session were provided for the later stages, but were found to be inadequate. The Select Committee on Procedure (Unofficial Members' Business) of 1927 concerned itself with this point, and recommended that four days should be given to the later stages.[1] The Standing Orders were revised accordingly,[2] and from 1928 until 1939 there were about ten Fridays each session for second readings and four Fridays for the later stages.

The Procedure Committee of 1945-6 showed itself in favour of a further redistribution, giving a still greater proportion of the time to the later stages, namely four out of a total of ten days allocated for private Members' bills.[3] The Committee's proposals have been followed ever since,[4] except in the session of 1948-9, when the later stages had priority on only three days.

The increases in the time given to the later days are significant because they indicate the desire of the House that private Members' bills should be constructive proposals for change, and that if approved at second reading their further progress in private Members' time should not be impeded by procedural obstacles. It is true that the Government has usually been ready to provide time for the later stages in the House, but the new arrangement reduces the dependence of private Members' bills on the Government's good will.

2. PRESENT PRACTICE: METHODS OTHER THAN THE BALLOT

A. *Indirect Legislative Proposals*

It is important to remember that the actual introduction of a bill is not the only form of legislative initiative open to Members of Parliament. Any Member may propose to insert a new clause or an amendment in a Government bill. Some individual amendments may themselves be more important and far-reaching than other complete bills, and may be tantamount to independent

[1] Report, op. cit., H.C. 102 of 1927, para. 11.
[2] C.J. (1927), p. 391. Cf. Campion, *Introduction to the Procedure of the House of Commons*, p. 116.
[3] Report of the Select Committee on Procedure, H.C. 189-1 of 1945-6, para. 51. Cf. Minutes of Evidence, Q. 3902-8.
[4] C.J. (1950-1), p. 13, etc.

bills. Thus, although there have been several private Members' bills proposing the abolition of capital punishment, the most important debate to have taken place on this subject so far was in 1948, when it was brought forward as a proposed new clause for insertion in a Government bill.[1] On the other hand, a proposal to insert an amendment in a bill already before the House can scarcely be counted as an exercise of the right of legislative initiative.

Members also have opportunities for indirectly advocating legislation on various other occasions, without proposing either bills or amendments to bills. The best of these opportunities are those afforded by the days given to private Members' motions. Under the present arrangements, ten Fridays each session are available for the moving of such motions. The distribution of this time among the private Members who wish to make proposals is arranged by means of a ballot like that for bills. Ballots for notices of motions are held periodically at suitable intervals before the Fridays which are to be available.[2] A motion may take the form of the expression of a wish that the Government would introduce a bill for some specific purpose or other. The use of motions for this purpose is not very popular, however; there seems to be a distinct preference for motions expressing rather general opinions, or calling for administrative action.

Occasionally the Government may agree to the provision of an ordinary day for a debate on the principles of a legislative proposal which it does not intend itself to bring forward. Thus the proposal to abolish capital punishment was debated in 1955, on a Government motion to 'take note' of a Royal Commission's report on the matter.[3]

Other opportunities for indirectly advocating legislation arise, or can be created,[4] during the annual debate on the reply to the

[1] H.C. Debs., 14th April 1948, vol. 449, cols. 979–1098.

[2] For each of the allotted days, on the Wednesday sixteen days before the day in question. If the House is not sitting sixteen days before one of the days for motions, the ballot for that day is generally held on the Wednesday nine days before it. Cf. Erskine May, *Parliamentary Practice*, 15th (1950) ed., p. 358.   [3] *Weekly Hansard*, 10th February 1955, cols. 2070–190.

[4] The prize for ingenuity in creating an opportunity for debate on the principles of a bill must probably go to Mr. Follick. He wanted to propose a bill to simplify the spelling of the English language. He entered the ballot for notices of motion on going into Committee of Supply, and won a place. So

Address at the beginning of each session, and at various other points during the session. These opportunities are of so little effective use that we need not take them into account for the purposes of our present study. The degree of their ineffectiveness needs to be recognized, however, before we can finally assess the value and the worthwhileness of our actual provision for private Members' bills. The most that a Member can do on these occasions is to indicate the general direction in which he would like to have Parliament proceed by way of legislation. He cannot bring about a debate on specific concrete proposals.

B. *Bills*

(i) *General Rules for the Introduction of Bills.* Before it can go to the Queen for the Royal Assent and final enactment, so that it becomes part of the law of the land, every bill must pass through five stages in each House of Parliament, namely first and second reading, committee, report and third reading. A bill may be introduced in either House of Parliament, and will normally be dealt with first in the House of origin.

The first reading is merely formal, and serves no further purpose than to place the bill on the calendar of Parliament for the session. It is only the title of the bill, not the bill itself, that is read out, and there is no debate. Indeed, the text of the bill is not printed until after the first reading. The second reading is the most important stage (in theory for all bills and in practice too for private Members' bills). It allows the House to debate the principles of the bill, and to decide for or against the principles.

After the House has approved the principles of a bill (and, if necessary, has shown itself ready to grant the money which will have to be spent if it is passed),[1] its next task is to examine the

as an amendment to the motion to consider the Navy Estimates he moved that 'this House is of the opinion that a great advantage would accrue, in the sending of despatches, signals, orders and messages, if some simplification of English spelling were introduced'. H.C. Debs., 6th March 1952, vol. 497, cols. 777–806.

[1] If a bill will impose a charge on the public funds the Standing Orders require that the proposal for the charge must originate in Committee of the whole House, to which the Queen's Recommendation can only be given by a Minister of the Crown. For a bill whose proposals will involve public expenditure, the Committee and Report Stages of the Financial Resolution normally follow the second reading. Cf. below, pp. 25 f.

details. This it does in Committee, debating and deciding on each clause and on any amendments that may be proposed.[1] The committee stage is normally taken by a Standing Committee of forty-five or fifty Members, but it may be taken by a Committee of the whole House.[2]

The report stage (technically the consideration by the House of the Report of its Committee) follows, and resembles the committee stage, with more formal rules in operation. In practice much of the work done at the report stage consists of clearing up and deciding upon amendments which have been withdrawn in Committee pending discussions in private outside.

The third reading, which follows the report stage (often without any interval), gives the House another chance of debating and deciding upon the bill as a whole, in its amended form as it has emerged from the committee and report stages. The debate at this stage must be confined to what is in the bill, and is generally shorter than that on the second reading.

Having passed through all its stages in the House of Commons a bill must pass through the same stages in the House of Lords. If the Lords return a bill to the Commons with amendments, the Lords amendments must be considered in the Commons. If the Commons disagree with any part of the Lords amendments, the bill is returned to the Lords and goes to and fro between the two Houses, if necesssary, until agreement is reached. Finally the bill goes for the Royal Assent.

At the end of each annual session,[3] Parliament is prorogued, and all business still pending is lost; the slate is wiped clean. Any bill which has not completed all its stages by the end of the session must start at the beginning again if it is to make any further progress.

[1] Subject to the Chairman's power to 'select' only some of the proposals for amendment that have been put down (and to pass over others) 'in such a way as to bring out the salient points of criticism, to prevent repetition and overlapping, and, where several amendments deal with the same point, to choose the more effective and better drafted'. (Erskine May, op. cit., p. 455; cf. S.O. Nos. 31 and 57(5).)   [2] Cf. below, pp. 33 ff.

[3] It is not strictly correct to speak of an 'annual' session, because a session may last for more or less than a year, and there may be more than one session in a particular year. Normally, however, a session now begins in November of one year and ends about a year later. Until 1928, the session normally began in January.

These rules of procedure apply to private Members' bills, but the limitation of private Members' time makes necessary special rules governing the conditions of debate on them.

(ii) *The Different Methods of Introducing Private Members' Bills.* To state the matter very briefly, there are two ways in which a private Member may introduce a bill: he may bring it in for an automatic first reading, either under the ballot or not, or he may move a motion for leave to bring it in under the so-called Ten Minutes Rule. An unofficial peer's bill may also be brought down to the Commons from the Lords, if it has successfully passed through all its stages there. It is, however, not much use bringing in a bill unless it has some chance of being passed, or at least of being debated. Because the time allowed for debate on private Members' proposals is strictly limited, it is more important to see under what conditions a bill may be debated than it is to see under what conditions it may be introduced.

In each session in which time is provided for private Members' bills, the distribution of this time among the Members who are competing for it is decided by the device of the ballot. Normally a bill has little chance of making any progress unless it is introduced under the ballot, and we shall be mainly concerned with bills brought in in this way. Something must be said, however, about the other ways of bringing in bills, either without preliminary proceedings or under the Ten Minutes Rule.

(*a*) *Unballoted Bills without Preliminary Proceedings.* Formally there is no difficulty whatever about introducing a bill; Standing Order No. 35, which dates back to 1902, provides that 'a Member may after notice present a Bill without previously obtaining leave from the House. . . .'[1] The bill shall be read the first time without any questions being put, and shall be ordered to be printed.'[2] In fact, however, if a bill is introduced in this way when its introducer has not won a place in the ballot for private Members' time, it can only hope to be discussed further, (*a*) if it is allowed to go forward for second reading as an 'unopposed' bill, or (*b*)

[1] A Member may act alone in introducing a bill. It is usual, however, for the introducer of a bill to be joined by other Members, whose names are put down jointly with his as 'supporters' of the bill; when the bill is printed, their names are printed on the back of it. There are often up to ten or eleven supporters, drawn if possible from both sides of the House.
[2] Cf. Erskine May, op. cit., pp. 490 and 493.

THE ORGANIZATION OF PRIVATE MEMBERS' TIME

if it is taken in the Government's time, or (c) on one of the private Members' Fridays if the balloted bills are all dealt with before the end of the day's sitting. A fairly large proportion of all the private Members' bills that have been passed into law have not been introduced under the ballot, but taken as unopposed business at second reading.[1] The procedure for this seems simple enough; the second reading is proposed at the close of the main debate on some pre-arranged Friday, under the rule which allows unopposed business to be taken then, even after 4 p.m. Provided that not a single Member objects, the question is put immediately and without debate. But any Member can prevent the question from being put by simply saying 'Object'.[2] The bill must then be either abandoned or brought forward again later on, after the objector has been persuaded to let it go through.

Bills are in fact allowed to go through the second reading stage under the 'unopposed' procedure only if the proposers have had full discussions with all Members and outside bodies who might conceivably be interested, and provided that every interest, including the Government, has shown itself satisfied that the bill should pass. If these preliminaries are neglected, someone is sure to object. The Government itself normally sees to it that someone objects, unless it has been fully consulted and satisfied.[3] It is probably fair to say that the House of Commons exercises ample vigilance in preventing measures from being rushed through. Even so, Mr. Herbert Morrison recently said that passing bills 'on the nod' was a poor way of legislating.[4]

[1] Eleven of the 49 private Members' bills enacted in 1948–54. Of these eleven, seven were introduced under the Ten Minutes Rule and four under S.O. No. 35. In addition, in the same period, 12 of the 38 balloted bills which became law received their second readings 'on the nod'. The proportion of non-balloted bills enacted was greater thirty years ago; e.g. in the Parliament of 1924–9, 29 balloted bills were finally passed, as compared with 11 Ten Minute bills and 20 other bills. Cf. Report of the Select Committee on Procedure, H.C. 161 of 1930–1, p. 439, and Sir W. I. Jennings, *Parliament* (Cambridge U.P., 1929), p. 233.

[2] Cf. S.O. Nos. 1 and 2; Erskine May, op. cit., pp. 309 f.

[3] Cf. Lord Hemingford, *What Parliament is and does* (Cambridge University Press, 2nd ed., 1948), p. 40.

[4] H.C. Debs., 8th November 1950, vol. 480, col. 973. It should be noticed that Mr. Morrison was here talking about bills first brought in under the Ten Minutes Rule. His remarks would apply even more, apparently, to bills first brought in with no discussion whatever.

PRESENT PRACTICE

The second possibility of an unballoted bill's getting a second reading, namely by being taken in Government time, may be said to exist only in theory and not in practice. The third possibility, that it should be taken on one of the private Members' Fridays, is rather remote, but it does exist. It sometimes happens that as many as three or four balloted bills, all very uncontroversial, are dealt with in quick succession on one of the private Members' days, so that, with the outstanding balloted bills all down already for some later day, there is still spare time available. An eventuality of this kind is generally foreseeable, and Members with bills which have already had their first reading will be ready waiting with their bills, in the hope that time will be available for them.

Non-Government bills brought down to the Commons after being passed by the House of Lords meet, in the Commons, the same difficulties as those which face private Members' bills brought in outside the ballot in the Commons.

(b) *The Ten Minutes Rule.* The Ten Minutes Rule is at first sight a rather curious device, in so far as it seems pointless to ask the House for leave to bring in a bill, when it is already permissible to bring the bill in anyway. The fact that the device survives, and is still fairly frequently used, is an indication of the uselessness of bringing in bills, other than wholly uncontroversial ones, in the ordinary way and not under the ballot. To move a motion for leave to introduce a bill under the Ten Minutes Rule does at least ensure that the proposal receives some publicity, and having failed to be introduced under the ballot that is really the most that it can expect during the current session, unless it is either wholly uncontroversial or very fortunate.

The rules for the introduction of Ten Minute bills are laid down in Standing Order No. 12:

'On Tuesdays and Wednesdays . . . notices of motions for leave to bring in bills . . . may be set down for consideration at the commencement of public business. If such motions be opposed, Mr. Speaker, after permitting, if he thinks fit, a brief explanatory statement from the Member who moves and from the Member who opposes any such motion respectively, shall put either the question thereon, or the question, that the debate be now adjourned.'

The 'short explanatory statement' is, by custom,[1] of no more than ten minutes' duration, and the opposing speech is of the same length, so that not more than twenty minutes are taken up by the debate. It is hardly fair to suggest that this does not give the House long enough to hear adequately the arguments for and against, because all that the House has to decide is whether or not leave shall be given to do something which can be done in any case without its leave. All the same, the vote may be regarded as a fair indication of the general feeling of the House towards the proposal.

If a motion under the Ten Minutes Rule is approved, the bill is given its first reading forthwith, and its ultimate fate depends on the same considerations as does the fate of any unballoted private Member's bill brought in in the ordinary way; it is in fact unlikely to be discussed any further.

In our study of private Members' bills we shall be concerned almost entirely with bills introduced under the ballot, and with the procedure whereby balloted bills are debated. A brief examination of the operation of the system of non-balloted bills and of indirect methods of proposing legislation will be undertaken in Chapter VII.

3. BALLOTED BILLS

A. *The Ballot*

Under the present system, ten Fridays a session are provided for private Members' bills.[2] On the first six Fridays, which are devoted to second readings, the order in which bills are taken is decided by a ballot. On the last four Fridays precedence is given to the later stages of bills which have already passed through their earlier stages, but any time still left over can be used for the second readings and, if possible, the later stages, of other bills whose second reading stages were not completed during the first

---

[1] Neither the Standing Order nor the text of Erskine May mentions any specific length of time, but May refers to the Speaker's definition of 'brief', given on 19th May 1931 (H.C. Debs., vol. 252, col. 1785). Cf. Erskine May, p. 369*n*. Speaker Fitzroy was not exact on this occasion, but he seemed to agree with Mr. Foot's point of order that fourteen minutes was too long for an opening speech.

[2] Cf. above, p. 12, and below, Appendix A (2).

six Fridays. The total number of days is thus a little less than it was before 1940.[1]

The ballot is normally held soon after the beginning of the session, at a suitable interval before the first of the private Members' days. In the session of 1953-4, for example, Mr. Crookshank, as Leader of the House, announced the times for private Members' days on 4th November,[2] the draw took place on 12th November, and the successful Members introduced their bills on 18th November,[3] ready to be debated on the allotted Fridays, of which the first was 4th December.

Any Member may take part in the ballot, although it would not be appropriate for holders of ministerial posts to compete, because they cannot divide their personalities, but must act and speak always as members of the Government, and never on behalf of their own personal views (cf. below, p. 87).

Members often take part in the ballot without having any idea what bills they will introduce if they are successful. Indeed, Whips are inclined to encourage their own people to take part in the ballot, in the hope of preventing members of the opposite party from winning too many places. The total number of Members participating in each session in the last few years has been 250 to 300.

B. *The Choice of a Day*

When the ballot is drawn, the winner of the first place will normally decide to be the first to propose a bill on the first Friday, the second will take the first place on the second Friday,

---

[1] The old arrangement allowed, in theory, for about fifteen days a session for private Members' bills, but in fact the average actually allowed, taking into account the peacetime sessions in which no time was given, was 11·4 days a year in the period 1906-38. (Cf. Sir Gilbert Campion's Memorandum to the Select Committee on Procedure, H.C. 189-1 of 1945-6, Appendix 1.)

[2] 4th December, 29th January, 12th and 26th February, 12th and 26th March for second readings; 9th April, 7th and 21st May and 25th June for the later stages (H.C. Debs., vol. 520, col. 152).

[3] H.C. Debs., vol. 520, cols. 1731 ff. In the past the interval between the ballot and the introduction and first reading of the bills was only one day. The interval was increased to six days in order to give Members more time to decide what bills they would introduce—a process which, as will be seen below, cannot without an inconvenient rush be completed in so short a time as one day. Members introducing bills must attend in person.

and so on down to the winner of the sixth place. The Member who gets the seventh place will have to be content with being the second to propose a bill on one of the Fridays, but he can take his pick of all the Fridays. He will choose, not necessarily the first, but the Friday on which he thinks there is the greatest likelihood that time will be available after the debate on the first bill. If the first place has been won by a Member who is known to have a bill which seems likely to take the whole day, the seventh man will avoid that Friday, and take one for which the first place has been won by someone whose bill seems likely to be disposed of quickly. Thus when the ballot was taken on 5th December 1951, and the first place was won by Mr. Lever, who intended to introduce a bill to amend the law of libel, there was no desire to have the second place on the first Friday, and that second place was in fact still left open until the winner of the nineteenth place had to make his choice. Again, the winner of the ninth place, on looking round, evidently decided that, although he could have been second on any of four days, his best bet was to take the third place on the third Friday. He chose wisely, because on that day the first two bills down were both disposed of by 1.20 p.m.

Even a Member who wins one of the first six places in the ballot cannot be sure that he will get a hearing for his bill. The day which he chooses may be lost because of an exceptionally long sitting on the previous day, or for some other reason. Two private Members' Fridays have been unforeseeably lost since 1948. The sitting which should have taken place on Friday, 12th March 1954, one of the private Members' days of the session, was entirely lost, because the debate on the Army Estimates, which began on the previous afternoon, continued until 1 p.m. on the Friday.[1] The sitting which should have taken place on Friday, 15th February 1952, was lost because the House then stood adjourned after the death of King George VI. Again, private Members' time may always be swept away because of a sudden crisis or because of a dissolution of Parliament. In the session of 1954-5 the decision to dissolve Parliament was taken when five days allotted to private Members' bills were still outstanding. These were all lost, including one day for second readings.

A Member who has won any place in the ballot outside the

[1] H.C. Debs., 11th March 1954, vol. 524, col. 2828. Cf. below, p. 68.

first six may in any case be unable to get a hearing at all if he decides to bring in a really controversial measure. Even if he has the seventh place, no matter how well he chooses the bill which he wishes to follow, there is a danger that his opponents will keep the debate on that first bill alive until 4 o'clock or just before, simply in order to prevent his controversial bill from getting a hearing. Thus in 1951, Labour Members kept a debate on the Common Informers Bill[1] alive until 3.45 in order to make impossible a debate on a bill to allow increased use of motor-cars for electoral purposes in rural constituencies. Alternatively, those who wish to prevent the controversial bill from getting a hearing may succeed in getting the first bill counted out,[2] so that the House stands adjourned for the day and all the remaining business is lost.

C. *The Choice of a Bill: Pressures on Members*

Participation in the ballot is personal. Many participants do not know, when they enter the ballot, what bills they will bring in if they are successful in the draw. A member who wins a good place is therefore besieged by other Members and by 'lobbyists', all anxious to get him to use his good fortune for the introduction of bills on their behalf. If he has entered the ballot without any fixed intention of using it in any particular way, he will presumably listen to these blandishments, and use his place for the cause which is most successful in winning his sympathy. In 1932 Sir Walter Smiles, who won the first place, referred to 'the long list of motions from which to choose . . . covering human activities from the cradle to the grave'. But he decided that he must please his constituents, and so he chose the Dog Racing (Local Option) Bill, because he 'thought that Lancashire in general and Blackburn in particular wanted it'.[3] Sir Alan Herbert tells how, in 1936, having been unsuccessful in the ballot himself, he prevailed upon Mr. (now Sir Rupert) De la Bère, who had won a good

---

[1] H.C. Debs., 9th February 1951, vol. 483, cols. 2110–62. During the last 2¾ hours of the debate eleven Labour Members spoke in succession. For some Conservatives' reactions to these tactics, cf. specially cols. 2134–8.
[2] Cf. below, pp. 30 f.
[3] H.C. Debs., 2nd December 1932, vol. 272, col. 1156. For further discussion on this point, cf. Sir W. I. Jennings, *Parliament* (Cambridge U.P., 1939), p. 184.

THE ORGANIZATION OF PRIVATE MEMBERS' TIME

place, to introduce Herbert's bill to authorize new grounds for divorce. (Herbert wanted it to be called the Marriage Bill, but it was eventually passed as the Matrimonial Causes Act.)[1]

If a winner of a place has not already made up his mind he may, alternatively, go to see his Whips, who will gladly supply him with a bill. Another possibility is to take a bill directly from a Minister. The Government always has a number of small measures which it would like to introduce, but which it cannot fit into its own legislative programme, either because of straightforward lack of time or because of hesitations on political grounds. Opposition leaders, too, are often glad to have a private Member introduce a bill on their behalf. In the Procedure Committee of 1930–1, Mr. Barr said, 'I think all the parties have a list of subjects which they count most ripe, and they even arrange them in order.'[2] To take a bill from the Whips, though, shows a certain lack of enterprise and imagination, and indeed may perhaps be said to defeat the main purpose of private Members' time.[3] There was a good deal of discussion on this point in the Select Committee on Procedure of 1945–6, where Lord Campion agreed with Mr. W. J. Brown in deploring the practice,[4] while Mr. Herbert Morrison, who has always been sceptical about the usefulness of private Members' bills, could see no objection to it at all, but rather the contrary.[5] It must be remembered in any case that it is very often the Members with low places in the ballot who bring in bills on behalf of the Government, and that such Members would not have much chance of getting very far with bills brought in on their own account. Furthermore, the bills inspired by the Government are nowadays never party measures, and are often pre-eminently suitable for treatment as private Members' bills.

---

[1] 1 Edw. 8 and 1 Geo. 6, ch. 57. Cf. *The Ayes Have It* (Methuen, 1937), pp. 81 ff.

[2] H.C. 161 of 1930–1, Minutes of Evidence, Q. 2877.

[3] Thus in 1928, when a bill was brought in to improve the administrative arrangements connected with the registration of births, marriages and deaths, Mr. Scurr complained that this bill 'ought in every sense to be a Government measure'. More generally he protested 'on behalf of private Members, against the increasing practice of parties . . . to bring in measures which are party measures instead of measures which deal with private Members' affairs'. (H.C. Debs, 20th April 1928, vol. 216, col. 532.)

[4] H.C. 189-1 of 1945–6, Minutes of Evidence, Q. 1842.

[5] Ibid., Q. 3606. Sir Ivor Jennings, writing in his *Parliament* (1939), discusses this practice (pp. 180, 350), but seems to find it quite acceptable.

There is one most important limitation on the right of private Members to introduce bills. In 1706 it was resolved 'that this House will receive no Petitions for any Sum of Money, relating to publick Service, but what is recommended by the Crown'. The rule was made a Standing Order in 1713.[1] The rules as they now stand with regard to this matter are set out in Standing Orders Nos. 78–80. Their effect is to debar any private Member from bringing in any bill whose main object is the creation of a charge. A private Member may, however, bring in a bill whose objects include incidentally the creation of a charge. In this case the parts of the bill relating to the spending of public money must be printed in italics, and may only be dealt with on the basis of a resolution moved in Committee of the whole House by a Minister of the Crown;[2] in other words, the approval of the Government is a necessary condition of the discussion of the clauses, or parts of clauses, which create new expenditure.

A new complication has been introduced in this matter by the Local Government Act of 1948.[3] In the past, the restrictions with regard to proposals for expenditure did not apply if the expenditure was to come out of the local rates. Under the Act of 1948, however, new burdens cannot in most cases be placed on Local Authorities without increasing grants from the Exchequer. Most proposals which involve an increase in Local Authority expenditure therefore now require money resolutions. It has however been agreed that the Government should not as a rule refuse a money resolution purely on this ground.

Mr. Kinley's New Streets Bill, which was given a second reading on 30th January 1951, contained a clause (Clause 6) which required to be based on a money resolution, and which was accordingly printed in italics. The motion for the House to go into Committee to consider a money resolution was accordingly put down on the Order Paper, but was passed over day after day, and had not yet been dealt with when the Bill came before Standing Committee 'B' on 13th February. In the Standing Committee Sir Herbert Williams at once moved[4] that the Committee should adjourn, on the ground that the Bill would, as he saw it, be useless

---

[1] Quoted by W. C. Costin and J. S. Watson, *The Law and Working of the Constitution, Documents 1660–1914*, vol. 1, p. 197.
[2] Erskine May, op. cit., p. 498.   [3] 11 & 12 Geo. 6, ch. 26.
[4] Official Report, Standing Committee 'B', New Streets Bill, col. 584.

without Clause 6, for which the Government apparently did not intend to move the necessary money resolution. The Chairman ruled,[1] however, that it would be out of order for the Committee to adjourn on this ground. But some twenty minutes of the time of the Committee had by then been spent on the point. The money resolution was in fact eventually brought in by the Government, and passed after a discussion of five minutes' duration, in Government time, on 22nd February.[2] The Standing Committee had by that time not reached Clause 6, which was in fact reached (and approved) at the Committee's next sitting, on 27th February.

D. *The Task of Drafting*

When he has decided on a subject, the next task for a Member with a place in the ballot is to get his bill drafted, if it has not been drafted already. In this task he has to rely on his own skill and on whatever professional legal advice he can get, or that the Association behind the bill has cared to provide (and pay for).[3] Fellow-Members of Parliament who are barristers or solicitors may be prepared to help with drafting. In some cases, but not very often, the Government may allow a private Member to use the services of the Parliamentary Counsel in drafting his bill, or at least in looking over and criticizing the draft which he has prepared or had prepared for him. Such help is usually given only after the House has given a bill a second reading.

4. PRIVATE MEMBERS' BILLS BEFORE PARLIAMENT AND THE DIFFICULTIES IN THEIR WAY

A. *Obstacles at Second Reading*

(i) *The Problem of Keeping a House.* When his bill reaches its second reading stage, the private Member faces a whole series of difficulties. As there are no party Whips to compel attendance,[4]

---

[1] Official Report, Standing Committee 'B', New Streets Bill, col. 589.
[2] H.C. Debs., 22nd February 1951, vol. 484, cols. 1489-91.
[3] In fact, very many private Members' bills are backed by Associations. On this point, cf. Jennings, *Parliament*, op. cit., pp. 180 ff.
[4] Private Members sometimes send out requests for attendance in the same form as the official 'Whips' emanating from the Party offices, but these unofficial requests have no authority.

and as the debate is on a Friday, there will probably be a fairly small attendance at the House. If at any time after 1 p.m. (except between 1.15 and 2.15) the number of Members in the Chamber falls below the quorum of forty, a count may be demanded, and if after two minutes there are still under forty Members present the House is adjourned for that sitting.[1] When this happens, not only is the bill under discussion likely to be irretrievably lost, but also the other bills still awaiting discussion on that day lose (for the time being) their chance of being dealt with. In some sense, the time spent up to that point is wasted, and it can well be argued that the day would have been better spent on Government business.

The fear of a count is well illustrated by the plea of Sir Bolton Eyres-Monsell in 1930, during the debate on a bill to facilitate control of rabbits. Just before 1 p.m. he asked that 'the House should now let us have the Bill', because after 1 o'clock someone or other would probably call for a count, and it would then be difficult to collect the necessary Members. But another Member insisted on speaking, and a count was indeed called at 1.10; on this occasion, however, a quorum was mustered and the Bill passed its second reading stage two minutes later.[2] Counts are not, and have never (in this century, at any rate)[3] been very frequent, but they happen often enough to constitute a danger to any Friday's business. In 1949, after ten years without any private Members' time at all, the House was sufficiently pleased with its newly-regained Rights to take the trouble to keep the debates alive; but now that the novelty has worn off, counts are becoming more frequent again.[4]

(ii) *The Problem of Getting a Decision.* There is also the difficulty of forcing a vote. Here a private Member has only rather feeble weapons at his disposal for dealing with obstruction. If there are a few Members who do not like his bill, but who are afraid that it will pass if it is put to the vote, they can try to talk it out. The debate must be brought to a close at four o'clock, and if a Member is still speaking when four o'clock comes, no vote can

[1] Standing Orders Nos. 27 and 28; Erskine May, op. cit., p. 317.
[2] H.C. Debs., 7th March 1930, vol. 236, col. 876.
[3] They were more frequent a hundred years ago. Cf. Redlich, op. cit., vol. I, p. 80.   [4] Cf. below, p. 81.

be taken.¹ The promoter of the bill (or indeed anyone else) can move the closure by proposing 'that the Question be now put', but he can succeed in this only if two conditions are fulfilled. The Speaker must be satisfied that the bill has been adequately debated, and at least 100 Members must vote for the closure.²

A fairly general practice has developed, according to which the Speaker is prepared to put the question on the closure on the second reading of a private Member's bill, provided that it has been debated for the whole of the sitting,³ but not if the debate has gone on for less time than this, unless there are special reasons why the closure should be accepted; for example, when the same bill has already been debated and given a second reading in a recent session.⁴ This has not always been so. Several times before and at least once after 1914 the Speaker prevented the taking of a vote by refusing to put the question on the closure even when a bill had been debated for the whole of a Friday's sitting. In 1907, for example, he refused a closure on the Women's Enfranchisement Bill,⁵ in 1908 on the Ecclesiastical Disorders Bill,⁶ in 1912 on the Acquisition of Land Bill⁷ and in 1913 on a bill providing for conscription for part-time military service.⁸ The most recent instance was in 1924, when Speaker Whitley

---

¹ S.O. Nos. 1(5) and 2.   ² And, of course, a majority. S.O. No. 30.

³ The Speaker is not absolutely bound to put the question on the closure even after a full day's debate, though by now it can be considered practically certain that he would not refuse to do so, particularly after the report of the Select Committee on Procedure (Unofficial Members' Business) (H.C. 102 of 1927, para. 8), which explicitly recognized 'the practice of the Chair' on this matter and implicitly approved that practice.

⁴ On 17th February 1928 the Speaker put the question on the closure on the Slaughter of Animals (Scotland) Bill after 2 hours (H.C. Debs., vol. 213, col. 1184), but it had had a second reading the previous year; on 23rd March 1934 he put it on the Methylated Spirits Bill after 3 hours (vol. 287, col. 1610), and on 26th January 1951 on the Deserted Wives Bill after it had been debated only 2¾ hours (vol. 483, col. 536). In the last case the closure was lost by 52 votes to 44. On 7th April 1933 (vol. 276, col. 2150) the Speaker put the question on the closure on a bill for the regulation of the slaughter of animals, after a mere five minutes. It was carried by 133 votes to 9. But the same bill had reached its committee stage in 1930, albeit in a previous Parliament.

⁵ Parl. Debs., 4th series, 8th March 1907, vol. 170, col. 1162.
⁶ Ibid., 17th February 1908, vol. 184, col. 379.
⁷ H.C. Debs., 19th April 1912, 5th series, vol. 37, col. 739.
⁸ Ibid., 11th April 1913, vol. 51, col. 1594.

refused the closure on a Scottish Home Rule Bill although it had been debated all day, but this was for a special reason. Sir Robert Horne, who was on his feet when the closure was moved, had been so much interrupted that the Speaker considered that he had not yet had a fair hearing and that therefore the closure should not be allowed. The Speaker's decision led to such an uproar that the House had to be adjourned owing to 'grave disorder'.[1]

A bill which has not the first place for a particular day may be talked out by a single hostile Member, and having suffered this fate its chances of getting another hearing later on are not very good. The examples of bills being talked out in this way are very numerous. It should be noticed, however, that some bills, after being talked out, have come back to the House and made further progress on a later day, and to judge from very recent experience it may be fair to say that the House is becoming more inclined

---

[1] H.C. Debs., 9th May 1924, vol. 173, col. 869-74.
It is worth quoting Hansard in part on this:

'Mr. Neil Maclean rose in his place, and claimed to move, "That the Question be now put", but Mr. Speaker withheld his assent, and declined to put that Question.

Mr. Buchanan : On a point of order, Mr. Speaker.
It being Four of the Clock, the Debate stood adjourned.
Mr. Buchanan: This is shameful. (Interruption.)
Mr. Speaker: Debate to be resumed. The clerk will now read the remaining Orders.
Mr. Kirkwood: There will be no orders read. You have no right, Mr. Speaker, to refuse the Closure. I move the Closure now (Interruption). We are going to have the Closure now.
Mr. Maclean: On a point of order. I understood, when arrangements were made for this Debate that the Closure was going to be accepted by you, Mr. Speaker. . . . I should like to know, Sir, whether that was a correct understanding, and if so why it was not carried out?
Mr. Speaker: I cannot allow . . . any right of hon. Members to put such a question as that. It is perfectly true that it was my intention in the earlier part of the Debate, but a right hon. Member (Sir Robert Horne) on the Opposition side was not allowed to address the House . . . (after some heated interchanges) . . . On the question of granting the Closure, if asked for, I am always guided by the proceedings up to the very last moment, and I give no promise or understanding beforehand. . . . The clerk will now proceed to read the remaining orders.
Mr. Maclean: There will be no orders read today. . . .
Mr. Speaker: The hon. Member persists in defying the Chair, and being of the opinion that grave disorder has arisen in the House, I adjourn the House without question put, pursuant to Standing Order No. 21.'

to let bills through without undue obstruction. Thus on 13th March 1953[1] Mr. Teeling's Dogs (Protection of Livestock) Bill, which came up for debate at 2.36 p.m. and was well received on all sides, was talked out by Mr. West, amid very indignant protest, but later on it was allowed to pass through this stage without opposition,[2] and eventually obtained the Royal Assent after its progress (always in private Members' time) had been made possible by 'co-operation and understanding ... from all parties in the House'.[3] Again in 1954 the Pool Betting Bill, after being talked out in much the same way (also amid vigorous protest) the first time it came up for second reading,[4] came up again a fortnight later,[5] as the fifth bill discussed on that particular day, and also eventually obtained the Royal Assent.

A prefectly innocuous bill may fall victim to the tactics of obstructionists who want to prevent the passage of some other bill. The first bill down for 28th March 1952 was the Intestates' Estates Bill, whose intentions most people would agree were both harmless and laudable,[6] and the second was the Housing (Temporary Prohibition of Sale) (Scotland) Bill, a highly controversial proposal to forbid the sale of council houses in Scotland. All that there was to be said at the second reading stages of the Intestates' Bill had been said in a very few minutes, but the debate (or rather the talk; there was no debate, because no one was against the Bill) went on and on, with one Conservative after another talking at great length about particular points to an almost empty House,[7]

[1] H.C. Debs., vol. 512, cols. 1757–84.
[2] Ibid., 1st May 1953, vol. 514, col. 2595.
[3] Ibid., 12th June 1953, vol. 516, col. 673.
[4] Ibid., 29th January 1954, vol. 522, cols. 2109–34.
[5] Ibid., 12th February 1954, vol. 523, cols. 1579–1607.
[6] H.C. Debs., vol. 498, cols. 1077–1147. It had been approved in substance by the House of Commons on 13th February 1931 (H.C. Debs., vol. 248, cols. 1641–1703). On that occasion there was a division, and the majority was 149 to 28.
[7] At one time in the debate (col. 1100) it was mentioned that only one Opposition Member was present, and at another time that there were only eight Members in the Chamber altogether. After the opening speeches there were ten speeches by Conservatives and none by Labour Members until the beginning of the last wrangle that was brought to an end by the final count. It is only fair to mention that on the Bill of 1931 the debate was of about the same duration as in 1952. The next bill in 1931, the Solicitors' Bill, was talked out (H.C. Debs., 20th February 1931, vol. 248, cols. 1703–24).

until at two o'clock Mr. Steele, who wanted a chance to introduce his bill to stop the sale of Local Authority houses in Scotland, plaintively asked the Deputy-Speaker to accept a motion for the closure, on the ground that the points being made were all committee points.[1] But the Deputy-Speaker refused, and the debate continued for another hour until Mr. Steele moved the closure again. He was supported by Mr. Wheatley, who claimed that the Attorney-General had been adopting the rôle of a Government Whip, and had been going round to try and persuade Conservative Members to speak. 'This debate has been kept going by Government supporters,' said Mr. Wheatley, 'largely with the intention of preventing the next measure being reached.'[2] This was apparently true, but nevertheless the Speaker (who had by then returned to the Chair) refused to put the question on the closure, and the Labour supporters took their revenge a few minutes later by demanding a count, at which there were under forty Members present. The debate on the Intestates' Estates Bill was accordingly adjourned, and a good cause, on which there was broad agreement, might well have been sacrificed. The Bill was, however, later allowed to go forward as an unopposed measure,[3] and eventually went on to receive the Royal Assent.

When the Speaker does put the question on the closure it may be easy enough to get a majority to support it, but nowadays, with the changing character of Friday debates, and the generally small attendance, it is often difficult to find one hundred Members to vote in support of it. Thus on 25th April 1952, when her Women's Disabilities Bill had been debated all day, Dr. Summerskill moved the closure, for which there was a good majority (fifty-four votes to twenty), but because the closure had not been supported by a hundred Members it could not be carried, and the debate had to be adjourned without a vote being taken.[4]

When there is no firm pressure on Members to be present to vote there is a strong tendency, particularly on Fridays, to be absent from the House, and on a recent Friday even the

---

[1] Col. 1128.
[2] Col. 1145.
[3] H.C. Debs., 28th April 1952, vol. 499, col. 1184.
[4] Ibid., col. 982. Cf. also *Weekly Hansard*, 18th March 1955, col. 1708.

Government could not raise the necessary hundred Members to carry the closure against an unexpected filibuster.[1]

The closure was only twice[2] successfully moved on a private Member's bill on a Friday in 1948–55, once with only two votes to spare. If we go back to an earlier period we find that it was often carried—twelve times on second readings in the five sessions of 1906–10 and fifteen times in the ten sessions of 1919–28.

B. *Obstacles after Second Reading*

(i) *Financial Resolution.* Once through the second reading stage, a bill has fresh similar obstacles to overcome at the later stages. If the passing of the bill will entail new expenditure from public funds or require payments into the Exchequer, the Government can prevent discussion of the money clauses by refusing to bring in the financial resolution. It must be remembered, however, that it is unusual for private Members to propose bills which entail new public expenditure. Normally there is no need for a financial resolution in any case.[3]

(ii) *The Committee Stage.* (a) *General Rules regarding Standing Committee.* Before we examine the particular problems of private Members' bills at the committee stage, we must briefly examine

---

[1] Cf. H.C. Debs., 20th November 1953, vol. 520, col. 2124. On the Cinematograph Film Production (Special Loans) Bill, on which the Government had expected no trouble, Mr. Lever spoke for over two hours, and at 4 p.m. the Government got a majority of only 91 to 8 votes for the closure. There are probably two parallel factors at work in accentuating the tendency of Members to be away from the House on Fridays. On the one hand there is a general tendency for Members to have more week-end engagements in their constituencies and elsewhere; on the other hand the temporary situation of 1950–5, produced by the smallness of the Government's majority and the consequent necessity for a high level of attendance on Mondays to Thursdays, made Members all the more inclined to be absent on Fridays.

[2] Cf. below, p. 62. One other closure motion produced no less than 116 favourable votes, but there were 124 votes against it (on the Press Council Bill, 28th November 1952).

[3] Cf. above, p. 25. Only two of the 36 private Members' bills enacted in 1948–53 had required financial resolutions.

the general rules relating to that stage.[1] During the nineteenth century the committee stage was nearly always taken on the floor of the House, with the House resolved for the time being into a committee. In 1882, however, two Standing Committees were set up, to which bills which were technically intricate and politically uncontroversial were sent.[2] In 1907 the number of Standing Committees was increased to five (one of them for Scottish bills), and it became the rule that all bills should go to Standing Committee unless the House should specifically decide otherwise.[3] (Since 1945 there has been no limit to the number of Standing Committees.)[4]

Each Standing Committee has twenty Members, appointed for the Session, to whom not more than thirty Members are added for the consideration of each of the bills which go in succession before the Committee. Since 1951 the number of added Members has been twenty-five.[5] The nomination of members of Standing Committees is the task of a body of Government and Opposition Members, the Committee of Selection, which in choosing the first twenty must 'have regard to the composition of the House', and must choose the added Members with regard to their 'qualifications'. This is always done in such a way that the balance of Parties in each Committee is as nearly as possible the same as that in the House.

In one of the Standing Committees appointed each session,

---

[1] For more detailed treatment of the rules, etc., relating to Standing Committees, cf. S.O. Nos. 57 and 58; Erskine May, op. cit., pp. 511 and 627 f.; A. L. Lowell, *The Government of England* (Macmillan, 1908), vol. 1, p. 269; and Jennings, op. cit., pp. 265 f.

[2] C.J. (1882), p. 520.   [3] C.J. (1907), pp. 119–22.

[4] C.J. (1945–6), pp. 81 f., etc.

[5] From 1907 to 1945 the permanent nucleus of each Standing Committee consisted of from 30 to 50 Members, to whom not less than ten or more than 35 Members were added for each bill. From 1945 to 1951 the number of added Members was usually 30, sometimes 25. The practice of invariably adding only 25 Members for every bill was instituted in 1951, when the Government's majority was so small that it could have no majority at all in a Committee of 50 members. The odd number gave it a majority of one.

The change was made after the Chairman of a Committee of 50 Members had had to give a casting vote. It so happened that the first bill for which a Committee of 45 Members was set up was a highly controversial private Member's bill. The Opposition, feeling itself robbed of a chance of embarrassing the Government, raised a storm of protest. (H.C. Debs., 8th March 1951, vol. 485, cols. 668 ff.) Cf. below, pp. 39 and 55.

private Members' bills have precedence, and are dealt with in order as they emerge from their second reading stages. It is through this Committee that private Members' bills (other than Scottish bills) must pass if they are to have any hope of going on to the later stages.[1] Scottish bills go to the Scottish Standing Committee, where they have no precedence.[2] A bill which affects private rights may be sent to a Select Committee.

(b) *The Choice between Standing Committee and a Committee of the Whole House.* One device, which seems to have become obsolete, for hindering a bill from getting beyond the second reading stage, is to propose, after the second reading, that it should go to a Committee of the whole House instead of to a Standing Committee.[3] If this motion is passed, the bill is almost certainly lost, because, if there is to be any discussion in committee, it cannot make any further progress unless its committee stage is taken either on one of the private Members' days reserved for the later stages of bills, or in time provided by the Government.[4] Neither of these conditions is likely to be fulfilled. On the last four private Members' days of each session precedence is given to the bills

[1] It has been known for the Speaker to allow a private Member's bill to be taken by one of the other Standing Committees, on which Government bills have precedence. Cf. Select Committee on Procedure, H.C. 161 of 1930–1, Minutes of Evidence, Q. 249. A recent instance was the Pet Animals Bill, taken by Standing Committee 'C' on 24th April 1952.

[2] The Scottish Standing Committee comprises all the Members for constituencies in Scotland (S.O. No. 59). The Committee of Selection adds to them not less than ten or more than fifteen other Members for each bill; in so doing it tries to make the party balance in the Scottish Committee the same as that in the House.

[3] Before 1907, if opponents wished to prevent a bill from going to one of the Standing Committees, they had only to vote against the motion to send it to such a committee. Since 1907, committal to a Standing Committee has been the normal procedure, and any bill goes to Standing Committee unless a motion is passed sending it to a Committee of the whole House.

[4] It should be mentioned that with a bill so uncontroversial that it seems certain to pass through its committee stage entirely without amendment or even discussion, it may be desirable to have the committee stage taken on the floor of the House, because it can be dealt with as unopposed business without occupying any time at all. Four bills were successfully treated in this way during the period 1948–53. All four had passed through second reading as unopposed bills. With three of the four the committee, report and third reading stages followed in succession immediately after the second reading. Cf. below, Appendix E.

PRIVATE MEMBERS' BILLS BEFORE PARLIAMENT

that have made the greatest amount of progress, and a committee stage of a bill would have to wait until all the outstanding report, third reading and Lords' amendments stages of other bills had been dealt with. In most sessions the whole of the time is exhausted before all these later stages have been completed. On the other hand, the Government is most unlikely to give of its own time to the committee stage of a private Member's bill.

The device of moving for a Committee of the whole House on a private Member's bill for the purpose of obstruction appears to have been abandoned because of its evident futility. In practice it rarely had any other effect than to send Members tramping through the lobbies a second (or even a third) time in succession. Almost all the Members who have voted for a bill's second reading will generally vote against a proposal to send it to a Committee of the whole House. There have been exceptions, however. In 1908 the Liberal Government's spokesman welcomed Sir Charles Dilke's bill to regulate working conditions in shops, and voted for the second reading, but then went on to move that the bill should go to a Committee of the whole House. The details were so complicated, he said, that the bill would fail to make progress in the Standing Committee, and would prevent other bills from passing. The Government Whips were put on to ensure that the motion for committal to a Commmittee of the whole House should pass.[1]

The device almost succeeded on the Racecourse Betting Bill in 1928, when many Members changed their alignment between the successive divisions. The motion for the closure was carried by 172 votes to 111, and that for the second reading by 149 to 134. The motion to commit to a Committee of the whole House, however, was defeated only by 128 votes to 126.[2]

The last occasions on which motions of this kind were moved were in 1930-1, on Mr. Chuter Ede's bill to provide for the admission of the Press to Local Authority meetings,[3] and on an I.L.P. minimum wage bill, which had been given a second reading with the support of Labour back-bench votes.[4]

---

[1] Parl. Debs., 1st May 1908, 4s, vol. 187, cols. 1598, 1610 (Mr. Herbert Samuel). Cf. below, p. 105, *n.* 1.
[2] H.C. Debs., 16th March 1928, vol. 214, col. 2360.
[3] Ibid., 5th December 1930, vol. 245, col. 2654.
[4] Ibid., 6th February 1931, vol. 247, col. 2354.

THE ORGANIZATION OF PRIVATE MEMBERS' TIME

(c) *The Composition of the Standing Committee.* In the Standing Committee there are important new difficulties, and most of the old difficulties come up again, sometimes in accentuated form. Some Members who have acquiesced in the second reading of a bill may become hostile at the later stages, because of belated complaints from constituents who had known nothing about the proposal beforehand.[1] Or again the hostile interests may have known about the bill, but preferred to remain silent at the second reading because they wanted time to prepare their arguments.[2]

Some further difficulties may arise owing to the composition of the Standing Committee to which the bill is sent. In making up the Standing Committee for a particular bill, the Committee of Selection cannot proceed according to any watertight plan in trying to achieve a fair balance between the opponents of the bill and those who are in favour of it.[3] There may be some difficulty in finding the twenty-five or thirty Members who are needed to fill up the Committee's complement, and as the enemies of the bill will probably be anxious to serve, the Committee may turn out to have an unduly large proportion of hostile Members.

(d) *Quorum in Standing Committee.* When the Committee sets to work, a relatively large proportion of its mildly well-disposed members may fail to attend at all. It is, moreover, sometimes difficult to raise the necessary quorum (now fifteen Members out of the total Committee strength of forty-five or fifty) in order that proceedings may begin, or to keep the quorum in being once the Committee has begun its sitting.

Furthermore, if on any bill the Standing Committee has to be adjourned through absence of a quorum at two successive sittings, that bill must be placed at the bottom of the list of bills awaiting consideration by the Committee.[4] The danger of losing time through failure to form or to keep a quorum is these days not very great, however. In the period from 1949 to 1953 only two

[1] Cf. Lord Hugh Cecil's question to Sir Robert Sanders in the Select Committee on Procedure (Unofficial Members' Business), H.C. 102 of 1927, Q. 94.
[2] A good example is provided by Major Legge-Bourke's intervention on the Docking of Horses Bill in 1949 (Official Report, Standing Committee 'E', 5th July 1949, col. 1463).
[3] Any Member who has spoken on the second reading is generally considered to have a special claim to be added to the Standing Committee.
[4] Erskine May, op. cit., p. 634.

out of fifty sittings of the Standing Committee dealing with private Members' bills were lost from this cause.[1]

(*e*) *The Committee Proceedings.* The character of the Committee proceedings also creates difficulties. The proposer of the bill must be in charge, fulfilling the rôle taken by the Minister with a Government bill, but lacking the Minister's power to use the weapon of party discipline in order to get a majority for the points which he favours. If his bill is at all controversial he may have to make large concessions to his opponents. Nor will he have any substantial chance of cancelling these concessions when the bill gets to the report stage, such as the Government has if it has had amendments passed against its wishes in the Standing Committee.

(*f*) *Obstruction in Standing Committee.* Furthermore, all the private Members' bills are dealt with by a single Standing Committee, and in this Committee the traffic may be blocked if one bill takes up a great deal of time there, and thus prevents any later bills from being discussed at all.[2] Thus in 1949 Standing Committee 'E', which was dealing with the private Members' bills that year, made slow progress on the first bill sent to it and later lost a day through the absence of a quorum. By June 23rd, when the summer recess was apparently only six weeks ahead, it had completed its discussion of five bills and five others remained to be discussed. Three bills did not come before the Committee until after 8th July, which was the last of the private Members' days in the House. None of these bills was able to make any progress beyond Committee.[3] In 1951-2 the Defamation Bill took a very long time (ten sittings, covering the period 21st February to 27th March) in the Standing Committee. In both these sessions, however, the Committee succeeded in disposing of all the bills which had come up to it.

Private Members have of course the weapon of the closure available at the committee and report stages, but each amendment (provided that it has been selected) must be thoroughly debated before the chairman can put the question on the closure.

---

[1] Cf. Appendix E. The sittings lost were those which should have been held on 27th November 1949 (on the Censorship of Plays (Repeal) Bill) and on 11th March 1952 (on the Defamation Bill).
[2] Cf. Jennings, *Parliament*, op. cit., p. 355.
[3] Cf. below, p. 58.

If many amendments have been put down, the closure is not very effective in expediting business. A Government which finds that one of its measures is being delayed in the Standing Committee can hasten its progress either by imposing a time-table or by proposing that the Committee should hold extra sittings in addition to the usual sittings on Tuesday and Thursday mornings.

There is no reason why a Standing Committee should not have additional sittings similarly when considering a private Member's bill, and this has sometimes been done.[1] On the other hand, the Government can get its way through the operation of party discipline, whereas a private Member has no weapon but his own persuasiveness to help him to coax the Committee's Members to accept the very disagreeable imposition of extra sittings.

It is at present almost inconceivable that a private Member in charge of a bill could carry the House with him in proposing a guillotine. Similarly the Standing Committee would probably not agree to a time-table for the discussion of the clauses. The Government's need to use these devices from time to time is recognized on the ground that it has a duty to fulfil its programme, but this argument could not be used to support a guillotine proposed by a private Member. At present there seems in fact to be little need for such weapons to hasten the passage of private Members' bills. Deliberate obstruction in Standing Committee is almost unknown; any Member who practised it would incur great odium because his action would spoil the chances of success of bills still awaiting discussion.[2]

(g) *The Power of a Committee to Destroy a Bill.* A Standing Com-

[1] Late in June 1949, when Standing Committee 'E', which was the private Members' bills committee that year, had taken a very long time over the Hairdressers' Bill and still had several more bills awaiting discussion, a motion for an additional sitting for the afternoon of Tuesday 28th June was accepted unanimously. The Committee did in fact sit from 4 p.m. to 6.42 p.m. that afternoon. A motion for further additional meetings, in the morning and afternoon of the following day (Wednesday), was rejected by 15 votes to 14 (Official Report, Standing Committee 'E', Analgesia in Childbirth Bill, 28th June 1949, cols. 1419 f.). As it turned out, however, the motion was unnecessary because the bill then under discussion was speedily disposed of without the need for another sitting.

[2] Sir Ivor Jennings, in his *Parliament*, p. 355, seems to suggest that on the basis of the experience of the years up to 1939, when he wrote, deliberate obstruction in the Standing Committee was then fairly frequent.

mittee can kill a bill by making a special report to the House to the effect that it cannot with advantage proceed further with the consideration of it, or by negativing all the clauses. There is, however, some doubt as to the proper limitations to a Standing Committee's powers in relation to a bill. If a Committee has been entrusted by a superior body, such as the House, with the task of examining a bill in detail, and of making such amendments as it deems necessary, it may be asked whether it can possibly be right for the Committee to take it upon itself to kill the bill. This argument was put forward very strongly in 1949 in the Standing Committee which considered the Hairdressers' Bill.[1] Yet neither law nor Standing Order nor convention prevents a Committee from killing a bill on the initiative of its own majority. In France and the United States, Standing Committees kill a large proportion of the bills which are sent to them.

The Annual Holiday Bill was killed by the Standing Committee in 1936. This was apparently because the Bill had passed its second reading stage mainly on Labour votes owing to the reluctance of Conservative Members to vote against it, whereas the Conservatives had their usual majority in the Standing Committee, where the Bill could be rendered innocuous rather more discreetly than by wholesale rejection.[2] In 1951 the Standing Committee killed Mr. Bevins' Road Transport Bill by voting against each of the clauses.[3] In 1951, also, Mrs. Eirene White, having become convinced that her own Matrimonial Causes Bill had no chance of reaching the statute book, and knowing that a Royal Commission was to be set up, moved that the Standing Committee should not proceed with the Bill, and her motion was carried.[4]

The introduction of very great changes in Standing Committee may lead to vigorous reactions at the report stage. It may be argued that the changes brought into a bill in the committee stage have so much altered the bill that the whole subject had better be

[1] Cf. below, Appendix B. Lord R. Cecil also argued this way in 1920, when a Standing Committee had reported unfavourably on a bill (H.C. Debs., 22nd August 1920, vol. 128, col. 576).
[2] Cf. below, pp. 106 f.
[3] Official Report, Standing Committee 'B', 21st March and 5th and 10th April 1951. Cf. above, p. 33, *n.* 5.
[4] Official Report, Standing Committee 'B', 17th April 1951. Cf. below, p. 109, *n.* 1.

reconsidered. In 1928, when the Racecourse Betting Bill came back from the Standing Committee, no less a person than the Leader of the Opposition, Mr. Ramsay MacDonald, called the Speaker's attention to the fact that the Bill had grown in length from seven operative lines to 141,[1] and Mr. Rhys Davies moved that it should be recommitted to a Select Committee.[2] The Leader of the Opposition and several of his front-bench colleagues voted for Mr. Davies' motion.

(iii) *The Later Stages.* (*a*) *Report and Third Reading.* In the past, one of the most serious obstacles to the eventual passage of a private Member's bill was the difficulty of finding time for the later stages, once the bill had gone through the Standing Committee. Since the introduction of the reforms of 1927 and (in 1950) of the new pattern proposed by the Procedure Committee of 1945–6,[3] however, with the four days for the later stages more or less guaranteed, this obstacle has become much less important, at least in so far as concerns the bills that have been given a second reading during the first six Fridays. The other obstacles at the later stages are still the same as those which the bill had to face in the early stages, but are probably greater rather than less.

A bill may itself be badly held up at the report stage, but no single bill can cause very serious obstruction to other bills. Standing Order No. 5, and the sessional orders which have replaced it in recent years, provide that if the report stage of a bill is begun but not completed on one Friday, its precedence on the next allotted Friday will be after all bills which are ready for the report stage but have not yet been dealt with.

The third reading stage also provides further opportunities for obstruction, but obstruction is somewhat rare here because the Speaker has always been ready to grant the closure after a short debate, as in 1923 when the closure was put and carried on the

[1] H.C. Debs., 6th July 1928, vol. 219, col. 1743.
[2] Ibid., col. 1753.
[3] Cf. above, p. 12. In the session of 1948–9 the three days allowed for the later stages were found to be inadequate. Three of the successful private Members' bills of the session were amended in the Lords, and the discussion by the House of Commons of the Lords' Amendments took place late in the autumn, in time provided by the Government (H.C. Debs., 5th December 1949, vol. 470, cols. 1576–1656).

PRIVATE MEMBERS' BILLS BEFORE PARLIAMENT

third reading of the Railway Fires Bill after a debate of only five minutes.[1]

(b) *The House of Lords.* While a bill is going through the House of Lords it is out of the ken of its original proposers altogether, and the peer who takes charge will probably not be ready to accept the same subordinate rôle as a peer piloting a Government bill; furthermore he will have no authority with his colleagues. The Lords will generally not reject or fail to deal with a private Member's bill which has passed the Commons,[2] but they may alter it substantially.

In the House of Lords there is no need for any ballot or other special device for the allocation of priorities among private Members' bills; the Upper House contrives to fit the bills into its time-table without undue difficulty or delay. In the whole of the period 1948-53 there were only three private Members' bills which occupied the House of Lords on second reading for more than an hour each, and the longest second reading debate lasted for under two hours. On the rest, the second reading would generally be disposed of after a speech from the peer in charge of the bill, and at the most two or three other speeches. There was no division on any second reading, but this was not very remarkable, in view of the fact that none of the bills which reached the Lords had produced a division on second reading in the Commons. The Lords were no less expeditious in dealing with the committee stages. The Defamation Bill took nearly four hours, but all the other private Members' bills together took under eight hours of debating time in all in the four sessions under review. Only six of the 36 bills gave rise to any discussion at all on report, and all but three passed through the third reading stage without debate.

[1] H.C. Debs., 15th June 1923, vol. 165, col. 942. The Government was so much in favour of the Bill that a few minutes earlier the Minister of Agriculture himself had moved the closure to the debate on a wrecking amendment which Sir F. Banbury had moved on Report (col. 936). On that occasion 40 Members voted against the closure, but only 13 for the amendment, so there was apparently some feeling, even among opponents of the amendment, that more might have been said on the subject.

[2] Since 1931 not a single private Member's bill has failed to be passed by the Lords after being passed by the House of Commons. In the eighteen peace-time sessions between 1910 and 1931, however, twelve private Members' bills which had been passed by the Commons failed to be passed by the Lords (House of Commons annual returns).

THE ORGANIZATION OF PRIVATE MEMBERS' TIME

Only the Defamation Bill was debated at any length on third reading, and it took under an hour.

One useful feature of the contribution of the House of Lords is that, with the great flexibility of the time-table, there is no need to have bills hustled through at second reading 'on the nod'. Of the 36 private Members' measures enacted in 1948–53, just half had had their second readings taken in the Commons under the unopposed procedure, without a word being said about them. All but two of these were debated, or at least introduced by short explanatory speeches, on second reading in the Lords, including all the four bills which had passed through all their stages in the Commons without a word being said about them.

If the Lords amend a bill, it often cannot be returned to the Commons for consideration of the Lords Amendments before the last of the days allotted to private Members' bills. If a bill has reached this stage, however, it is almost inconceivable that the Government should fail to provide the necessary time in the Commons.

5. SOME POSSIBLE REFORMS OF PROCEDURE ON PRIVATE MEMBERS' BILLS

A. *The Device of a Steering Committee*

If we once accept the principle that private Members' bills have a useful function to perform, there seem to be good grounds for arguing that our methods of dealing with them fail to make a sound distribution of the limited time available between the different proposals that are brought forward. The problem is not insoluble; indeed several possible solutions have been put forward and discussed, particularly in the Procedure Committee of 1931. Instead of leaving the allocation of priorities to chance we could put the task into the hands of some suitable body of persons. The French Conférence des Présidents and the Aeltestenrat of the West German Bundestag draw up the whole of the programmes of their respective Assemblies, planning the debates on questions of all types; but our Parliament, with its two major Parties and its lack of permanent Standing Committees, could not furnish a body equivalent to either of these. We have, of course, already our 'usual channels', the Leader of the House and the Chief Whips, who are responsible, in an informal way, for allocating all time other than private Members' time, but the essence of the 'usual channels' is their partisan character. Their task is to reconcile the claims of the Government and of the Opposition, of which they are the spokesmen and negotiators. It would, for obvious reasons, not be feasible to impose on them the task of adjudicating between private Members' bills.

If, then, a body were to be set up for the allocation of priorities, it would have to be a special committee of some kind, such as was proposed by Professor Ramsay Muir in 1930.[1] There is much to be said for this solution, in theory at least, and there is no reason why the committee should not draw up a detailed time-table, as Ramsay Muir proposed, in such a way that each bill was divided upon.[2] But the committee's task would be invidious and difficult.

B. *Priority According to Volume of Support*

Another device would be to have bills placed in order according to the amount of support they obtain. Lord Campion advocated a scheme of this type in 1945.[3] This might be arranged in any of several ways, of which the simplest would probably be for bills to be laid before the House for a period expiring on a given day, and for Members to be allowed to append their signatures to bills during this period. The bills would them be arranged in order, according to the number of signatures appended to each bill. The method could, alternatively, be made to work the other way round, with priority given to bills according to the smallness of the number of votes cast against them at some preliminary sifting stage. If this method, in either of its forms, were adopted, various points of detail would have to be decided, such as whether or not a limit should be set to the number of bills which a Member could support or oppose.

The adoption of a device such as this has a great deal to recommend it. It is simple, and it would not involve the creation of a

---

[1] Select Committee on Procedure, H.C. 161 of 1930–1, Minutes of Evidence, Q. 2642, para. 5.

[2] Cf. Michael Stewart, *The British Approach to Politics*, 2nd edn. (Allen & Unwin, 1949), p. 130.

[3] Cf. para. 29 of his Memorandum to the Select Committee on Procedure, H.C. 189–1 of 1945–6, and Minutes of Evidence, Q. 2881 ff. Speaker Clifton Brown, in his Notes to the Committee (Q. 5179, para. 10) thought that volume of support would be an 'unreliable and unsteady factor'.

committee with awkward duties. On the other hand, there is some doubt whether the bills which got the greatest quantitative support or aroused the smallest opposition would necessarily be those most deserving the attention of Parliament. Again, the system might lead to 'log-rolling' and to various difficulties over personalities. It would, furthermore, attempt to settle only the problem of the order in which bills were taken, and would leave untouched the distribution of the time in debate and in committee. Another possibility would be to empower the Speaker to certify bills as non-contentious if certain stipulated conditions were fulfilled, and special facilities could be provided for bills so certified.[1]

C. *General Considerations*

The problem of bills being talked out is indeed an intractable one, and could only be dealt with adequately by a business committee or steering committee of the type suggested by Professor Muir. A less cumbersome solution would be for the Speaker to grant the closure more readily than at present. Probably the former solution would be the better, because a new restriction of the right of minorities to obstruct business would be more acceptable if the power were in the hands of a committee.

When we come to look at the committee stage and at the later stages we find problems of much the same kind, and the possible solutions are similar to those which we have already examined. Here again, either we continue as we are, leaving substantial powers of obstruction in the hands of individual Members or groups, or we must accept the institution of some kind of steering committee. What has been said about a steering committee in relation to its potentialities as an organizer of second reading debates applies also to its potentialities as an organizer of the later stages; there are obvious disadvantages, but they would not be intolerable.

This discussion of possible reform suggests that it is no use

[1] A suggestion on these lines was favoured by Mr. Scott Lindsay, then Secretary of the Parliamentary Labour Party, in the Select Committee of 1927 (H.C. 102 of 1927, Q. 161). But the Committee in its Report, at para. 11, rejected this suggestion on the ground that it was too difficult to distinguish between controversial and non-controversial bills. The division of bills into two distinct classes in this way would be over-rigid.

SOME POSSIBLE REFORMS OF PROCEDURE

advocating the abolition of private Members' time simply because of the evil effects of its inefficient organization. If these effects are evil, and if private Members' time is intrinsically worth having, then the solution would seem to be to consider adopting reform of the machinery. In any case, it still remains doubtful whether the existing machinery, for all its haphazard character, really is so very inefficient in relation to the achievement of the tasks which it sets out to perform. The ballot itself turns out to be a less haphazard way of selecting measures than it appears to be at first sight. So many of those who win places are ready to introduce bills on behalf of others, that an interesting proposal has a reasonable chance of getting a hearing. The selection of measures is not necessarily inefficient for its lack of conscious plan. Perhaps the most serious complaint that can be brought against the present system is that second reading debates tend to be longer than they need to be, and this complaint is becoming less serious in view of the current tendency to take second readings more quickly than in the past.

Finally, it should be observed that on two recent private Members' days the adjournment has been moved well before 4 p.m. because there has been no further business to transact. On 8th May 1952 all the outstanding business was completed by 1.20 p.m., and on 21st May 1954 the business was completed at 2.14 p.m. On either of these days there would have been plenty of time for a second reading debate on a bill not yet dealt with. In neither of the two sessions concerned could it be justly complained that Members without places in the ballot were denied the opportunity of bringing proposals forward.

Chapter II

A HISTORICAL SURVEY OF PRIVATE MEMBERS' BILLS SINCE 1900

1. GENERAL TRENDS: TOWARDS A CONCEPTION OF A DISTINCTIVE FUNCTION

IN this chapter it is proposed to attempt a broad and general survey of the private Members' bills dealt with by Parliament in the past fifty years, observing the trends suggested by the survey. As the survey comes down to examine the events of recent years, there will be more attention to detail and fuller examination of some typical bills as examples.

Private Members' bills have undergone changes of many different kinds during the past fifty years. The character of the bills themselves, the character of the parliamentary process with respect to them, the form and atmosphere of the debates, the manner of making the decisions—all have undergone fundamental changes while remaining superficially the same. There have of course always been many relatively uncontroversial measures brought in on Fridays, and there has been a fairly steady flow of such measures going forward to receive the Royal Assent. In the early years of the century, however, the bills dealt often with points which were at the very centre of political and social controversy; the debates were conducted often with much feeling and party controversy, and with leading members of the Government and Opposition taking part. The final decision was often made in a division in which a very large number of Members, including the Party leaders, voted; indeed, the feelings were often so strong that the opponents of a bill would find pretexts for dividing the House three or four times on each bill—once on the closure, once on the amendment, once on the main question, once, if the bill had not been thrown out, on the almost inevitable motion to commit to a Committee of the whole House instead of to a Standing Committee.[1] The great aspirations for social reform and improvement which were current in the early years of the century are reflected in private Members' legislative proposals, each of which would be introduced year after year and earnestly debated from time to time as a matter of great national importance.

As time went by it became more and more widely recognized that modest proposals were more constructive and more suited than great ones to private Members' Fridays. In the words of Ellen Wilkinson, as she explained her motives for a choice which she had made after a success in the draw, 'if you win the ballot, you can either try some big reform and have a good day till 4 p.m.; or you can bring in a minor reform, and preferably get agreement first'. She had decided on the constructive minor reform, and brought in a bill to regulate hire-purchase agreements—a reform concerned only with a tiny corner of the life of the community, but one which was clearly needed to protect guileless people against a few unscrupulous traders. She had, furthermore, drawn up her bill in consultation with the Hire Purchase Trade Association, the organization most nearly concerned by her proposal, and the Association had sent a letter to Members of Parliament expressing its approval of the bill.[2]

The decline of the practice of bringing forward great questions as private Members' bills was gradual, and reflected a developing recognition of the changes taking place in the relations between Government and Parliament. Probably the most authoritative and influential condemnation of the old practice was that made by Mr. Baldwin in 1925,[3] and in 1927 we find Lord Hugh Cecil putting forward the view that 'nothing is worse, both in the interest of the House of Commons generally, and in the interest of

---

[1] Before 1907, a bill was committed to a Standing Committee only on a positive motion. Cf. above, p. 34, *n.* 3.

[2] H.C. Debs., 10th December 1937, vol. 330, col. 729. Her bill passed as the Hire-Purchase Act, 1938 (1 & 2 Geo. 6, ch. 53).

[3] Cf. below, p. 54.

A HISTORICAL SURVEY OF PRIVATE MEMBERS' BILLS

private Members themselves, than that private Members should be tempted to deal in private Members' time with large controversial issues'.[1]

Since 1948, Lord Hugh Cecil's views have almost wholly prevailed. The bills brought forward have nearly all dealt with questions which, from the point of view of the nation's history as a whole, are of secondary interest. The debates have usually been rather quiet discussions, in which most of the participants have been concerned to indicate possible difficulties or to suggest improvements, rather than to produce rhetorical arguments, favourable or hostile, which would clearly be out of place in relation to proposals of the kind which have been put forward. There is still a contribution from the Government front bench, but it is usually made by a junior Minister and seems to bear the imprint of the civil servant rather than the politician. Opposition leaders do not very often speak, and when they do, they tend to speak as individuals or as men with special administrative experience, and not in a partisan way. The decision on the second or third reading is generally made without a division, and when there is a division the leaders of the main parties rarely vote. There is still indeed from time to time some controversy at the committee stage, but the battles in Committee are often concerned with points of very restricted importance, and conducted between spokesmen of rival interest groups who have not succeeded in settling their differences by private discussions outside Parliament.

2. TYPES OF BILL BEFORE 1914

When we look back over the history of the past fifty years, it seems as though we are following a process by which the natural inclinations of men have been tamed and restrained by experience of political reality. If a man is elected to Parliament with powerful ideals and with a strong desire to have the life of the community improved by some great reform, it can be expected that he will wish to propose his reform to Parliament on every occasion, so that at least he may have an opportunity of trying to persuade the rest of the House, and through it the country at large, that his reform is a good one. Thus in the earlier years of the twentieth

[1] Select Committee on Procedure (Unofficial Members' Business), H.C. 102 of 1927, Q. 45.

century, both Irish and Labour Members found it quite normal to bring in bills relating to Home Rule or land reform, on the one hand, or to restriction of the hours of work on the other hand. It did not seem to these Members that they were wasting their own time or the time of the House with their proposals; on the contrary, the debates were in their opinion very valuable, perhaps even the most valuable of the debates in the House at that period.

The Irish Members had one dominating interest—Home Rule —and other ancillary interests such as land reform, and they almost all were inclined to concentrate all their parliamentary activities on subjects of this type. Each year they would move an amendment to the Address, regretting the absence of Irish Home Rule proposals from the Government's programme, and every Irish Member who won a place on the ballot for private Members' bills or on any other ballot thought it perfectly natural that he should use that place to initiate a debate on some aspect of the subject that interested him and all other Irish Members to the exclusion almost of everything else.[1]

The Labour Members of pre-war days were in a somewhat similar position, and they thought it perfectly natural that they should miss no opportunity of bringing about debates on the grievances over which their feelings were so strong. Among the great mass of the Liberal Members too there were powerful and urgent aspirations towards many great reforms, social, moral and rational. Before 1914 there were several questions which, though essentially non-political in character, aroused feelings and controversies no less violent than those produced by the burning political questions. In some cases it happened too that opinion was divided mainly on party lines. The most obvious instance was the whole question of the control of drinking, with regard to which the Liberals were on the whole in favour of stronger measures of restriction, while the Conservatives were against them. There was a flood of proposals for 'local option', some of them relating to Wales or to Scotland only, by which machinery was to be set up to make possible the establishment of prohibition on a local basis.

Until 1914, then, the House of Commons spent many of its private Members' Fridays in debates, conducted with all the panoply of ardent political conflict, on great constitutional,

[1] Cf. F. S. L. Lyons, *The Irish Parliamentary Party, 1896–1910* (Faber, 1951), p. 222.

economic and social questions. The change came for the most part later on.

3. TRENDS AND INFLUENCES AT WORK, 1918-39

In the years between the wars there appear to have been two main factors in the situation, on the one hand the use to which Labour Members generally put good fortune in the ballot, and on the other hand the steady movement, which we have already noticed, on the part of Parliament as a whole towards a habitual restriction of balloted private Members' bills to narrower classes of uncontroversial subjects. In the long run, it was the second factor which was the predominant one.

A. *The Labour Members and their Party Bills*

The Labour Members of the 1920s and 1930s resembled their Irish predecessors in that they too most ardently desired certain reforms which they were themselves powerless to put into effect in the existing balance of the Parties. Even when Labour was in office, the Government could not pass measures through the Commons unless they were approved by the Liberals. The Labour Members had little opportunity for using Parliament for the education of public opinion except through the use of chances presented by the ballot for private Members' time—apart of course from the innumerable debates on unemployment that were initiated by amendments to the Address, etc., year after year.

During the 1920s and 1930s, then, it was the rule rather than the exception for the Labour Members who had obtained the highest places in the ballot to introduce bills which represented fundamental Labour Party policy. Indeed so well-accepted among them was the idea that Friday was a day for first-class debates on the pet projects of the Opposition that as late as 1936 so experienced a politician as Mr. Kirkwood apparently assumed that the debates should be closed, like any ordinary debate, by front-bench speeches, the only difference being that on the private Members' day the Opposition spokesman should have the last word.[1]

In 1945 some Labour Members still thought that the debates on the old Coal Nationalization Bills and other big party measures

---

[1] H.C. Debs., 27th November 1936, vol. 318, col. 781. Cf. below, p. 88.

INFLUENCES AT WORK IN 1918-39

had been very useful and had contributed towards 'a continuous education of the public and evolution of the idea'.[1] As late as 1949, one writer, himself a Labour Member, in an edition of a book published on the eve of the reintroduction of private Members' time, in dealing with the history of private Members' bills, remarked that it was the settled practice of the Labour Party to prepare a list of its own bills, and suggested that this habit was becoming general.[2] Mr. Herbert Morrison, on the other hand, who looked back with some scorn at the old nationalization debates on bills 'drafted by politicians',[3] held that if a matter was a live issue and really worth discussing, the Opposition could always get a debate through the usual channels.

A Prevention of Unemployment Bill was brought in in each of the sessions 1919, 1922, 1923, 1925, 1926 and 1927, and a bill for the nationalization of coal mines in 1924, 1925, 1936 and 1938. There were also in the 1920s and 1930s Labour bills aiming to prescribe conditions of employment, in relation to wages and to hours of work, in particular occupations and, in some cases, in general.

A certain shift in the objectives of Labour Members may be discerned after 1931. Instead of using good places in the ballot to declare, over and over again, to the people rather than to Parliament or to the Government, their articles of belief and their conviction that the whole economic system should be changed, they now tried to achieve more limited objectives by persuading the existing Government within the framework of the existing political situation.

Thus the Prevention of Unemployment Bill was heard of no more after 1930. But in each session from 1932 until the war, either the first or the second Labour Member in the ballot introduced a Workmen's Compensation Bill. Again, while in 1925 and 1926 Labour Members with good places in the ballot brought in bills providing for maximum hours of work in all industrial employment, the later maximum hours bills related to particular types of employment—that of 1928 for coal mines, one of 1933

---

[1] Select Committee on Procedure, H.C. 189-1 of 1945-6, Minutes of Evidence, Q. 3581. Cf. Q. 3598, 3656-63.
[2] Michael Stewart, *The British Approach to Politics*, 2nd edition, 1949, p. 130.
[3] H.C. 189-1 of 1945-6, op. cit., Q. 3586-7.

for shops, bills of 1934 and 1936 for offices, of 1937 for certain types of institutions, of 1938 for bakeries.

B. *Major Bills brought in by non-Labour Members*

The Labour Members did indeed set the pace in proposing large party bills in the 1920s and 30s, but they were not by any means alone in doing this at the beginning of the period. During the early 1920s Conservative back-benchers were fairly persistent in bringing forward bills to regulate Trade Unions in various ways, and particularly by preventing them from collecting contributions to political funds from members who did not specifically contract out of the political levy. Indeed, in 1925, before the ballot for private Members' time was held, it was announced that all the members of the Conservative Industrial group (of whom there were nearly 100) would take part, and that the Member who won the best place would bring in the Trade Union Bill.[1]

There were also some bills concerned with incidental issues of the great problem of Free Trade and Protection. A bill to compel the special marking of certain classes of imported goods, such as 'foreign' eggs, was frequently brought in in the 1920s, and in 1923 it passed its second reading by the substantial vote of 183 to 100, with the Government supporting it.[2] It was treated largely as a party matter. Mr. Graham moved the rejection of the bill and acted as a teller in the division. Similarly, a bill to encourage the use of British ingredients in the brewing of beer was introduced in 1930. Here the Labour Government, while approving the objectives, thought that the method proposed was unduly cumbersome. (Brewers who showed that they had used the specified quantities of British materials were to be allowed to use special labels.)[3] The Minister undertook to do what he could by unofficial action.

From various parts of the House there were proposals for

[1] *The Times*, 6th February 1925.
[2] H.C. Debs., 16th March 1923, vol. 161, col. 2046. The Labour and Liberal Members felt strongly enough against this measure to divide the House on a motion for a Committee of the whole House. The bill duly went to Standing Committee and was reported. The Government eventually took it over, but had to drop it through lack of time (H.C. Debs., 30th and 31st July, vol. 167, cols. 1031 and 1301).
[3] Ibid., 21st November 1930, vol. 245, col. 831.

major constitutional reforms, such as the extension of the franchise,[1] the introduction of Proportional Representation, and the regulation of the manner of voting in national and local elections. But these major proposals were heard of no more after 1927, partly for practical reasons, but partly, it may be, because the general conception, outside the Labour Party, of the proper function of private Members' bills was changing, and the views expressed by Mr. Baldwin in 1925 and by Lord Hugh Cecil in 1927 were winning general acceptance. The fact that the Conservative Party was securely in office, either alone or as the dominant partner in a coalition, with only slight interruptions during a long period, probably contributed something to this development. The majority of Conservative Members had comparatively little incentive for bringing forward partisan proposals.

C. *Summary*

In retrospect the tendency to use private Members' time in a more restricted way seems to have represented the true direction of parliamentary practice. The evidence for this is to be found not only from a study of the trend in the matter of the type of bills introduced, but also in other ways. We see the tendency for the number of Members voting to decline, for Ministers and Opposition leaders to take less and less part in the divisions,[2] and for the whole atmosphere of the debates to become less and less controversial. On many occasions, in discussions in committees on Procedure and in the debates on the bills themselves, we find the view put forward that private Members' bills are best when they deal with small and non-controversial problems. More and more the argument is brought forward, on bill after bill, that the matter in question is too important, too controversial, too difficult, or too complicated, to be dealt with in any other way than by a Government bill.

[1] On Mr. W. M. Adamson's big franchise bill of 1924, which proposed to give the vote to all women over 21, to abolish the business premises qualification, and to assimilate the local government franchise to that at parliamentary elections, the Duchess of Atholl unsuccessfully moved a reasoned amendment to the effect that such reforms should be introduced only after a conference between party spokesmen. The bill was given a second reading by the large majority of 288 votes to 72 (H.C. Debs., 29th February 1924, vol. 170, cols. 859-944). [2] Cf. Chapter III, below.

We may perhaps look to the 1920s as the period in which the evolution proceeded with almost revolutionary speed. Certainly it must be hard to find any individual speech in the history of Parliament which had so profound an effect on the habits and customs of politics as Mr. Baldwin's speech on the Trade Union Bill of 1925. The Bill, which sought to abolish 'contracting-out' and to regulate Trade Unions in other ways, was strongly supported by the mass of Conservative Members, but immediately after the opening speeches at the second reading debate Mr. Baldwin rose and moved an amendment to the effect that big and controversial measures such as this should not be brought forward as private Members' bills. Curiously enough, the text of Mr. Baldwin's motion was not, at the time, considered to be of much importance. Contemporary comment seems to have assumed that he was seeking to deal with a particular problem, and not to lay down a general principle with regard to the proper scope of private Members' bills; indeed, in the leading article of *The Times* on the day after the debate it was said merely that the terms of the Government motion were 'as good a ground for the purpose (of securing the bill's rejection) as any other'. The general principle was, then, considered as nothing more than something to serve the immediate purpose. The fact remains, however, that Mr. Baldwin carried the whole of his party with him on his amendment, and the rule which he expounded at that time, that big and controversial measures should not be introduced as private Members' bills, was generally obeyed by Conservatives throughout the rest of the inter-war period. We may, then, be justified in regarding Mr. Baldwin's speech as a turning point. It would of course be wrong to regard Mr. Baldwin as an innovator. On the one hand the principle which he laid down in 1925 had already found fairly wide acceptance before then, and on the other hand the Labour members did not, at the time at any rate, feel themselves to be bound by it.

The setting up of the Select Committee on Procedure (Unofficial Members' Business) of 1927, and the alteration of the distribution of the private Members' days in accordance with the Committee's recommendations, have an obvious importance in relation to the change in the character of the bills.[1] On the one hand it was because of a widespread feeling that private Members'

[1] Cf. above, p. 12.

bills should have a better chance of being passed into law without the need for the granting of facilities by the Government, that it was decided to give more days to the later stages; on the other hand the reform did in fact encourage Members to bring in bills of a 'constructive' type, which would have a real hope of being accepted by the House.

4. PRIVATE MEMBERS' BILLS SINCE 1948[1]

For ten years during and after the second world war no time at all was allowed for private Members' business, and when the time was at last restored in the session of 1948-9 it was soon clear which conception of its proper use had, for the time being at any rate, prevailed. Of the first twenty bills brought in, seven dealt with the welfare of animals, and among the rest there was not one which could be called a party-political matter, or indeed (except perhaps for two bills which aimed at forbidding hunting or coursing in various forms) which seemed likely to arouse really serious controversy of any kind. In the years since 1949 the same pattern can be observed, although Labour Members have kept the old traditions partly alive by their persistence in bringing in bills dealing with the intricate problems connected with industrial accidents. In 1951 there was indeed a party bill brought in by a Conservative, aiming to amend the recently-passed Transport Act so as to allow privately-owned lorries to ply for hire within a radius of sixty miles instead of twenty-five miles,[2] but this was little more than a piece of sport at the expense of the expiring Labour Government with its tiny majority. In fact the Conservatives succeeded in beating their opponents in the division on the second reading, and it was only by good attendance of their own supporters in the Standing Committee[3] that the Socialists were able to prevent the bill from making any further progress. (The Committee voted against each of the clauses.)

Apart from this and two other slight exceptions there were, up

---

[1] For a list of all the private Members' bills enacted in 1948-54, giving a brief statement of the purport of each bill, cf. Appendix D. For an analysis of the debates, cf. Appendix E.

[2] H.C. Debs., 23rd February 1951, vol. 484, cols. 1615-1708.

[3] The Government had a majority of one in the Standing Committee to which the bill was committed, instead of no majority as in the earlier Standing Committees of the 1950 Parliament. Cf. above, p. 33.

to the end of 1954, no partisan measures; nearly all the private Members' bills were genuine attempts to bring about reforms, sometimes of considerable social importance, in fields which are not the concern of the Parties as such. There was however a suggestion of a reverse in the trend in 1954-5, when some Labour Members' bills dealt with party matters.

It would be unwise to go so far as to assert that the habits of the last few years have established anything like a firm convention. It has to be recognized that the revolution in the political situation since 1945 would alone explain the change in practice since that time. Since 1945 there has been no longer an opposition party with the pre-war Labour Party's passionate faith in the necessity for social changes. During its five years in power, the Labour Government was able to carry out the great reforms about which it felt strongly, and since 1951 the Party has no longer had motives of the same order as before 1939 for pressing party measures in private Members' time. It is conceivable that the situation of the period between the wars may arise again at some time in the future, though it is perhaps only likely to arise through the presence of a large party which has been for a long time excluded from power, or which has never been in power.

A. *Examination of the Bills in Detail*

In 1949, when private Members' time was allowed for the first time since the war, it was not long before a small incident took place which most strikingly indicated the effects of ten years of control by the party machines. A bill to forbid the docking and nicking of horses' tails had passed its second reading, and in the Standing Committee the Members in charge of the bill, having taken official advice, proposed an amendment to exclude the operation of 'nicking' from the terms of the bill. The form of amendment was to omit the words 'docking and nicking', and to insert the word 'docking' only. The Committee accepted the first part of the amendment, by agreeing to negative the motion 'that the words proposed to be left out stand part', but some of those who voted were a little confused about the procedure. The Chairman had to explain the necessity for a second amendment (to insert 'docking'), but even so the Committee did not altogether follow what was happening, and in a division the new amendment was defeated by ten votes to five, mainly it would seem because there had been doubt about the purport of the first vote. At all events, this new decision had the effect of making the clause meaningless, and the sitting had to be suspended for a quarter of an hour to clear up the muddle. Such was the result when Members, after years of guidance and instruction from the Whips, had to fend for themselves amid the intricacies of committee procedure.[1]

Taking the bills of the session of 1948–9 first, we find that, of the 22 introduced, five were eventually passed. Two of the five were so uncontroversial that they demanded hardly any discussion at all,[2] and two others were passed with almost as little trouble in the House.[3] The Adoption Bill, when it was passed, made a fairly substantial change in the law, but it had for some time been generally agreed that a new law on these lines was necessary in order to make clearer the legal position with reference to the adoption of children.

The agreement on these five bills was so general, and their objects were so praiseworthy, that we might say in each case that the introducers were simply relieving the Government of a burden.

The majority of the private Members' bills of 1948–9, and all the controversial ones, failed to receive the Royal Assent. Two never had any chance at all, because of lack of time. These were the Statutory Instruments (Control) Bill and the Public Bodies (Admission of Press) Bill. Each of these appeared for second reading only two or three minutes before 4 o'clock, and could only have passed if, as with the Slaughter of Animals (Scotland) Bill, every Member present in the House had been prepared to let it go by without discussion. In fact the bills were both talked out, and no decision was ever taken on them.

[1] Official Report, Standing Committee 'E', 5th July 1949, cols. 4–6.
[2] Mr. Manningham-Buller's Law Reform (Miscellaneous Provisions) Bill and Major Ramsay's Slaughter of Animals (Scotland) Bill. Neither of these was debated on second reading in the Commons, though the Law Reform Bill did produce some discussion at its later stages. It was amended in the Lords, and the Lords' amendments were discussed in the Commons in Government time just before the end of the session.
[3] These were the Docking and Nicking of Horses Bill and the Married Women (Maintenance) Bill. The latter occupied the Standing Committee for three days.

One other bill that had a very short hearing at a second reading debate at the end of the day was Sir Thomas Moore's bill for the better protection of pit ponies. In this case the four minutes that were left for the bill were long enough for the Parliamentary Secretary to say that he already had the power, under existing laws, to make regulations to cover the proposals of the bill, and indeed that regulations were actually being prepared.[1] The bill may then be said to have achieved its object of goading the Government to make better use of the powers it already had. Although this is strictly speaking not the proper function of a bill, it is one that the proposer often intends.

Three bills were passed at the second reading, and went through the Standing Committee very late in the session, but made no further progress because no time was found for their later stages on the floor of the House.[2] These were the Pet Animals Bill, which the Government believed to be unnecessary, because the power to control pet shops already existed; the War Damage (Amendment) Bill, which the Government strongly resisted; and the Censorship of Plays Bill, on which the Government was neutral.

Each of these has its points of interest. Brigadier Peto's Pet Animals Bill aimed at regulating the conditions in pet shops, and he was able to cite many instances in which shameful cruelty and deliberate neglect of animals had gone unpunished under the existing law. The Bill was based on the extensive observations of the R.S.P.C.A., by which it was strongly supported. Mr. Younger, the Under-Secretary at the Home Office, replying on behalf of the Government, said that he was very doubtful whether there was any need for the Bill, with the 'rather considerable apparatus' that it sought to create for the repression of offences which he did not believe to be widespread.[3] He considered that the law should be as simple as possible, and for this reason was sceptical about this new proposal to circumscribe the liberty of the subject by statute, and to create a new apparatus of licences and inspecting officers with powers of entry. In spite of the Government's doubts, the Bill

[1] H.C. Debs., 18th March 1949, vol. 462, col. 2532.
[2] Cf. above, p. 37.
[3] H.C. Debs., 18th March 1949, vol. 462, col. 2472. The sponsors of the Bill mentioned several instances of cruelty or neglect, but Mr. Younger was impressed also by the fact that the police in London had not found any cause for complaints of this type.

was given a second reading without a division, but, as it never reached the report stage, there was no need for the Government later on to make any decision on the matter.

This was not the end of the affair. A bill backed by the R.S.P.C.A. will often have many supporters, and this bill was taken up by one of the Members successful in the ballot for the 1950–1 session (Mr. Russell). It eventually passed, with the Government's blessing, although the new Under-Secretary of State, Mr. de Freitas, repeated the same doubts as had been expressed by Mr. Younger.[1]

The Government did not find itself unduly embarrassed over the Spelling Reform Bill, which it opposed uncompromisingly. This was of course a genuinely non-party matter, and there was not even any concealed or implied party feeling about it. It happened too that Mr. Pitman, who proposed the Spelling Reform Bill, was a Conservative. In this case the Government's view was put forward by the Minister of Education, who mentioned the private discussions in which he had already been engaged. He had received Mr. Pitman and his friends, 'not enthusiastically, but I hope . . . courteously', and he had listened to all that Mr. Pitman had to say. He had undertaken to consider setting up a committee inside his Department to advise him about Mr. Pitman's ideas, but after hearing the opinion of his own experts informally he had decided not to set up any committee; he could already see the force of the arguments against any attempt to impose changes in English spelling by legislation. It is interesting, as we read the Minister's speech, to notice that he did not so much put forward arguments of the 'official' type, about the administrative difficulties involved, but rather met Mr. Pitman on his own ground, and argued against the proposal on the ground that it was essentially misconceived.[2]

Although the Minister had opposed the Bill so strongly in the debate, the Government evidently did not think it necessary to take any particular steps to kill it. Only two Ministers voted, both of them against the Bill, which was defeated by the very narrow

[1] It is interesting that for this bill, both in 1949 and in 1951, the proposer and seconder came from opposite sides of the House. This is a device which can usefully be employed with bills of this type, in order to emphasize their non-partisan character (H.C. Debs., 6th April 1951, vol. 486, cols. 519–609).
[2] H.C. Debs., 11th March 1949, vol. 462, cols. 1660–74.

margin of 87 votes to 84.¹ Perhaps this is an example of a case where a small but enthusiastic minority nearly carried its will; the great majority of Members were too little interested to bother to stay for the vote at all.

This bill too reappeared at a later session. Mr. Follick, who had already inaugurated another debate on spelling reform on the Navy Estimates, by moving that naval signals should be sent out in reformed spelling,² won the fifth place in the ballot for private Members' bills in the session of 1952–3, and this time there was a majority of 65 to 53 in favour of the second reading in spite of the fact that seventeen office-holders voted against it.³ The Conservative Government, like its predecessor, did not favour the introduction of such reforms in this way, but this time the Bill could only be stopped during the committee stage.

One of the private Members' bills of 1949 was withdrawn when the Government undertook itself to introduce a measure along the same lines and having the same objectives. This was the Safety of Employment (Employers' Liability) Bill, introduced by Mr. Piratin, one of the two Communists in the House, who won the first place in the ballot. The Bill's aim was to strengthen the law with reference to the duty of employers to take proper steps for protecting their employees against the danger of accident. The Minister of Labour, Mr. Isaacs, asked for the Bill to be withdrawn on the ground that its objects could be better achieved under legislation of the Government's own devising. As he put it: 'The Government feel that if we are going to legislate in that wide field with further protection for those already covered, it ought to be done by way of a Government bill prepared and produced by the Government with all the opportunities for consultation, examination and so on available to them.'⁴ The matter was already being considered by a committee appointed by the Home Office and the Scottish Office. Later on Mr. Isaacs gave an undertaking, not merely that the Government would make every effort to introduce the desired legislation during the current session, but also that, as Minister, he would, in preparing the Government's Bill, 'take into consultation any hon. Members who are interested in workmen's

---

¹ H.C. Debs., 11th March 1949, vol. 462, col. 1686.
² Ibid., 6th March 1952, vol. 497, cols. 777 ff. Cf. above, p. 14, *n.* 4.
³ Ibid., 27th February 1953, vol. 511, cols. 2417–500.
⁴ Ibid., 11th February 1949, vol. 461, col. 688.

compensation and get their views'.[1] In view of these undertakings, Mr. Piratin withdrew the Bill.[2]

Among other bills of 1948–9 we may notice the Analgesia in Childbirth Bill, which was ardently supported by a few Labour Members but opposed by the Government because it might upset the balance of the National Health Service which the Minister of Health wished to treat as a single whole. The Bill was in general well received by Conservatives, who saw the debate on it as an opportunity for drawing attention to shortcomings in the actual working of the Health Service. Something of a partisan tone crept into the debate for this reason, and during the later stages it was as though the Bill had been an Opposition measure. Two of its leading Socialist supporters, Mrs. Castle and Mrs. Manning, took no part in the proceedings in the Standing Committee (of which they were members), and Mrs. Manning, having spoken for the third reading, abstained from voting in the final division, which was on party lines, and in which the Bill was defeated.[3]

There were also two bills backed mainly by Labour Members but opposed by the Government. The Hairdressers' Registration Bill caused the Government a good deal of trouble before it was defeated at the third reading stage, but the Hunting and Coursing Bill aroused such strong opposition among Conservatives that it was easily defeated. The proceedings on these two bills present so many interesting features that they seem to merit fuller examination than can conveniently be given here. (Cf. Appendix B.)

There was no time for private Members' bills in the short session of 1950. The next session, in which the Labour Government, in the last year of its life, was faced by a triumphant Conservative minority, produced three partisan measures proposed by Conservatives. The first of these was Mr. J. R. Bevins' Transport (Amendment) Bill, which has already been mentioned.[4] The second was Mr. N. Davies' Trade Union Bill, which was brought forward in order to attack the principle of the closed shop. Little was heard of the Bill, however, because Mr. Davies did not have a good place in the ballot, and had to be content with the second place on 6th April, on which day the debate on the Pet Animals

---

[1] Ibid., col. 717. [2] Ibid., col. 718.
[3] Ibid., 8th July 1949, vol. 466, col. 2588.
[4] Cf. above, p. 55.

Bill was kept alive until just before 4 p.m., so that Mr. Davies only had time to say a few sentences before the adjournment. A similar fate befell Mr. Marples' Representation of the People Bill, whose object was to make less rigid the restriction on the use of motor-cars at election time in certain types of constituency. However much its proposers might protest that this was not a partisan measure, it was inevitably regarded as such by Labour Members. It received a fifteen-minute hearing on 9th February, after the Common Informers Bill, before being talked out, and then had the good fortune to get a second hearing, this time of an hour's duration, on one of the last four private Members' days, after the two other bills down for that day had passed through their report and third reading stages.[1] It was again talked out.

Mrs. White's Bill to bring in some reforms of the divorce laws was given a second reading by a good majority (131 votes to 60), after the closure had been carried by the narrowest of margins (102 votes to 99). The Attorney-General thought that the bill attempted to deal with only a part of a large problem which should be treated as a whole, after a good deal more consideration than could be given in the parliamentary stages of a bill.[2] Although the bill had a good majority in the division on the second reading, it was abandoned at the committee stage.

For the rest, the successful bills of 1950–1 were mainly good examples of constructive, useful, uncontroversial proposals. The first, second, third and sixth places in the ballot were won by Mr. Monslow, Mr. Kinley, Mr. Heald and Mr. Russell, who brought in respectively the Fraudulent Mediums Bill, the New Streets Bill, the Common Informers Bill and the Pet Animals Bill. All these measures were passed into law, helped on their way by the goodwill of the House and the collaboration of the Government.

Four other private Members' bills were enacted during the session without having been debated on second reading in the Commons. Of these the Slaughter of Animals Bill and the Fireworks Bill dealt with matters of general import, but went forward without much difficulty. The Slaughter of Animals Bill had a

---

[1] H.C. Debs., 9th February 1951, vol. 483, cols. 2162–7 and 20th April 1951, vol. 486, cols. 2227–50.
[2] Ibid., 9th March 1951, vol. 485, cols. 1003–6. Cf. below, pp. 104 and 124.

third reading debate of over an hour and a half's duration; the Fireworks Bill was amended in the House of Lords after the last of the private Members' days in the Commons, so the consideration of the Lords' amendments had to be taken in Government time just before the summer recess. The two other bills which received the Royal Assent dealt with very narrow issues. The Criminal Law Bill was concerned with the 'white slave' traffic, and the National Assistance Bill gave the appropriate authorities power to remove a person from his home without a court order in certain circumstances if the Medical Officer of Health and one other doctor certified that such removal without delay was necessary. The Bill arose out of a case in which a lady had died after she had refused the urgently-needed assistance which had been offered her, and which under the existing law she could not be compelled to accept until a week had elapsed.

For the rest, the session was peculiarly unkind to bills introduced on low places in the ballot. The winner of the eighth place, Mrs. Hill, brought in the Deserted Wives Bill, on which the closure was defeated after a debate of nearly three hours, and Major McCallum and Colonel Hutchison saw their bills talked out. Apart from the bills which have already been mentioned, none of the other balloted bills was debated at all. It is only fair to mention, however, that on 4th May, the second of the days on which precedence was given to the later stages of bills, the House adjourned at 1.20 p.m., having by then disposed of the later stages of four bills and the second readings of two others. It would presumably have been possible for at least one of the nine bills still awaiting second reading to be brought forward and dealt with on that day.

In 1951–2 the most interesting of the bills brought in was Mr. Lever's Defamation Bill, whose aim was to clear up some of the anomalies in the law of libel. It eventually received the Royal Assent amid plenteous eulogy, and was even called by one commentator 'the most important measure of the whole session'. Certainly it has by common consent taken its place along with Sir Alan Herbert's Matrimonial Proceedings Bill as an example of a really important Act of Parliament brought in originally as a private Members' bill.

The need for legislation in this sphere had been widely felt for a considerable time, and as long before as 1948 the Government had been asked, at Question time, what measures it intended to take to implement the recommendations of the Porter Committee.[1] On that occasion the Prime Minister replied that the Government had not yet decided which, if any, of those recommendations ought to be accepted. There was no action from the Government for three years, and the initiative was left to private Members.

Mr. Lever's Bill was given a second reading without a division.[2] In the Standing Committee, however, the discussion of clauses and amendments occupied ten sittings and a total time of some 24 hours. Although its sponsor was a Labour Member, nearly all the difficulties were brought up by Members on the Labour benches. Mr. Silverman's interventions occupied about 53 columns of the Official Report, and Mr. Hale's about 26, as compared with the Attorney-General's 15 columns and the Solicitor-General's 21. Sir L. Ungoed-Thomas, a former Labour Solicitor-General, was responsible for 27 columns, and Mr. Lever himself, in dealing with the points brought forward, for 88. In all, the speeches of the Labour Members of the Committee, excluding Mr. Lever, occupied some 183 columns, as compared with 37 columns taken by unofficial Conservative Members.

There were altogether ten divisions in the Standing Committee, of which none except those concerned with group libel produced votes entirely on party lines. The proposal to make it possible for a statement to be a libel against a whole group or class of people, such as 'the Jews', was defeated by a solid block of Conservatives against Labour Members, with Mr. Lever himself abstaining.

The report stage occupied the whole of the sitting of 9th May, which was the first of the days provided for the later stages of private Members' bills, and was still incomplete at 4 p.m.[3] On the second day, the other bills which had already emerged from the Standing Committee had precedence. The report and third reading stages of three of them were disposed of by 1.49 p.m., but on the fourth the House was counted out. The next day for the later stages of private Members' bills was not until 27th June, by

[1] H.C. Debs., 1st November 1948, vol. 457, col. 512. The Report of the Committee on the Law of Defamation (Cmd. 7536) had then been recently published.
[2] Ibid., 1st February 1952, vol. 495, cols. 507–94.
[3] Ibid., 9th May 1952, vol. 500, cols. 723–800.

PRIVATE MEMBERS' BILLS SINCE 1948

which time a large number of bills had accumulated. They were all uncontroversial, however, and on only one of the six was anything at all said on report. They were all finally disposed of in under one hour, and the Defamation Bill had almost four hours left for its report and third reading stages.[1] The report stage took until almost 4 o'clock, but the third reading was approved without a debate, and the Bill thus passed through the Commons without needing to rely on the provision of time by the Government.

By this time it was clear that the Bill could not be returned from the Lords to the Commons in time to have the Lords' amendments, if any, taken on the last of the private Members' days, 11th July, which was then only a fortnight ahead. The second reading in the Lords was in fact taken on 15th July, the committee stage on the 28th and the report on the 31st. Lords Jowitt and Silkin proposed numerous amendments, but withdrew most of them. Some amendments were put into the Bill, however, particularly one to restore a provision which had already been defeated in the Commons, to extend qualified privilege to reports of proceedings in foreign Parliaments, provided that the reports should be fair, accurate and without malice.

The Lords' amendments were debated in the House of Commons on 24th October, in Government time provided during the last few days before prorogation. The amendment on the extension of qualified privilege was negatived without a division after an hour's debate, in which the Attorney General had suggested that this should be done.[2]

Apart from the Defamation Act, the session of 1951-2 produced several praiseworthy minor reforms, relating to the compulsory provision of fireguards on heating appliances, to the regulation of the practice of hypnotism, and to the further extension of the powers of the authorities to take measures to prevent cock-fighting, a 'sport' which had first been made illegal a hundred years before. The session also produced the first successful attempt since the war to have the House counted out through lack of a quorum on a private Members' bill.

One of the successful measures of the session deserves special mention because it evidently supplied a rather urgent need, which might well have been attended to earlier by the Government. A

[1] H.C. Debs., 27th June 1952, vol. 502, cols. 2712-86.
[2] Ibid., 24th October 1952, vol. 505, col. 1537.

A HISTORICAL SURVEY OF PRIVATE MEMBERS' BILLS

case argued in the Courts in 1947 had shown that Crown property was not covered by the Rent Restriction Acts. Since then certain persons had been buying up the leases of some houses in the South-East suburbs of London, evicting the tenants and reletting the properties at whatever rents they would command on a free market. The Government might have been expected to do something to prevent such an evident abuse, but found no opportunity for doing so. Finally, in the session of 1951-2, when Sir Austin Hudson, the Member for one of the constituencies affected, won a place in the ballot (for the first time since he entered Parliament in 1922), he used it for the introduction of a bill on the subject.[1] In his second reading speech he acknowledged that he could not have produced the bill, with its complicated drafting, unless he had had 'the goodwill and friendly co-operation of the Department concerned'.

The session of 1952-3 produced several bills involving lively controversy on matters of fairly substantial importance. These were the Press Council Bill, the Sunday Observance Bill, the Criminal Justice Bill, and the Simplified Spelling Bill. The last of these has already been mentioned above.[2] The other three were all defeated at the second reading, each having been debated for a whole sitting. With the Press Council Bill the opponents were so strenuous in their opposition that the proposers had to move the closure, which was lost by a narrow majority. The voting was entirely on party lines. With the other two the main interest was in the voting at the division.

The Sunday Observance Bill, which proposed to relax the existing law on Sabbath observance, was defeated on second reading by 281 votes to 57, with both Conservatives and Labour Members showing majorities against the Bill, but another division was held on Mr. Eric Fletcher's proposal that there should be a broad enquiry into the question of the laws on the Sabbath. Mr. Fletcher had argued that Parliament should not embark on such a reform as this without first taking steps to inform itself on the state of public feeling on the matter. His proposal for an enquiry was defeated, on a free vote, by the narrow margin of 172 votes to 164. This vote has a special interest, because it strikingly illus-

[1] H.C. Debs., 29th February 1952, vol. 496, col. 1583. The debate on the second reading of this bill took one and a half hours.
[2] P. 60.

PRIVATE MEMBERS' BILLS SINCE 1948

trates an anomaly in the British system of government which is produced by the fact that Scottish and Northern Irish Members can and do vote on questions which concern England and Wales only. (The anomaly works the other way round, too.) 21 of the Members who voted against Mr. Fletcher's proposal, but only 11 of those who voted for it, represented constituencies outside England and Wales. Thus if all Scottish and Northern Irish Members had abstained, the proposal for an enquiry, instead of being defeated, would have been carried by 153 votes to 151. Among English and Welsh Labour Members the voting was mainly on party lines; the 164 in favour included only 33 Conservatives and the 172 against only 15 Labour Members, of whom ten were from Wales and two from Scotland.[1]

The voting on the Criminal Justice Bill, which came up for second reading on 13th February, was interesting because this, like the Hunting and Coursing Bill of three years earlier, was well supported on the Government back benches but opposed by the Government itself and by many Opposition Members. The Bill proposed to restore the power of the Courts to order corporal punishment for certain offences. 63 Conservatives voted for it and 52 against it. The 52 included the Home Secretary, and no office-holders voted for the Bill. But while among Conservatives there was a majority in favour, the Labour Members were solidly against the Bill. 106 of them voted against it, and not one in its favour.[2]

Some less contentious measures received the Royal Assent. These were a bill to safeguard farmers and others who might shoot dogs for chasing sheep, a bill to permit the parking of vehicles at night without lights in certain circumstances in lighted streets, a bill for the regulation of the wills of personnel of the Navy and Marines, and a measure for the reorganization of the Royal Pharmaceutical Society. The session was noteworthy for the fact that while only one of the first six bills introduced under the ballot went on to receive the Royal Assent, the bills introduced by winners of low places were on the whole very successful. Six of these passed into law, besides four bills which had not been introduced under the ballot at all. Of the total of eleven private Members' bills enacted, all but four passed through second reading unopposed.

[1] H.C. Debs., 30th January 1953, vol. 510, cols. 1337-438.
[2] Ibid., 13th February 1953, vol. 511, cols. 758-846.

The session of 1953–4 seems, in retrospect, to have been remarkable above all for the expeditiousness with which the balloted bills were disposed of, although one of the days allotted for second readings was lost because the previous day's sitting lasted all of Thursday night and on into the Friday morning.[1] One of the remaining five days was taken up entirely with a bill which was in some ways in the tradition of the old Labour Members' bills of the 1930s (though hardly of the 1920s). This was Mr. William Paling's bill to bring in a large and ambitious reform of the rules for the promotion of safety in employment. The debate continued until just before 4 o'clock, when it became evident that a Conservative intended to talk the measure out. The closure was therefore moved and the question on it was put, just as had happened on the party bills of the pre-war years. The voting was entirely on party lines, and several Labour leaders, including Mr. Attlee and Mr. Bevan, took the trouble to vote, but the general enthusiasm of Labour Members was so slight that they could not muster the 100 votes needed for the closure, which was lost by 82 votes to 75.[2] On the remaining four days for second readings 13 bills were disposed of after debate. On the third day, 12th February, no less than four bills were given their second reading by 2.36 p.m.[3] and the Pool Betting Bill, which had been talked out on an earlier day, was able to get another hearing and to pass its second reading stage as the fifth bill of the day.

The committee, report and the third reading stages were in general dealt with no less quickly. The whole programme of bills which had come up for second reading during the first six allotted days was completed by 1.53 p.m. on 21st May, the next to last of the days given to the later stages.[4] The last day, 25th June, was therefore used for second readings of bills not yet reached.[5]

[1] Cf. above, p. 22.
[2] H.C. Debs., 26th February 1954, vol. 524, cols. 706–96.
[3] Ibid., 12th February 1954, vol. 523, cols. 1513–79. The four bills dealt with by 2.36 were the Protection of Animals (Anæsthetics) Bill (79 minutes), the Protection of Animals (Amendment) Bill (which aimed to strengthen the sanctions against cruelty) (60 minutes), the Coroners Bill (31 minutes) and the Law Reform (Miscellaneous Provisions) Bill (40 minutes).
[4] H.C. Debs., 21st May 1954, vol. 527, col. 2523.
[5] The Ministers of the Crown (Fisheries) Bill, which was given a second reading, and the Theatrical Companies Bill, which was talked out (H.C. Debs., 5s, vol. 529, cols. 765–860).

PRIVATE MEMBERS' BILLS SINCE 1948

One very striking point about this session is that among many quiet and generally uncontroversial measures the only bill to arouse little enough interest to be counted out was one on a subject which was an old favourite among the stormy and exciting first-class debates of the years before 1914 and the 1920s. This was Mr. Grimston's Representation of the People Bill, whose aim was to introduce Proportional Representation, not, admittedly, in the country as a whole, but in Mr. Grimston's own constituency of St. Albans. The House showed its indifference (and perhaps hostility) by not even giving Mr. Grimston a chance to set forth his arguments. Within ten minutes of the opening of his speech the Speaker's attention was called to the absence of a quorum, and after two minutes more the necessary forty Members were still not in the Chamber.[1] The House was adjourned and half a sitting was lost.

One bill of the session aroused a great deal of public attention and controversy. This was the Pool Betting Bill which, as has been seen, received a second reading after the unauspicious adventure of being talked out the first time it came up. Its aim was to compel the promoters of football pools to publish their accounts so that the public might have some information about the proportion of their investment that found its way back into the pockets of the investors. The proceedings on this Bill illustrate the importance of private transactions between the proposers of a reform and the interests most closely concerned with it. The pool promoters could hardly be expected to welcome the Bill, and during its early stages there was a battle of public questionnaires, conducted by the pool promoters and by newspapers. The pool promoters claimed that the replies which they received showed that their investors evidently did not feel the need of the protection that the Bill sought to give them, but other questionnaires, conducted in other ways, produced different results. At any rate, after the Bill had been given a second reading in the Commons, and a generally good reception by the Press, the promoters decided to collaborate in making the Bill workable, and they agreed to meet the backers of the Bill. Eventually the Bill was passed in a form which the promoters declared to be acceptable to themselves.[2]

[1] H.C. Debs., 26th March 1954, vol. 525, col. 1602.
[2] It received the Royal Assent on 4th June 1954 (H.C. Debs., vol. 528, col. 1600).

The session of 1954-5 was brought to a premature conclusion by the dissolution of Parliament on 6th May 1955. By this time only the first five of the Fridays allocated for private Members' bills had been used for such bills; on 20th April an order was passed taking all the remaining time for the Government. Nevertheless, the Government provided facilities for some of the private Members' bills which had already passed through their earlier stages.

The bills of the session showed a certain tendency to revert to subjects rather larger and more controversial than had been usual in 1949-54. On four of the five days the first bill down was debated for the whole sitting. Four of the first six places in the ballot were won by Labour Members, all of whom introduced bills backed only by party colleagues and unlikely to be received with much enthusiasm by the Government. Two of these bills were distinctly controversial in their aims. Of the two Conservatives among the first six in the ballot the only one to get a hearing was Mr. Nabarro, who for years had been fighting determinedly for the better use of fuel. His Clean Air Bill, though not in essence controversial, dealt with large and complicated questions.

The two most controversial measures both produced debates leading to divisions. The Government of Wales Bill, though in one sense of limited interest, in another sense raised fundamental issues. This revival, the first for many years, of the issue of home rule for a part of the kingdom, might have been expected to produce the same kind of enthusiasm on both sides as had been produced by the home rule bills of the past. Public discussion of the subject in Scotland and Wales has, after all, been very widespread in recent years. Scottish Members interested in Scottish home rule were sympathetic to the bill, and six of them, all Labour Members, put their names down in support. The debate on the second reading did indeed last all day, but aroused so little general interest that only 62 Members voted in the division, 48 of them against the Bill.[1] The reply to the debate on behalf of the Government was at least given by the Home Secretary, but he was Major Lloyd-George, who would hardly be expected to delegate his function in a Welsh debate.

The Leasehold Enfranchisement Bill dealt with a controversial matter, and in this case one about which the Labour Party had

[1] *Weekly Hansard*, 4th March 1955, cols. 2447-536.

been concerning itself for some time. The organization of the debate, with the Attorney-General beginning to speak just before 3 p.m., followed by Mr. David Grenfell and Sir Lynn Ungoed-Thomas, a former Solicitor-General, had some of the features of an Opposition, rather than of a private Member's, occasion.[1] On this Bill the closure was moved. Only 38 Conservatives (including three members of the Cabinet) voted against it, and they were easily outnumbered by the 85 Labour and two Liberal Members who voted for it in a division which entirely followed party lines. It is noteworthy, however, that even on this matter the Labour Members as a whole were so lukewarm in their enthusiasm that there were not the 100 present who would have been needed if the closure was to be carried.

Mr. Short's bill to empower Local Authorities to run contract carriages and to subsidize the travel of certain deserving classes of people was debated mainly on party lines and received rather unsympathetically by the Government spokesman, but it was nevertheless allowed to be given a second reading without a division.[2] During his speech Mr. Short stated most emphatically that 'neither the Transport group of the Labour Party, nor any other person in the Labour Party or outside', had advised him on what the Bill should contain, or how it should be arranged. The Bill went forward and passed through Standing Committee, and the Government, which could easily have let the Bill die a natural death owing to the dissolution, provided facilities for the later stages. The Bill received the Royal Assent on 6th May, just before prorogation.[3]

The Non-Industrial Employment Bill, proposed by Mr. H. Davies, was a measure of enormous scope.[4] Its aim was no less than 'to make statutory provisions relating to the health, welfare and safety at places of employment other than those regulated by the Factories Acts or the Mines and Quarries Act of 1954'. It was based on the report of the Gowers Committee, which was issued in 1949 after three years of enquiry and consultation. For the past six years, in the words of Mr. Davies, 'the T.U.C. and the unions concerned had been urging Governments to introduce

[1] *Weekly Hansard*, 18th March 1955, cols. 1623–710.
[2] Ibid., 18th February 1955, cols. 757–816.
[3] Ibid., 6th May 1955, col. 2053.
[4] Ibid., 1st April 1955, cols. 685–782.

legislation'. On the Government side the debate was treated as an important one. The Home Secretary was unable to be present, but made his apologies; the reply from the Government front bench was made by the Minister of Agriculture. Not surprisingly, he said that he thought that the subject could best be dealt with in a Government bill, and indeed that the Government did intend to introduce a bill itself as soon as it could manage to do so. Just before 4 o'clock a Conservative Member suggested that the Bill might be withdrawn, but the proposers preferred to let it go forward. The questions on the closure and on the second reading were put and agreed to without any division.

As the Non-Industrial Employment Bill was given its second reading on the last of the private Members' days before the announcement of the dissolution, its passage through second reading did not raise any difficulties with the committee and later stages. If the session had proceeded in the ordinary way, however, and if the Bill had had to be fully dealt with in the Standing Committee, the Committee would have had before it a more complicated and difficult subject than has ever been successfully dealt with in committee as a private Member's bill. In the previous session the Mines and Quarries Bill, a Government measure involving probably less difficulty than Mr. Davies' bill, had occupied the Standing Committee for 26 sittings. The Non-Industrial Employment Bill could hardly have been dealt with more expeditiously than this, so if it had continued on its way it might well have occupied the private Members' bills Standing Committee for the whole of the rest of the session.

Mr. Nabarro's Clean Air Bill, which came up for second reading on the first of the private Members' days,[1] was also most ambitious in scope. But the Bill was brought in with the purpose of urging the Government to take action itself; it would hardly be practicable for a measure involving so many interests, creating such extensive new powers of inspection and control, and requiring such careful and detailed preparation, to be dealt with entirely as a private Members' bill. Mr. Nabarro did say in his introductory speech that he would only withdraw the Bill if the Government would give an assurance that they would introduce a comprehensive measure during the current session. That assurance was given, and Mr. Nabarro, having gained what he wanted,

[1] *Weekly Hansard*, 4th February 1955, cols. 1426–514. Cf. below, pp. 131 f.

withdrew his Bill, but the session ended before the Government had had time to fulfil its promise. (See note on p. 74.)

The only other bill to get a hearing was Sir Eric Errington's Lotteries Bill, which was talked out after a debate of an hour and a half.[1] A highly controversial Agricultural and Industrial Rates Bill was brought in one minute before 4 o'clock on 4th February, but this can scarcely be counted as a debate. For the rest, a few uncontroversial measures were allowed to go forward as unopposed bills.

B. *Conclusions*

The experience since 1945 is perhaps as yet too short for us to attempt to draw from it any firm conclusion about the trend of parliamentary institutions, but at any rate such evidence as there is points mainly in the same direction. The tendency towards concentration on non-partisan measures, which we already observed before 1939, seemed, until 1954–5, to have been maintained and reinforced. The suggestion of a reversal in that session, however, shows how dangerous it is to attempt to predict the behaviour of the House of Commons. Even these bills can hardly be said to represent a return to the habits of the 1920s or even of the 1930s. The debates have still conformed to the peculiar pattern of most modern private Members' debates, without party speeches from the Opposition front bench. It is conceivable that we will at some future time be faced again with a situation in which a group passionately desires big reforms, so that its members use places in the ballot to propose those reforms; for the present, however, it appears that the long-run tendency is for private Members' bills to be removed from the sphere of party controversy. This tendency is an aspect of a general development in the character of Parliament, itself related to the increase in the strength of party discipline. As the Government comes to have firmer control over the process of decision in all matters, so the House of Commons comes less and less to feel itself able to make large decisions on its own account. Whenever there is a point of any really serious difficulty raised on a private Member's bill, somebody says at some stage 'This is too large a matter for the House to decide itself. Let the Government establish a committee or some other

[1] *Weekly Hansard*, 18th February 1955, cols. 816–42.

machinery whereby it may find out for itself what are all the arguments and the opinions on both sides of the question, let it allow opponents to confront one another in argument, and then let it finally decide, as far as possible in accordance with the wishes of the interested parties, and come to Parliament with recommendations based on its discussions and on the arguments that it has heard.' Although we often hear complaints against the stifling discipline of the division lobbies, it is by now fairly widely recognized that a free vote of the House, not founded on a responsible opinion of the Government, is too haphazard a way of deciding a difficult or complicated problem, and indeed has defects of the same order as the referendum.

Note on the Session of 1955-6.

It was in the following session, less than a year after the debate on Mr. Nabarro's bill, that the Government fulfilled its promise to bring in a Clean Air Bill of its own. The Bill received a second reading without a division on 3rd November 1955 (*Weekly Hansard*, cols. 1225-337), though Mr. Nabarro and many of his supporters complained that the Bill was inadequate in many respects.

Chapter III

THE INTEREST SHOWN IN THE DEBATES

THE changes in the character of the bills introduced, and of the debates on them, are well illustrated by a consideration of some concrete facts about them. A controversial measure is obviously more likely to be decided by a division than an uncontroversial one, and is also more likely to produce a debate lasting all day on the second reading. Again, the more controversial the bill, the greater, as a rule, the number of Members likely to vote in the division.

It is proposed in this chapter to try to illustrate graphically the changes of the last fifty years, by presenting tables based on comparative figures relating to such matters as the length of the debates on particular bills, the readiness of the House to divide, the number of Members voting in the divisions, and the frequency with which the House has been counted out.

1. THE INCIDENCE OF ALL-DAY DEBATES

On the whole the more controversial bills lead to longer debates than the less controversial. A really controversial measure, whether it relates to party differences or not, is likely to produce a debate lasting all day. A measure of the more 'constructive' type, which does not arouse violent opposition and which has a real chance of being passed into law, is likely to have its second reading stage disposed of more quickly.

THE INTEREST SHOWN IN THE DEBATES

The tendency towards a greater concentration on uncontroversial bills is clearly illustrated by Table 1, which shows for each session since 1903 the number of days devoted to second readings of private Members' bills, and the number of such days on which the first bill down for debate was debated for the whole of the sitting. The same table also shows, for each Parliament in the period under review, the number of all-day second reading debates expressed as a proportion of the total number of Fridays devoted to the second readings of private Members' bills.

The table shows that, in the long run, there has been a fairly steady decline in the incidence of long debates. In the twelve sessions before 1914 nearly three-quarters of the Fridays devoted to second readings produced in each case an all-day debate on the first bill brought forward on the day, while between the wars the proportion declined to about half. Since 1948 it has declined to about a third.

When we look at the figures in greater detail, we can observe some short-term fluctuations. Before 1914 the proportion of all-day debates was highest in 1909–14, which was a period of particularly acute controversy between the Parties. The increase of all-day debates on private Members' bills during these years probably reflects this fact to some extent. Between the wars the general picture is one of fluctuations between Parliaments rather than of a steady decline, with a tendency for the proportion of all-day debates to be high in the years 1923–6 and again, though to a somewhat smaller extent, in 1935–9. Reasons for this will be suggested later.

2. THE INCIDENCE OF DIVISIONS

If we turn from a study of the number of private Members' Fridays producing all-day debates on single bills to a study of the incidence of divisions, and of the numbers voting in the divisions, the figures tell much the same story. Table 2 shows in its second column, for each Parliament, the average number of private Members' bills decided by a division on second reading in each session. The third and fourth columns show the incidence of divisions producing large numbers of Members voting.

Before we examine the figures, a word must be said about the method used in compiling them. It has seemed, in the first place,

TABLE I
THE DECLINE IN THE TENDENCY OF PARTICULAR PRIVATE MEMBERS'
BILLS TO PRODUCE ALL-DAY DEBATES, 1903–54

Session.	No. of Fridays on which second readings of private Members' bills had precedence.	Days spent entirely on one bill No.	%
1903	9	6	
4	10	5	58·2
5	12	7	
6	10	6	
7	11	5	
8	13	8	63·0
9	9	8	
10	3	2	
11	6	4	
12	9	8	
13	6	6	84·8
14	12	10	
20	11	5	
21	5	2	
22	6	2	50·0
23	9	7	
24	12	10	83·3
24–25	11	6	
26	10	6	
27	11	5	50·0
28	10	4	
29–30	14	6	
30–31	13	4	37·0
32–33	12	4	
33–34	10	6	45·5
35–36	7	4	
36–37	11	6	
37–38	13	10	53·5
38–39	12	6	
48–49	7	2	
50–51	6	2	30·8
51–52	5	1	
52–53	6	3	
53–54	5	1	37·5
54–55	5	4	

Notes: The precentages are expressed for each Parliament separately, except for the short Parliaments of 1910, 1923, and 1950–51, which are taken jointly with their predecessors.

Sessions in which there were no balloted private Members' bills are excluded.

more useful to indicate the number of divisions in which over 200 and over 300 Members voted, than simply to give the averages session by session. In the second place, we must remember that a particular bill often produces two or three, and occasionally even more, divisions on second reading. There may be a division on the closure, one on the main question, and one on a motion to commit to a Committee of the whole House. We want to take into account only one division on each bill. In cases where there are several divisions on the same bill, the number voting generally varies a little between the divisions.

Particularly if there is a big majority on one side, some of the Members who have voted in the first division may decide that it is clear which way the final result will go, and accordingly depart rather than go through the same tedious process of passing through the lobby a second or a third time. Again, the second division may sometimes produce a bigger number voting than the first. If the first is on the closure there may be some Members who abstain, but then, the closure having been carried, vote on the second reading. In some cases there may be a successful division on the closure and no division at all on the question on the second reading or on the amendment to the main question. In view of these difficulties, we have followed a procedure which may seem to be a little arbitrary, and based the table on whichever division produced the largest number of Members voting, except in a few cases where it has seemed that considerations unrelated to the merits of the bill in question have been responsible for the size of the vote. For the sake of convenience, this division, which is generally the first of a series, can be called the 'crucial' division on the bill in question. The matter is of little importance for the main results of the survey, because the differences between the successive divisions on any bill are very slight—in the order of one or two per cent.

The table shows that the proportion of Fridays producing divisions declined in much the same way as the proportion producing all-day debates. From over three-quarters of the days in the years before 1914 it fell to about two-thirds during the period between the wars and to two-fifths after 1948. Here too there were temporary increases in the middle 1920s and after the general election of 1935.

It is when we look at the number of bills which produced

votes of over 200 and over 300, that we notice the most striking change over the years. Before 1914 well over half the Fridays under consideration produced divisions in which over 200 Members voted. During the 1920s and 1930s the proportion was well under half, but the fluctuations which we have already noticed with regard to the total number of divisions were much more

TABLE 2

NUMBERS OF DIVISIONS AND NUMBERS VOTING ON PRIVATE MEMBERS' BILLS ON FRIDAYS

Period.	Average no. of days per session for second readings of P.M. bills.	No. of second readings of P.M. bills decided by divisions. Average per session.	Average no. of 'crucial' divisions on P.M. bills (second readings) per session producing	
			over 300 votes	over 200 votes
1903–5	10·3	9	4 (3·3)	7·7 (6·0)
1906–10	9·2	7·2	2 (1·2)	5·6 (5·0)
1910–14	8·25	6	1·5 (1·5)	4·25 (2·5)
1920–23	8·75	6·5	0·75	2·75
1924	12	10	8	10
1924/5–28	10·5	6·5	2·5	5·25
1929/30–30/1	13·5	5	0	1
1932/3–33/4	11	6	0	0·5
1935/6–38/9	10·75	7	0·5	4·5
1948/9–50/1	6·5	2·5	1·0	1·0
1951/2–54/5	5·25	2·0	0·25	0·5

Notes: Sessions in which there was no time allotted for private Members' bills are excluded from these calculations.

The figures in brackets after the numbers voting for the period before 1914 are the figures obtained by taking 330 and 220 as the basis of the calculations, instead of 300 and 200 respectively.

Before 1914, on the most controversial bills debated, the Speaker refused to put the question on the closure, so no division could take place. Had it not been for this, the figures for this period would presumably have been higher.

violent. In 1920–3 just over a third of the private Members' days for second readings brought out over 200 Members to vote, but the proportion rose greatly in 1924 and remained high in the first part of Mr. Baldwin's second administration. It fell to almost nothing at all from 1929 to 1935, and then rose again to nearly half in the 1935 Parliament. After 1948 it fell again so much that only an occasional exceptional bill produced a vote of as many as 200 Members.

When we turn to column 4, which shows the incidence of

divisions in which over 300 Members voted, we find a similar decline, with the difference that the 1935 Parliament this time failed to produce any striking increase. Since 1929 divisions bringing out half the House to vote have been almost unknown. It must be remembered, of course, that before 1914 the membership of the House of Commons was larger than after the Great War, when the Irish Members had withdrawn. But if, to make allowance for this fact, we substitute 220 for 200 and 330 for 300 as the basic figures for our calculations for the pre-war period, the relative result is not materially altered. The fact remains that the figures illustrate very clearly the change from a time when the House treated private Members' days in much the same way as it treated ordinary days, to the present, when it regards Friday debates very much as second-class debates from which most Members normally absent themselves.

A word of caution is necessary in relation to the number of Members voting, particularly in the past few sessions. In 1950–5 the House of Commons worked with Governments enjoying very small majorities. This meant that on all days except private Members' days there was exceptionally heavy pressure on all Members to be at the House, ready to vote in divisions. It seems reasonable to expect this pressure to make Members all the less ready to be at the House to vote at 4 p.m. on private Members' Fridays, on non-party topics. On the other hand, the smallness of Government majorities might have been expected to act as an incentive to enthusiastic Opposition parties to bring in party bills on Fridays, both for the purpose of harassing the Government's supporters by making them feel a duty to stay at the House on Friday, and also in the hope of securing majorities for the second readings of their own bills against the Government's wishes. We might, therefore, well have expected to see an increase in party measures proposed by Opposition Members as a result of a temporary electoral situation; such measures could, furthermore, be expected to produce divisions with large numbers of Members voting. The fact that there was only one real party measure in the four sessions of 1950–4 is, in relation to these considerations, perhaps significant of the force of the changes in habit. An alternative interpretation might, however, ascribe the quietness of the Labour Opposition in 1951–4 to lassitude following the Party's great reforms during its time in office.

LABOUR MEMBERS' BILLS AND OTHER BILLS

3. THE FREQUENCY WITH WHICH THE HOUSE HAS BEEN COUNTED OUT ON PRIVATE MEMBERS' BILLS

Another concrete indication of the amount of interest in debates can be obtained by enquiring how often the House was counted out on private Members' Fridays. There is nothing to be gained by tabulating the occasions on which the Speaker's attention was drawn to the absence of a quorum, because the attendance of Members may fall below forty at some time during almost any debate; but it is worth while to enquire how frequently the attendance failed to reach forty even at the moment when the count was taken, after the required interval of two minutes. If the House is frequently counted out on private Members' days it is a sign that the interest in the debates is really very low indeed.

Up to and including 1927 the number of successful counts was negligible. The House was counted out on days for second readings twice in 1908, once in 1912, and once each in 1921 and 1922 —a total of only five times in some twenty sessions. After 1927, however, the new tendency to concentrate on non-controversial measures produced unfortunate results for a time, and there were no less than fifteen successful counts in the next five sessions. Three of these were in 1928, six in 1930-1, and four in 1932-3. In the 1935 Parliament, along with the increase in the number of contentious bills went a decline in the number of days on which the House was counted out; there were only five successful counts on second reading days during the four sessions. Since 1948, although there have been very few controversial bills, the House has generally been interested enough in the 'constructive' measures to keep the debates alive. The quorum was maintained during all the days for private Members' bills during the first two sessions in which time was provided, but there were four successful counts during the next three sessions, two of them in 1951-2.

4. THE DIFFERENCE BETWEEN LABOUR MEMBERS' BILLS AND OTHER BILLS WITH RESPECT TO ALL-DAY DEBATES AND DIVISIONS, 1920-39

We have already noticed the difference between Labour and Conservative Members' bills in the 1920s and 1930s. If, in enquiring how many days produced all-day debates and how many

THE INTEREST SHOWN IN THE DEBATES

produced divisions, we list the Labour Members' bills separately from the others, we find that, as we would expect, the Labour

TABLE 3

Session.	Days on which the first place was won by a Labour Member.			Days on which the first place was not won by a Labour Member.	
	Total.	No. leading to an all-day debate.	Proportion leading to all-day debate.	Total.	No. leading to an all-day debate.
			%		No. %
1920	4	2 ⎫		6	2 ⎫
21	–	– ⎬ 71·4		5	3 ⎬ 45·8
22	1	1 ⎬		5	1 ⎬
23	2	2 ⎭		8	5 ⎭
24	6	5	83·3	6	6 100
24–25	6	6 ⎫		5	2 ⎫
26	3	3 ⎬ 100		7	3 ⎬ 38·7
27	1	1 ⎬		10	4 ⎬
28	1	1 ⎭		9	3 ⎭
29–30	7	4 ⎫ 50		7	2 ⎫ 26·7
30–31	5	2 ⎭		8	2 ⎭
32–33	3	3 ⎫ 100		9	1 ⎫ 33·3
33–34	1	1 ⎭		9	5 ⎭
35–36	3	2 ⎫		5	2 ⎫
36–37	5	4 ⎬ 81·8		6	2 ⎬ 36·4
37–38	8	7 ⎬		5	3 ⎬
38–39	6	5 ⎭		6	1 ⎭

Notes. In the session of 1935–36 one of the Labour Members' bills down to be taken first on its day, the Workmen's Compensation Bill, was not taken then, because the day was lost owing to a long sitting the previous day. The bill did come forward on one of the later days, and was then debated for the whole of that day. It is included in this table.
In this table and in Table 4, 'Labour' includes I.L.P., etc.

Members' bills produced far more all-day debates and more divisions than those brought in by Members of other Parties.

During the whole of the period between the wars, there were 62 Fridays for second readings on which Labour Members had the first place. On 49 of these days (or 79 per cent), the debate on the first bill occupied the whole of the sitting. Non-Labour Members had the first place on 116 days, and between them introduced 47 bills taking a whole day each. As we would expect, the proportion of their bills producing all-day debates declined a little after the middle 1920s; up to and including 1924 the figure was 17 out of 32, as compared with 30 out of 86 for the remainder of the period. With the bills brought in by Labour Members we do not notice any change, except during Mr. Ramsay MacDonald's second administration, when only half the Labour Members' bills produced all-day debates. (Table 3).

A study of the number of bills producing divisions, according to the party allegiance of the Members introducing them, produces almost the same result. During the period between the wars (counting only the bills which were the first to be dealt with on their respective days) over four-fifths of the Labour Members' bills produced divisions, as against two-fifths of the bills brought in by other Members. With the Labour Members' bills the proportion was more or less constant all through the period, except for a temporary decline in 1929–31. During those two years only seven of the twelve Labour Members' bills produced divisions, but during the rest of the period there was almost invariably a division on a 'first' bill brought in by a Labour Member; in no session was there more than one Labour Member's bill which failed to produce a division, and in all there were 43 such bills on which the House divided, out of a total of 50.

With the bills brought in by non-Labour Members there was a striking decline in the number of divisions during the years between the wars. Up to and including 1926, three-fifths of their bills produced divisions (almost four-fifths in 1923–6), but after that the proportion fell to below half, and remained low until 1939. In the first four years of the 1935 Parliament it was just over a quarter (Table 4).

In relation to these comparisons between the behaviour of Labour and non-Labour Members we must recognize the effect of the party situation. Most (but not by any means all) of the controversial bills leading to all-day debates and divisions involved party differences. Members whose party is in power have less incentive to bring in partisan measures than have Members whose party is in opposition. Thus in 1924, when Labour was in office, all the non-Labour Members' bills with good places in the

THE INTEREST SHOWN IN THE DEBATES

ballot produced all-day debates, and five of the six were decided by divisions. We have already noticed the temporary change in emphasis of the Labour Members' bills in 1929–31 (though by

TABLE 4

THE FREQUENCY OF DIVISIONS ON PRIVATE MEMBERS' BILLS, YEAR BY YEAR, ACCORDING TO THE PARTY ALLEGIANCE OF MEMBERS INTRODUCING THEM, 1920–39

Days on which the first place in the ballot was won by a:

	Labour Member.			Non-Labour Member.		
Session.	Total.	Leading to divisions.	Proportion in each Parliament leading to divisions.	Total	Leading to divisions.	Proportion leading to divisions.
		No.	%		No.	%
1920	4	3		6	3	
21	–	–	71·4	5	1	50
22	1	1		5	1	
23	2	1		8	5	
24	6	5	83·3	6	5	83·3
24–25	6	6		5	2	
26	3	3	100	7	3	48·4
27	1	1		10	4	
28	1	1		9	3	
29–30	7	4	58·3	7	2	33·3
30–31	5	3		8	3	
32–33	3	3	100	9	2	38·9
33–34	1	1		9	5	
35–36	2	2		5	1	
36–37	3	3	86·4	6	1	27·3
37–38	8	7		5	3	
38–39	6	4		6	1	

'Labour' includes I.L.P., etc.

then the non-Labour Members seem to have been fairly well converted to the new interpretation of the proper function of private Members' bills). Of the Labour Members' bills decided by divisions during these two sessions, six were given a second reading; during the whole of the rest of the years between the wars all but three were rejected.

These figures relating to the incidence of all-day debates, and of divisions, and to the numbers voting in the divisions, taken together, seem to have some significance in relation to our general conclusions about the long-term trends.

Chapter IV

THE GOVERNMENT AND PRIVATE MEMBERS' BILLS

1. GENERAL PRINCIPLES GUIDING THE GOVERNMENT'S ATTITUDE

IN this chapter an attempt will be made to define the principles which form the basis of the attitude of the Government to private Members' bills. We can begin by enunciating two very simple rules, the first that the Government does take some part in the debates, and the second that it does not put the Whips on at divisions,[1] but there is a great deal more to be said than this, and the implications of these two rules have not been by any means static during the past half-century.

The convention of the collective responsibility of the Cabinet has long been established and has often been defined. The Ministers are supposed to be jointly responsible for the Cabinet's policy, but not to be bound to speak or to vote together on matters about which there is no Cabinet policy. It is doubtful whether we can accept this as an adequate account of the situation today, however. A study of recent practice suggests that the conception of Cabinet responsibility is becoming more far-reaching and more rigid; the field within which a Minister feels justified in acting independently in political matters is very narrow

[1] For a discussion of the general principles governing free votes in the House of Commons, cf. the present author's article on the subject in the *Durham University Journal* for June 1953, vol. XLV, pp. 104-13.

indeed. Although private Members' bills are normally decided by free votes of the House, and although there is thus apparently no Cabinet responsibility with regard to these bills, it has become almost unknown for Ministers to vote against one another, even in private Members' debates.

A. *Ministers do not propose Bills as Private Members*

A Minister (and this term, for our present purpose, includes any person holding office in the Government) by custom may not introduce a bill in his capacity as a private Member.[1] The existence of a convention to this effect seems to be suggested by the action of Sir Hugh Lucas-Tooth in 1952. Having received no office at the beginning of Mr. Churchill's new Government in the autumn of 1951, he won the fifth place in the ballot which was held soon after the beginning of the session, and introduced the Intestates' Estates Bill. Before the Bill came up for second reading he was appointed to the office of Under-Secretary of State for the Home Department, and when the Bill came up for debate he announced that he would take no part in the discussions.[2] (A suggestion that the Bill should be withdrawn was rejected by the Speaker, who pointed out that by being given a first reading the Bill had become the property of the House.)

A member of the Government may not even put his name down among the supporters of a private Members' bill. There is no formal rule to this effect, but it appears that such abstinence has been practised for so long that it can be regarded as an established convention. The last occasions on which a Minister acted as a supporter of a private Member's bill were in 1919, when Mr. Walter Long, who was then First Lord of the Admiralty, put his name down as one of the supporters of Colonel Yate's Statement of Rates Bill,[3] and in 1924, when Colonel Wedgwood, Chancellor of the Duchy of Lancaster, supported a Rent Restriction Bill. It seems that by the spontaneous action of successive generations of Ministers, itself suggested by the Ministers' feelings about their own position in parliamentary life, a practice has

---

[1] There appears to be no written authority for this statement, but it seems nevertheless to be justified both by common sense and by the evidence.
[2] H.C. Debs., 28th March 1952, vol. 498, col. 1079.
[3] Ibid., 18th March 1919, vol. 113, col. 1924.

grown up which agrees with the general theory of collective responsibility and which has by now been hallowed by time.

B. *Rôle of Ministers in the Debates*

(i) *The Duty of Participation.* Of more substantial interest are the form and objectives of the participation of Ministers and their assistants in debates and divisions. One custom seems to have remained unchanged over a long period. It is that a Minister or junior Minister should normally take part in the debate on behalf of the Government but exert no pressure on Members with regard to the manner in which they are to exercise their votes. Within the confines set by this general rule, there is room for a good deal of flexibility, and there have been some modifications in practice in the past thirty years, not, in all probability, as a result of any deliberate plan of any Government, but rather imperceptibly and in accord with the gradual changes in political habits which come about quietly and as a result of changing circumstances.

(ii) *The Timing of the Minister's Intervention.* There is no rule or fixed custom about the time during the debate on a bill at which the Government spokesman should intervene, although he may prefer to wait until it appears that the debate has nearly run its course, in order that he may reply to points that have been made in the House. In 1936 the Speaker corrected Mr. Kirkwood, who had claimed that the Minister always refrained from speaking before 3 p.m. In fact, the Speaker told him, the timing of the Minister's intervention would generally depend on the character of the bill under discussion.[1] Since 1948 the most usual time for the speech from the Government front bench has been around 1 p.m.

(iii) *The Duty of Attendance by a Departmental Representative.* The

---

[1] H.C. Debs., 27th November 1936, vol. 318, col. 782. Cf. above, p. 50. The incident provoked by Mr. Kirkwood on this occasion gave the Government spokesman the opportunity of mentioning that, before deciding exactly at what time he should rise to speak, he had referred to the report, in Hansard, of an earlier debate on the same subject six years previously. He had found that in that debate the Minister had risen at the same time as he had now chosen himself for his contribution.

House has always expected the Minister concerned or his assistant to be present at least. In 1924 there was no representative of the Ministry of Agriculture present at the debate on a Merchandise Marks Bill, and Sir Henry Cautley complained that this was 'almost an outrage'.[1] The Lord Privy Seal, Mr. Clynes, replied that the Government was neutral and that the Minister had nothing to say,[2] but this explanation did not please the House.

(iv) *Which Minister should speak?* (*a*) *General.* The task of stating the Government's opinion on a bill is normally left to one spokesman, although if circumstances should seem to demand more than one speech from the Government front bench there is no reason why there should not be more than one speech. In the days when first-class debates were common on Fridays, the nature of the subjects discussed sometimes demanded the intervention of the Prime Minister as well as the Minister concerned. In 1925, on Mr. Whiteley's bill to extend the franchise to women of between 21 and 30, the debate was wound up by the leader of the Opposition and the Prime Minister, although the Home Secretary (and his predecessor for the Opposition) had already spoken.[3]

In present conditions, however, a matter of the kind that in 1925 seemed to require the intervention of the Prime Minister as well as the Home Secretary would probably not be brought in as a private Member's bill, and even if such a subject were brought in it would hardly be thought to merit such treatment.

The Government's spokesman is normally the Minister or junior Minister at the Department concerned; it would be contrary to normal practice for another Minister to act as a substitute. On the Re-election of Ministers Bill of 1926, which went on to receive the Royal Assent, Mr. Baldwin was the only Minister to speak; apparently he felt that as the proposal was one affecting the constitution, and as its subject matter was in the province of the Prime Minister rather than of any other Minister, he should state the Government's opinion. It is noteworthy that in his speech he apologized several times for intervening, as Prime Minister, on a private Members' day.[4]

[1] H.C. Debs., 7th March 1924, vol. 170, col. 1807.
[2] Ibid., col. 1818.
[3] Ibid., 20th February 1925, vol. 180, cols. 1479–562.
[4] Ibid., 12th February 1926, vol. 191, cols. 1436–40.

(b) *The Modern Tendency for Junior Ministers to speak in Private Members' Debates.* An interesting development has been the establishment of the custom that the reply on behalf of the Government to the debate on a private Member's bill should in general be made by the Under-Secretary of State or Parliamentary Secretary, as the case may be, of the appropriate Department rather than by the Minister himself. This is in agreement with the wider development of a general principle that the Minister's deputy generally deals with matters of secondary importance raised by private Members;[1] for example, the reply to the adjournment debate at the end of each day's business is almost always made by a junior Minister.

In this matter the change in habit took place during the period between the wars, and the new custom seems by now to have become thoroughly established. As recently as 1923, under a Conservative Government, the Government's attitude was stated by the Minister, and not by his deputy, on the second reading of every balloted private Member's bill debated first on its day during the session, and in 1924 the Labour Government put up junior Ministers as its spokesmen on only two out of eleven such bills. Under Mr. Baldwin's second Government, deputy Ministers spoke on two private Members' bills of 1925, two of 1926 and three of 1927—some of them controversial measures and some not. By the session of 1936–7 the change in practice had been pretty well completed. Although there were five substantial measures, each debated all day and closed by a division in which over 200 Members voted, none of them was dealt with by a departmental chief.[2] It is noteworthy, however, that on the Annual Holiday Bill a Labour Member complained about the fact that the Minister had deputed his task.[3] For the rest, with the exception of the Minister of Agriculture,[4] whose deputy was in the House of

[1] Mr. Crookshank recognized and approved of this development in his evidence before the Select Committee on Procedure of 1945–6 (H.C. 189–1 of 1945–6, Q. 3668).

[2] Unless we count the Secretary for Mines of those days as a departmental chief; Mr. Crookshank, who then held that office, replied on a nationalization bill on 12th February 1937. H.C. Debs., 12th February 1937, vol. 320, cols. 780–7.

[3] H.C. Debs., 27th November 1936, vol. 318, col. 791 (Mr. Rhys Davies).

[4] He spoke on the Exportation of Horses Bill on 5th March 1937 (H.C. Debs., vol. 321, cols. 753–62).

Lords, no Minister of higher rank than the Attorney-General spoke on any private Member's bill of the session. Since 1948 the Government's speech has most often been made by a junior Minister, although there have been many exceptions. Indeed in the session of 1954–5, the Government's contribution was made by a junior Minister on only one of the five bills which were taken first on their several days.

(v) *The Character of the Minister's Intervention.* The character of the Minister's intervention is not easily to be described, as it does not follow any universal pattern. Essentially it must be regarded as an official pronouncement, in which the Minister should be stating the view of his Department and of the Government as a whole, and not his own personal opinion. It would be abhorrent to our conception of governmental responsibility that a Minister should speak in a purely personal capacity about any matter falling within the sphere of his own Department.

The Government's official attitude may be one of complete neutrality, and we can find many instances of a Minister making a speech in which he expresses no actual opinion whatever, hostile or favourable, but merely presents or summarizes arguments which seem to him to be relevant. Such an attitude need not be regarded as an evasion of responsibility; it is quite legitimate for the Government, having its responsibilities in mind, to be indifferent which way a particular question is decided, and to leave the decision entirely to the House. In such a case it might be permissible for the Minister to express a personal opinion one way or the other, as distinct from his official indifference. He might say in effect, 'As Minister, looking at the question from the point of view of one who has responsibility for the promotion of the national good in this sphere, my official opinion is that it does not matter which way this question is decided. But because I am indifferent in my official capacity, I permit myself to say that my personal view is . . .'

On one occasion in 1926, on a bill which aimed to simplify the procedure whereby Local Authorities could obtain powers to run their own public transport services, Colonel Ashley, the Minister of Transport, not only said that he would express no opinion and that he would abstain from voting in the division, but also enunciated a principle of a much more far-reaching kind. 'On

Fridays ... private Members should discuss a Bill and come to a conclusion unfettered by any expression of opinion from the Government—the less interference the better.'[1] It is doubtful whether his argument would be very widely accepted. In so far as the issues were primarily concerned with local government, there were special reasons for the Minister's attitude in this case. Also there was the feeling within the Government itself.[2] The bill was indeed generally favoured by the Left but opposed by Conservatives because of its tendency to promote municipal enterprise, and in the two divisions, on the closure and on the second reading, the voting was mainly on party lines. Although one Cabinet Minister (Mr. Walter Guinness) voted against the bill, the Parliamentary Secretary to the Ministry of Transport, Colonel Moore-Brabazon, voted for it.[3]

Another example of complete abdication of responsibility by the Government was in connection with the Hotels and Restaurants Bill in 1934, on which Mr. Douglas Hacking, the Under-Secretary of State at the Home Office, twice asserted that everyone, including himself, was free to vote according to the dictates of his own conscience.[4] Ministers did in fact vote on opposite sides.

In 1936, on a bill designed to protect the position of widows and children under wills, the Solicitor-General said that the Government had no opinion whatever on the matter, but that if the House should approve the principle of the bill the Government would then give its full co-operation in the later stages, and do what it could to ensure that the bill if passed was workable and generally sound.[5] But the Government's attitude was not universally approved; one Member (Lt.-Col. Heneage) thought this matter too large for treatment in a private Member's bill at all.[6]

---

[1] H.C. Debs., 12th March 1926, vol. 192, col. 2817.

[2] Colonel Ashley himself, President of the Anti-Socialist Union, seems on other occasions to have found the Government's policies rather leftish for him. Mr. Attlee notices this (*As it Happened*, Heinemann, 1954, p. 55), and also suggests that the attitude of the Under-Secretary may not have been in full agreement with that of the Minister.

[3] H.C. Debs., 12th March 1926, vol. 192, cols. 2783–862. The result of the voting was very close. After the closure had been carried by a majority of only 138 votes to 134, the second reading was defeated by 133 to 128.

[4] H.C. Debs., 9th February 1934, vol. 285, cols. 1533–8.

[5] Ibid., 22nd January 1937, vol. 319, col. 534.

[6] Ibid., col. 521.

In a more recent instance too a Minister's statement (on a minor committee point) that the Government 'had a fairly open mind and would wish to be guided by the views of the Committee as a whole,' was met with the rebuke: 'I dislike Governments which have open minds.'[1]

It is conceivable, but unlikely, that a private Member's bill should be discussed in advance by the Cabinet, and that the Cabinet should find itself so deeply divided that it feels unable to express any 'official' view at all. Thus on a Proportional Representation Bill in 1921 the only Government spokesman to take part in the debate did so to say very briefly that the Government was divided over the matter and could not pledge itself to grant facilities for the Bill.[2] The Minister to whom this task fell was the Minister of Pensions.

Although the Minister's intervention must be regarded as the expression of the official opinion of the Government on the measure under discussion, the position of the Government is not the same as with respect to ordinary business. As *The Times* commented with regard to the Transport (Amendment) Bill in 1951, 'no question of a Government defeat can arise on private Members' Bills, however strongly they might be opposed to them'. It is, indeed, not quite clear how far this argument can be regarded as fully and universally valid. One can imagine a hypothetical case in which it would apparently not be so. A Conservative Opposition might, for example, press an amendment to a Labour Government's bill and be defeated, with the Government making it quite clear that it regarded the matter as a fundamental issue involving the confidence of the House in the Government. If the very same proposal were brought forward later on by a Conservative as a separate private Member's bill and passed through all its stages in the House of Commons, with the evident assumption that it would also pass in the House of Lords, the Government would apparently be guilty of inconsistency if it were now prepared to remain in office while having the duty of putting into effect a measure which it had a short time before said that it could not possibly enforce.

Although the Government customarily leaves the various

[1] Official Report, Standing Committee 'B', 1951–2, Affiliation Orders Bill, cols. 5 f.
[2] H.C. Debs., 8th April 1921, vol. 140, col. 677.

stages[1] of private Members' bills to be decided by free votes, the Minister is in no way precluded from expressing a strongly favourable or hostile opinion, and he may with perfect propriety say that he hopes the House will by its vote endorse his opinion.

(vi) *Should a second Minister contribute?* (*a*) *Officially.* With regard to the conduct of Ministers other than the official departmental spokesman, the rules are not at all easy to define, and must be deduced from our observations of recent practice. It is now very unusual for any outside Minister to take part in the debate, as the official opinion is normally indivisible, and if it is stated by the departmental Minister, there is no room for other members of the Government to add contributions of their own. Two possible exceptions suggest themselves. In the first place, if a bill covers the field of interest of several Departments, it may be appropriate for spokesmen of these Departments each to give the House his views, though nowadays this is not normally done. The most likely occasion for such an intervention would be an ancillary legal issue on which the advice to the House of one of the Law Officers would be useful. In the second place, if one Minister should have a special personal contribution to make on an uncontroversial subject in which he was specially interested, or a strong personal opinion which was at variance with the opinion of the Department directly concerned, he might just conceivably take part in the debate in his personal capacity. Technically, seeing that the responsibility of the Government is not supposed to be engaged over a private Member's bill, there seems to be no reason why a Minister should not express an independent or even a dissident opinion; on the other hand, with the strengthening of our feelings about the collective responsibility of the Cabinet, we have come to expect Ministers not to speak against one another on any political topic whatsoever. As the Government's opinion is supposed to be one and indivisible we would by now not expect to hear independent or personal contributions from any Minister, even on uncontroversial matters.

(*b*) *Unofficially.* There have indeed been such interventions in the past, but they were many years ago. In 1923, Mr. Neville Chamberlain, while Postmaster-General, spoke in the debate on the Legitimacy Bill, although the Government's speech was made

[1] Even on amendments proposed by the Government in Committee.

GUIDING THE GOVERNMENT'S ATTITUDE

by the Attorney-General. Mr. Chamberlain justified his intervention on the ground that he was specially interested in the wholly non-political subject of the Bill.[1] Mr. Philip Snowden's intervention from the Government front bench in the debate on the Temperance (Wales) Bill in 1924 comes near to providing us with an example of an independent speech by a Minister, although the opinion which he expressed was not actually at variance with the official opinion. Mr. Rhys Davies, the Under-Secretary at the Home Office, had said that the Government was on the whole in favour of the most important of the bill's objectives (the provision for local option), but opposed to some other sections.[2] Mr. Snowden, however, expressed the most vehement support for the whole bill and claimed that he supported it 'as a private Member', and because 'it had for twenty years been a part of the Labour programme'.[3] The inherent contradiction between these two aspects of his reasons for giving his support did not appear to trouble him, but it is unlikely that even on a matter of this kind a Minister would now claim so great an independence as this. A third member of the Government, the Parliamentary Secretary to the Board of Education, also contributed to the debate, apparently in his capacity as a Welsh representative.

In 1928 there was an admitted difference of opinion in the Cabinet on the Racecourse Betting Bill, which aimed to allow totalizators to be installed for betting at racecourses. Mr. Churchill, as Chancellor of the Exchequer, wound up the debate by saying that the Government itself was at sixes and sevens on the matter, and that it would 'refer for guidance to the sound, and, I might also go so far as to say, the unerring instinct of the House of Commons on large and vague general issues of this character'.[4] In view of the Government's attitude the Minister of Agriculture had permitted himself to rise earlier in the day to speak in his capacity 'as the Member representing the constituency in which is situated the town of Newmarket'.[5] In this

[1] H.C. Debs., 2nd March 1923, vol. 160, col. 2426.
[2] Ibid., 15th February 1924, vol. 169, col. 1217.
[3] Ibid., col. 1270. It must be remembered that these events took place on the fourth parliamentary day, and the first private Members' day, in the life of a new and inexperienced Ministry. Mr. Snowden did not think them of sufficient interest to warrant mention in his long and detailed autobiography.
[4] Ibid., 16th March 1928, vol. 214, col. 2347. Cf. below, p. 98.
[5] Ibid., cols. 2330 ff.

THE GOVERNMENT AND PRIVATE MEMBERS' BILLS

capacity he not only favoured the Bill very strongly but had evidently devoted much energy to the task of ascertaining the opinion of racing people on the matter, and to examining the validity of a poll conducted by the opponents of the Bill.

Apart from the notorious agreement to differ over tariffs in 1931–2 there seem to have been no instances of individual Ministers making speeches in Parliament against the official policy, even on non-political matters, since the debate on the proposed new Prayer-Book for the Anglican Church in 1928. This was not a private Member's bill, but Church measures do in some ways resemble private Members' bills in their constitutional status. In this case the Home Secretary, Sir William Joynson-Hicks, was perhaps the most forceful and prominent parliamentary opponent of the measure, and spoke and voted against it although it had the blessing of the Prime Minister and indeed of most of the Government.[1]

C. Unanimity of Ministers in Divisions

The custom which seems to prevent dissentient Ministers from speaking against the 'official' opinion does not necessarily prevent them from voting according to their own inclinations, although the degree of freedom which they permit themselves varies according to the importance of the topic in question. It also seems to have tended in practice to diminish in recent years. The only instance since 1945 of Ministers voting on opposite sides was on a question which, as it happens, was not put forward by private Members, namely the Government's proposal to allow the Festival of Britain fun-fair to be opened on Sundays.[2] If we go back to the 1920s, however, we find many instances in relation to private Members' bills. In 1921 Mr. Austen Chamberlain voted against a Proportional Representation Bill, which was supported in the division by Dr. Addison and Mr. Fisher.[3] In the same year Mr. Baldwin, who was then Chancellor of the Exchequer, voted on the opposite side to three other Ministers on an amendment

---

[1] H.C. Debs., 15th December 1927; 14th June 1928.
[2] Ibid., 28th November 1950, vol. 481, col. 1072. Cf. P. A. Bromhead, *Free votes in the House of Commons*, Durham University Journal (June 1953), vol. XLV, p. 107.
[3] H.C. Debs., 8th April 1921, vol. 140, col. 690.

which was moved on the report stage of the Criminal Justice Bill.[1]

In the Labour Government of 1924 Mr. Wheatley and Mr. Webb opposed the majority of their colleagues by voting against a bill proposing to introduce Proportional Representation. The bill was sponsored by a member of the Liberal Party, which had by now made this type of electoral reform one of the main planks in its platform. The Labour Party as a whole was clearly divided on this matter, and the amendment to the second reading was seconded by Mr. Herbert Morrison.[2] Labour Ministers also voted on opposite sides on the Temperance (Wales) Bill of 1924.[3]

Again in the same year Labour Ministers voted on opposite sides on the Summer Time Bill. Most of the Cabinet, including the Prime Minister, voted for the second reading, but some holders of minor offices, none of them in the Cabinet, took the opposite side.[4] Mr. Buxton, the Minister of Agriculture, whose Department was obviously closely interested in the Bill, did not vote. In 1925, in the division on the second reading of the Summer Time Bill of that year, which eventually passed into law, the Conservative Ministers were divided, with the Minister of Agriculture voting against the Bill in spite of the fact that the Government evidently thought it of substantial importance.[5] Eight members of the Cabinet, including the Prime Minister, voted for it and Mr. Baldwin made a speech on the matter.[6]

In 1926 a religious issue provided another example of cross-voting by Ministers. A Roman Catholic Relief Bill, which began its career by being introduced under the Ten Minutes Rule, was given a second reading without debate, but in the course of a full Friday's debate on the report stage an amendment was moved to expunge the proposed legalization of processions carrying images through the streets. In the division, in which the amendment was heavily defeated, three office-holders voted with the

[1] H.C. Debs., 4th August 1921, vol. 145, col. 1830.
[2] Ibid., 2nd May 1924, vol. 172, col. 2070.
[3] Ibid., 15th February 1924, vol. 169, col. 1272. Cf. above, p. 95.
[4] Ibid., 11th April 1924, vol. 172, col. 886.
[5] Ibid., 13th March 1925, vol. 181, cols. 1737–1820.
[6] (On the report stage) (H.C. Debs., 17th July 1925, vol. 186, col. 1720). On these bills cf. below, p. 99.

minority, on the opposite side to several of their colleagues, including the Prime Minister.[1]

On the Racecourse Betting Bill of 1928 five Ministers, including Mr. Baldwin and Mr. Churchill, voted in favour of the second reading,[2] and Lord E. Percy and Sir T. Inskip against it. In view of the early differences between Ministers it is remarkable that the Bill was eventually taken over by the Government. It completed its report stage in Government time with the Government Whips on, and went on to receive the Royal Assent. The Ministers naturally now showed complete solidarity, both at the report stage[3] and on the third reading, when Mr. Snowden accused the Home Secretary, Sir William Joynson-Hicks, of sacrificing his principles after being over-ruled in the Cabinet.[4]

On the Hotels and Restaurants Bill of 1934, Ministers voted on opposite sides.[5]

It can be seen that there are many precedents from a generation ago for cross-voting by Ministers on private Members' bills, but in the changed conditions of today it may be doubted whether these precedents can still be regarded as valid guides to ministerial conduct. There has indeed been no such cross-voting since 1945, although there have been at least two divisions (on the Hunting and Coursing Bill of 1949 and on the amendment to the Sunday Observance Bill of 1953) on which it is almost certain that some Ministers would have been personally inclined to vote on the opposite side to that which the Government as a whole favoured. This fact does not entitle us to say that cross-voting by Ministers is a thing of the past, however; the cross-voting on the Sunday opening of the Festival of Britain fun-fair might well be repeated over some similar question.

D. *How the Government forms its Opinions*

It is impossible for us to generalize about the process by which the appropriate Minister arrives at the decision as to his attitude

---

[1] H.C. Debs., 3rd December 1926, vol. 200, col. 1624.
[2] Ibid., 16th March 1928, vol. 214, col. 2358. Cf. above, p. 45.
[3] Ibid., 6th, 18th, and 19th July 1928, vol. 219, cols. 1743–1818, and vol. 220, cols. 439–568 and 647–772.
[4] Ibid., 19th July 1928, col. 731. Sir William Joynson-Hicks, within whose province the Bill apparently fell, neither spoke nor voted on the second reading.   [5] Ibid., 9th February 1934, vol. 285, col. 1554.

to a private Member's bill. The questions which suggest themselves are such as these: how far do Ministers accept the views of their civil servants in deciding what their attitudes are to be? How far does the Department concerned feel obliged to discuss the problems involved with the interested persons outside Parliament and with the promoters of the bill before arriving at its opinion? How far does the Cabinet discuss private Members' bills, and, in the absence of discussion in the Cabinet, how much informal discussion is there between Ministers? Finally, and most important of all, how far are individual Ministers, particularly those directly concerned, free to evolve their own opinions and to act on them?

The answers to all these questions, which may be asked in relation to most of the processes of government, remain particularly obscure with regard to private Members' bills, because the only sources of published information with regard to them, namely contemporary press comments and the memoirs of politicians, tend to concentrate on the more important political matters and to leave these comparatively humdrum activities unexplained.

The rule of collective responsibility and its corollary, the invariable duty of unanimity among all Ministers in their parliamentary utterances and votes, of course conceal not only the differences which exist between them as individual politicians, but also the substantial differences between them as heads of Departments which are at loggerheads with one another. The term 'departmental policy' may not be easy to define or to distinguish exactly from 'governmental policy', but the term has nevertheless some recognizable intent.

Thus, as we have seen, in both 1924 and 1925, when agricultural interests were generally opposed to the introduction of permanent legislation on Summer Time, the successive Ministers of Agriculture did not support their ministerial colleagues in voting for the Bill. In 1924 the Socialist Minister, Mr. Buxton, abstained, and in 1925 his Conservative successor, Mr. Wood, actually voted against his Cabinet colleagues.

We have some information at least about the circumstances which led up to Mr. Baldwin's famous intervention on the Trade Union (Political Fund) Bill early in 1925, soon after he had taken office as Prime Minister.[1] After the Bill had been introduced, an

[1] H.C. Debs., 6th March 1925, vol. 181, col. 833. Cf. above, pp. 53 f.

informal Conservative Party Committee was set up to advise the Government about the Party's attitude,[1] and it was generally assumed that the Government had a duty to declare a clear opinion, which should then be followed by the Party as a whole.[2] At a special Cabinet meeting, the Prime Minister made it clear that he intended to oppose the Bill in the House, and 'doubtfully and reluctantly the Ministers yielded to the fixed resolution of their leader'.[3] Mr. Baldwin not only undertook to state the Government's opinion on the Bill but himself spoke just after the seconder and moved the amendment, which was eventually the subject of a vote on party lines with the Whips on.

This example is interesting for its illustration of the extent of the Government's power in relation to its own parliamentary supporters. Action of this kind on the part of the Government is of course exceptional, but the fact that it has this power available for use if necessary enables it to adapt its course of action on each bill to the circumstances. It would probably be fair to say that the Government's chief contribution is very often as a mediator and arbitrator.

2. THE AMOUNT OF PARTICIPATION BY MINISTERS IN DIVISIONS

In the past generation there has been a striking decline in the readiness of Ministers to vote in divisions on private Members' bills. This development is not surprising, as it agrees with, and indeed illustrates, the tendency for the Ministers and their assistants to become more and more conscious of themselves as members of the Government rather than of Parliament. If a Minister feels that his main tasks are to administer his Department, to deal with matters concerning his Department in Parliament, and to take an appropriate part in the decisions on general governmental policy towards which he contributes when he attends meetings of the Cabinet and of ministerial committees, he can be expected to consider that to vote in private Members' debates on matters remote from his departmental responsibility is irrelevant to his main functions.

[1] Cf. *The Times*, 20th February 1925.
[2] Ibid., 26th February 1925.
[3] G. M. Young, *Stanley Baldwin* (Rupert Hart-Davis, 1952), pp. 91 f. Cf. *The Times*, 28th February 1925, and 7th March 1928, leading article.

PARTICIPATION BY MINISTERS IN DIVISIONS

Thus, although it was formerly quite usual for many or even most of the members of the Cabinet to take part in a division on a private Members' day, it is now rare for more than one or two to do so. We have already noticed that there was an important decline in the number of Members voting in the divisions on private Members' bills after about 1927.[1] When we come to look at the voting behaviour of Ministers we find a similar result. If we examine the voting record of members of the Cabinet in each Parliament, taking into account the 'crucial' divisions on the second readings of bills dealt with under the ballot, we find that during the period 1903-14, between a third and half of all the

TABLE 5

THE PARTICIPATION OF MINISTERS IN DIVISIONS ON PRIVATE MEMBERS' BILLS

	No. of Fridays spent on second readings.	No. of private Members' bills divided against at 2nd reading.	Number of 'crucial' divisions on private Members' bills in which at least one-third of the Ministers in the Cabinet with seats in the House of Commons voted.			
			Total.	Average per session.	As a proportion of all second reading Fridays.	As a proportion of all bills divided against on second reading.
					%	%
1903-13*	89	62	33	3·7	37·0	53·2
1923-8	63	43	27	5·4	42·3	62·8
1948-55	34	13	3	0·5	8·8	23·1

* Excluding 1910 and 1911.

days (four or five a session) produced divisions in which at least a third of the Ministers voted, and that after a decline to a tenth in 1920-2 the proportion rose again to around forty per cent. during the period 1923-8. Mr. Balfour voted in divisions on seven private Members' bills in 1903, Mr. Asquith on five in 1908. Mr. Baldwin voted on many Fridays in the middle 1920s. Like the total number of Members voting, the number of Ministers voting was at a peak in the years 1923-6, and declined again in the last half of Mr. Baldwin's second administration. In the Parliaments of 1929, 1931 and 1935 there was not a single division in which as many as a third of the Ministers voted, and since 1945 extensive participation by Ministers has only occurred on rare and

[1] Cf. above, Chapter III.

THE GOVERNMENT AND PRIVATE MEMBERS' BILLS

exceptional occasions. Only three bills since the war have brought out a third of the Cabinet Ministers to vote on second reading, two under the Labour Government (the Hunting and Coursing Bill of 1949 and the Transport Bill of 1951), and one (the Sunday Observance Bill of 1953) under the Conservative Government. (The big turn-out of Labour Ministers on the Hairdressers' Bill in 1949 was on the third reading.) In addition, the members of the Labour Opposition front bench turned out in considerable force to vote for the Press Council Bill in 1953.

Only one division, called for convenience the 'crucial' division, on each bill is taken into account. (For the definition of the 'crucial' division, cf. above, p. 78.) A bill which produced a division on the closure, but none on the question on the second reading, is treated, for the purpose of these calculations, as having been divided against.

3. THE GOVERNMENT'S USE OF ITS POWERS

A. *Weapons for use against Unacceptable Bills*

The rôle of the Ministers in relation to private Members' bills is not restricted to speaking and voting in the main debates. The Government often wishes to take measures to secure the amendment or defeat of a bill, and, in the absence of the usual weapons of party discipline, it has to decide on the most appropriate tactics in each particular case.[1]

If a proposal is put forward by an Opposition Member and embodies some main item of Opposition policy, the Government will probably have little difficulty in defeating it through a sufficient muster, spontaneous or cajoled, of its own supporters. All the party measures introduced by Labour Members during the periods of office of Conservative and National Governments in the 1920s and 1930s,[2] were more or less spontaneously defeated in this way. It sometimes happens, though, that an Opposition bill which the Government dislikes cannot be defeated quite so easily, particularly if the Government's majority is very small; the

---

[1] No bill has been passed into law against the declared wishes of the Government for half a century, though some individual amendments have gone against the Government.

[2] Except the Annual Holiday Bill of 1936, which was given a second reading but killed in the Standing Committee. Cf. below, p. 106.

THE GOVERNMENT'S USE OF ITS POWERS

Transport Bill of 1951 was in fact carried by the Opposition against the Government on second reading, because the Government was not able to muster enough supporters to outnumber the vast crowd of enthusiastic Conservatives who stayed at the House on that Friday in the hope that they would be able to humiliate and annoy the Government by giving the bill a second reading. Circumstances such as those which led to this defeat are rare, although we have now experienced two Parliaments, and five sessions with time for private Members' bills, in which the Government of the day has had a majority which most commentators in 1950 said was unworkable. Even so, there has been no serious attempt, apart from the Transport Bill, on the part of the Opposition, Labour or Conservative, to bring forward a purely party measure for the Government's discomfiture.

Sometimes the Government may wish to secure the rejection of a measure brought forward by some of its own back-benchers. Curiously enough, rebellious bills have been more frequent since 1948 than before; the Labour Government in particular found that in some instances its back-benchers were impatient. As the new distribution of time has increased the possibility of bills passing without help from the Government, such bills may become more frequent still in the future. Two Labour Members' bills which the Labour Government disliked were the Hairdressers' Bill and the Hunting and Coursing Bill, whose parliamentary stages are examined in detail in Appendix B, below.

In the last resort a Government which wishes to defeat a private Member's bill can put the Whips on against it. This was done fairly often before 1914, and in the atmosphere of the debates of those days did not seem abnormal, but during the 1920s it became usual to allow free votes on private Members' Fridays. By now, an attempt by the Government to coerce its back-benchers on a Friday would be regarded by many as an intolerable and an improper use of the authority of the party machine, and it is quite possible that many Government supporters would disobey the Whips; in such a case, the Government might be defeated, and although it would not necessarily have to resign, it would be severely humiliated. Members of the Government may on occasion use direct persuasion even if the Whips are not put on. Thus in 1951, on the second reading of the Matrimonial Causes Bill, the Attorney-General said that he thought a Royal

Commission should be set up before any new legislation was brought in, but that on the present bill everyone should vote according to his conscience.[1] But when the closure was moved, and a division took place, the Attorney-General himself, according to a Member who raised a point of order, stood in the gangway shouting, 'If you want a Royal Commission, vote "no".'[2] This manœuvre did not succeed. The closure was carried by 102 votes to 99, and the second reading by 131 votes to 60. Many Members who voted against the closure then voted for the second reading—a rather unusual circumstance.

The Government Whips can exert their influence behind the scenes in various ways, though it is rare for them to intervene. They can try to dissuade their party supporters from going into the Chamber when a count has been called,[3] or they can organize a filibuster and so prevent a bill from being discussed at all,[4] or they can try to build up a hostile majority by private appeals to supporters. A new device, seen for the first time only recently, is that of getting the Members who hold office in the Government to come down in such large numbers that they swamp the House.[5] It is only in contemporary conditions, when so few Members vote on Fridays, that this device can be of any use.

If a bill does get a second reading against the Government's wishes, other devices are available. If the bill involves expenditure from public funds, the Government can prevent the discussion of the money clauses by failing to move the necessary financial resolution. Otherwise there are still several possibilities. If the Government does not wish to incur odium for opposing a bill, it can support the second reading and then support, or itself move, a motion for committal to a Committee of the whole House. If such a motion is passed, the bill can only proceed in Government time.[6] This device has not been used for many

---

[1] Cf. above, p. 62. H.C. Debs., 9th March 1951, vol. 485, cols. 1001–6.
[2] Ibid., col. 1018.
[3] In the Select Committee on Procedure, H.C. 189-1 of 1945–6, Minutes of Evidence, Q. 3625–8, Mr. Herbert Morrison agreed with Mr. Cocks that this device was sometimes used, deplorable though it might be. There does not seem to be any evidence of such activities since 1945, however.
[4] They were accused, perhaps unfairly, of doing this on the Intestates' Estates Bill on 28th March 1952. Cf. above, pp. 30 f.
[5] Cf. below, Appendix B, p. 187.
[6] Cf. above, pp. 34 f.

years, but it was successfully employed twice by Mr. Asquith's Government in 1908.[1] Neither of the bills concerned made any further progress in that session, but the main provisions of both were later embodied in Government bills.

The Government can try to persuade the members of the Standing Committee to destroy a bill by reporting adversely on it, or by negativing all the clauses. This method is perhaps most likely to succeed against a bill of limited importance, which has passed its second reading simply because its supporters, though few, have been present, while the indifferent and potentially hostile majority have not been at the House at all. In the Standing Committee the enthusiasts may find it less easy to outnumber the indifferent, who may be willing to follow the Government's wishes.

There have been instances of bills making substantial progress in the face of the Government's hostility, and even passing the House of Commons with the Whips put on against them. Thus in 1919 the Government was defeated on the third reading of the Women's Emancipation Bill, whose aim was to give the vote to all women aged between 21 and 30. The Government, apparently recognizing the strength of the feeling for the Bill, did not oppose the second reading, which was taken without a division, after the closure had been carried by the narrow margin of 119 votes to 32.[2] At the third reading stage, however, the Government actually put the Whips on against the Bill, but to no avail. Even with 19 office-holders as well as two Whips (apart from the Whips who acted as tellers) voting against the Bill, the Government could only muster 85 Members, not enough to defeat the 100 who voted in favour of the Bill.[3] Nevertheless, the Bill failed to pass the House of Lords, where it was negatived without a division after a very short debate.[4]

In the next year, 1920, the same Bill again passed its second

[1] On Sir Charles Dilke's Shops Bill, a comprehensive proposal for the regulation of working conditions in shops, and on the Liquor Traffic (Local Option) (Scotland) Bill. Parl. Debs., 4s., 1st May 1908, vol. 187, col. 1610, and 22nd May 1908, vol. 189, col. 682.

[2] Narrow in the sense that the closure would not have been carried if under 100 Members had voted for it (H.C. Debs., 4th April 1919, vol. 114, col. 1628). Cf. above, p. 28.

[3] H.C. Debs., 4th July 1919, vol. 117, col. 1344.

[4] Ibid., 24th July 1919, vol. 35, cols. 1045-51.

reading stage in the Commons, in much the same way as in 1919, but this time the Standing Committee, following the Government's advice, decided to proceed no further with the Bill because it had no chance of passing into law. Mr. Bonar Law, Leader of the House, when he was later criticized for the Government's action in the Committee, defended himself on the ground that the Government was not obliged to provide facilities for private Members' bills.[1]

In 1936 a bill to compel all employers to grant their workers annual holidays with pay, though proposed and backed by Labour Members, was given a second reading against the Government's advice. The Government, although it opposed the Bill on technical grounds,[2] was unable to muster much support from its own back-benchers, and only managed to get 58 Members into the lobbies against the closure, on which the division was taken. A far larger body of Labour Members on the other side, joined by 24 Conservatives, easily carried the closure, and on the main question the Government allowed the Bill to go through without a division.[3] In the Standing Committee, however, a Conservative proposed an amendment, whose effect was to destroy the obligatory character of the Bill, and on the third day of the Committee's proceedings the amendment was carried by 20 votes to 18. As the whole Bill had now been wrecked, the Committee decided to proceed no further with it.[4] The Government did, however, undertake to appoint a special committee to hold an enquiry on the subject, and after the Committee had made its report,[5] a Government bill was passed in the following session.[6]

The stages through which a bill has to pass in the House of Lords provide the Government with further opportunities for the defeat of a measure which they do not like. If there are strong

---

[1] H.C. Debs., 22nd April 1920, vol. 128, cols. 565 f.

[2] Mainly because it considered that any new advance in this field should be made only after collective negotiation and agreement among the interests concerned, rather than by independent parliamentary action. Cf. the speech of the Parliamentary Secretary to the Ministry of Labour, H.C. Debs., 25th November 1936, vol. 318, col. 790.

[3] H.C. Debs., 27th November 1936, vol. 318, cols. 806-9.

[4] House of Commons, Reports from Committees, 1936-7, Standing Committee 'A', Annual Holiday Bill, 3rd March 1937, pp. 7 f.

[5] Cmd. 5724 of 1938.

[6] The Holidays with Pay Act, 1938, 1 & 2 Geo. 6, ch. 70.

administrative arguments against the measure the Government will stand a good chance of getting a majority of the Peers to defeat the bill. Indeed it is with private Members' bills passed by the Commons against the Government's wishes that the House of Lords as a body can still be regarded in fact as a bulwark against over-hasty and irresponsible legislation.[1] The Lords may save a Labour Government from possible indiscretions of its own left wing in the Commons, though perhaps not a Conservative Government from the excesses of its right wing. All this is somewhat hypothetical. The Upper House has not been used for this purpose in recent times, although the part that it played (without prompting from the Government)[2] in securing the final omission of the death penalty amendment from the Labour Government's Criminal Justice Bill in 1948 gives a clear indication of its potentialities.

B. *The Government's Positive Contribution on Matters of Detail*

(i) *General Considerations.* The Government's attitude to a private Member's bill is not necessarily hostile. Indeed these days most bills moved by private Members seem to be looked on with favour, if not with enthusiasm, by the Government of the day, no matter from which side of the House the bills emanate. We have already seen, furthermore, that many constructive and uncontroversial private Members' bills are really inspired by the Government. If a Minister wants to bring in a minor bill concerning his own Department, and is told that the Government's legislative time-table is so full that no room can be found for his bill, he may try, either himself or through the Whips, to get a private Member to use a place in the ballot for the bill.[3]

Special consideration must be given to the problem of the Government's attitude over matters of detail. The Government may be neutral about a private Member's bill in the sense that, while it is not convinced that the bill is essential, it is ready to accept the free decision of Parliament and, if necessary, to take

---

[1] Cf. above, p. 105.

[2] In this case the Lord Chancellor, Lord Jowitt, said that although he personally thought that the death penalty should be retained, it was his duty, as a member of the Government, to advise the House of Lords not to reverse the decision of the Commons.

[3] Cf. above, p. 24.

responsibility for making that decision effective. Such is the character of governmental responsibility that the Government, though it may be neutral, can rarely be wholly indifferent. If the passing of the bill will impose new duties upon it, it is concerned to see that the duties are such that it is prepared to accept the responsibility for them. Even if the bill does no more than make a change in the law, without adding to or in any way modifying the Government's administrative responsibilities, it must be remembered that the statute book is regarded as a single whole, and that the Government of the day ought to try to prevent Parliament from vitiating its quality by the introduction of inconsistency or obscurity of meaning. If a badly drafted bill is passed and creates difficulties in the courts, the Government of the day tends to be blamed, however much the passage of the bill may technically have been the responsibility of the Legislature alone.

Often, when the House has given a bill a second reading, the Government, even if it has been neutral at first, comes in with full offers of assistance, both by making available the expert advice of the parliamentary draftsmen, and by giving political and administrative advice. Thus when Sir Rupert De la Bère and Sir A. P. Herbert introduced their Bill to change the law on divorce in 1936, the Government, though neutral, considered that it had some responsibility for seeing that, if the Bill were passed, it should be passed as good law. Sir Alan Herbert tells how he was helped by the Attorney-General and the Treasury Solicitor, and how Parliamentary Counsel went through the draft with him, suggesting amendments, after the Bill had been given a second reading and before its committee stage began.[1]

It is perfectly possible for the Government to concern itself with the technical aspects of a private Member's bill without committing itself on the principles. To quote Sir A. P. Herbert again: 'The Bill would strictly remain a private Member's Bill, and with questions of policy the Government would have nothing to do in a positive manner. If, for example, we chose to include in our Bill a clause for the encouragement of bigamy, or the abolition of the King's Proctor, that would be our own affair, though of course there would always be the risk of incurring the active hostility of the Government.' It must be recognized that the

[1] A. P. Herbert, *The Ayes Have it* (Methuen, 1937), pp. 103 ff.

definition of 'questions of policy' is not clear and may be the subject of some disagreement.

(ii) *The Government in Standing Committee.* It is normal for at least one Government representative, generally the Parliamentary Secretary at the Ministry immediately concerned, to be appointed an added member of the Standing Committee which is to consider a bill. We would probably be justified in saying that there is a convention that the Government should have some officeholder to act as its spokesman.

An exception to this rule may be made in the case of a bill which the promoters have agreed to drop. Thus in 1951 Mrs. Eirene White's Matrimonial Causes Bill was given a second reading against the Government's wishes, and before the opening of the Committee proceedings Mrs. White had been persuaded to move that the Committee should proceed no further. No officeholder was appointed to Standing Committee 'B' for the purpose of the consideration of the bill.[1] It has also been known for a Government spokesman to be appointed to a Standing Committee for a particular bill, to attend for long enough to say that he does not intend to co-operate, and then to go away, leaving the Committee to its own devices.[2]

It is by no means unknown for the Government to have two or more office-holders added to a Standing Committee to represent it during the proceedings on a particular private Member's bill. If a bill is particularly interesting both the Minister and his deputy may go on to the Standing Committee; if the bill concerns both an English Department and the Scottish Office, both may be represented. Thus in the session of 1952-3 the Ministry of Agriculture and the Scottish Office were each represented by a junior Minister for the Standing Committee's proceedings on the Dogs (Protection of Livestock) Bill.[3] For the rather more controversial

[1] Official Report, Standing Committee 'B', 1950-1, cols. 879 f. The Government was perhaps taking a risk in this case. It could not be sure that the Committee would accept Mrs. White's motion not to proceed with the Bill. In the event, however, the motion was approved, at a division, by 20 votes to 8. It is noteworthy that although this decision was supposed to have been agreed in advance, eight Labour Members voted against it and eight for it. Cf. above, p. 39.
[2] Cf. below, Appendix B.
[3] Official Report, Standing Committee 'B', 1952-3, col. 1088.

Simplified Spelling Bill the Ministry of Education was represented by both the Minister and the Parliamentary Secretary, and there was in addition the Scottish Under-Secretary of State concerned with education in Scotland.[1]

On committee points the Government often finds itself impelled to take up a more definite and positive position than it would wish to take with regard to a second reading. With Government bills we hear more and more often the reply, to an amendment moved in Committee, that the matter has already been fully discussed with the interested bodies, and that it would be better for Parliament not to interfere with the solution that has been reached. With private Members' bills too this argument is often put forward, as with the Poor Prisoners' Defence Bill in 1930. Sir John Withers, in opposing an amendment, pointed out that the Bill had been thoroughly examined by the Home Office, together with the interested bodies, under the previous Government, and that the Home Office had again approved of the existing form under the new Government. He begged the House to be very chary of interfering with the balance that had been struck.[2] Later, in replying to another proposal for amendment, he said that he had himself at first favoured its objects, but that he had given way before the objections of the Home Office. At this stage he would prefer to leave it to the Government to decide; if they persisted in their attitude he would not support them.[3] The amendment was accordingly negatived without a division, although not without a protest at Sir John Withers' 'amazing confession'. 'Are we to be ruled by Government officials,' asked Mr. Grace, a little unrealistically perhaps, 'or by Parliament?'[4]

Silence on the Government's part over any point, although it reinstates Parliament, as it were, in its position as the true Legislature of the Kingdom, is not always welcomed by the members of a committee. Sir Alan Herbert has an interesting comment to make in this connection. His Matrimonial Causes Bill, which was passed during the session 1936-7, originally contained a provision to allow divorce on the ground that the respondent was 'an incurable habitual drunkard, and had for a period of at least three years been separated from the petitioner in consequence of

---

[1] Official Report, Standing Committee 'B', 1952-3, col. 708.
[2] H.C. Debs., 2nd May 1930, vol. 238, cols. 531 ff.
[3] Ibid., col. 558.   [4] Ibid., col. 559.

habitual drunkenness'. In the Standing Committee an amendment was proposed for the omission of this paragraph, and in the absence of any definite guidance from the Government, Sir Alan Herbert, the chief promoter of the Bill, had to decide for himself whether to combat the amendment or not. After hearing the arguments, he decided not to challenge a division, but to let the amendment go through. Any other member of the Committee could of course have forced a division, but even on a private Members' bill there is some feeling that the sponsor's decision to accept an amendment had better not be interfered with. So we find Sir Alan saying, 'for the omission of that important paragraph I accept entire responsibility'. He does comment though that 'a private Member should not be left by the Government to make such big decisions',[1] and thereby implies that, though himself an Independent, he would prefer that, on a technical question such as this, the responsibility for making decisions should rest with the Government. There is no inconsistency in his view. His contention would imply that, while the general questions about divorce which were decided at the second reading are such purely moral questions that the Government should not interfere, the question whether divorce should be allowed for drunkenness is, though important, so dependent on technical considerations that, within the general context of the bill, the decision as to how the Committee should be advised could best be made by experts.

C. *Conclusion*

It should now be possible to attempt an evaluation of the rôle of the Government in connection with private Members' bills. On the general principles of such bills Parliament has by now firmly established its claim to be allowed to vote without coercion from the party machines. This has been possible, at a time when the Government's domination over Parliament has been increasing, because private Members' bills have come to be restricted to non-political questions; the two movements have gone together. In exchange, however, the Government's rôle as mediator, conciliator and adviser in relation to matters of detail has become more positive, and on such matters the Government's authority

[1] *The Ayes Have it*, op. cit., p. 124.

THE GOVERNMENT AND PRIVATE MEMBERS' BILLS

is so well recognized that its advice is generally sure to be followed by the House. Without explicitly intending it, and almost without knowing it, Parliament has struck a balance between subservience and excessive independence. On matters which are unsuitable for decision by straightforward numerical majorities it has shown itself ready to accept guidance and advice; on simple questions of principle, so long as they do not involve party controversy, it has successfully asserted its right to decide itself by majority vote.

4. THE RÔLE OF THE OPPOSITION LEADERS

The leaders of the Opposition seem to let themselves be guided by rules or customs closely corresponding with those which Ministers follow, but less rigid. In this matter there have been noticeable changes in practice during the past thirty years. When the Labour Party regarded private Members' days as opportunities for bringing forward their chief party measures, the leaders not unnaturally balloted along with the rank and file. Occasionally they won good places and brought in party bills. Thus in 1923 Mr. William Graham brought in the Prevention of Unemployment Bill and Mr. J. H. Thomas the Workmen's Compensation Bill. In recent years there have never been more than a few Opposition leaders taking part in the ballot, and the only one to have had the opportunity of introducing a bill has been Dr. Edith Summerskill, who has twice proposed a Women's Disabilities Bill.[1] It would perhaps be rash to assert that no party leader would ever bring in a party bill, but it is at any rate thirty years since such a thing was last done.

With regard to participation in debate, there is more room for variation in practice than there is in the case of Ministers. In the past, and particularly before 1914, it was quite usual for one of the Opposition leaders to speak on a private Member's bill, but recently such participation has become rare except in the case of a former Minister who has advice to give on the basis of his experience. This change in practice is a further indication of the broader and more fundamental changes which have already been noticed. It is unusual for more than one Opposition leader to intervene in a private Members' debate. As we become more and

[1] H.C. Debs., 25th April 1952, vol. 499, cols. 899–982, and 8th May 1953, vol. 515, cols. 807–41.

THE RÔLE OF THE OPPOSITION LEADERS

more accustomed to the notion that every utterance of a recognized Opposition leader necessarily represents the considered view of Her Majesty's Opposition, so it becomes difficult for opposing opinions or even concurring but distinct opinions to be expressed in Parliament by members of the 'shadow cabinet'.

With regard to voting, it is becoming more and more rare for Opposition leaders to vote at all on private Members' bills, and when they do vote they tend (though not to the same extent as Ministers) to avoid voting against one another. On the old party bills proposed from the Opposition benches there was often a big turn-out of Opposition leaders. Thus on the Labour bills of 1920–39 Mr. MacDonald (before 1931) and later Mr. Lansbury and Mr. Attlee nearly always voted, along with almost all their front-bench colleagues. On the only purely party measure since 1948 the Opposition leaders turned out to vote in full force; seven of the ten Conservative members of the House of Commons who were to receive Cabinet rank on the formation of Mr. Churchill's Government voted for Mr. Bevins' Transport Bill on 23rd February 1951. In the division on the closure on the Press Council Bill, in 1952, thirteen former Labour Cabinet Ministers voted, including Mr. Attlee, Mr. Morrison, Mr. Gaitskell and Mr. Ede.[1]

When we turn from specifically 'party' bills to private Members' bills in general, we find that the decline in voting by Opposition leaders has corresponded with the decline in voting by Ministers.

In its earlier days the Labour Party tended to decide at its meetings on its attitude even to private Members' bills. In the 1920s there was regularly a Labour spokesman in most such debates, even when he merely announced, as Colonel Wedgwood did once in 1922, that the Labour Party, as a party, had not considered a bill and that it had therefore no corporate attitude to it.[2]

When there is no discussion in a party conclave, there may be informal discussion and if possible agreement among the members of the Opposition front bench, even when there is to be a free vote. In the past, such advance agreement was not necessarily binding. Mr. Tom Johnston, writing of the debate on the proposed new Anglican Prayer-Book in 1928, tells us: 'The Scots

[1] Cf. above, p. 66.
[2] Cf. Colonel Wedgwood's speech on the Rating of Machinery Bill, H.C. Debs., 28th April 1922, vol. 153, col. 886.

Members of the Opposition front bench decided that as it was almost entirely an English issue, it would be unjust and improper for us to vote.' But this is not the end of the story. Four of them, Messrs. Adamson, Graham, Kennedy and Johnston, listened to the debate, and Tom Johnston relates how one speaker deeply impressed Willie Adamson, who whispered, 'Tom, I couldna' look ma forefolks in the face if I didna' vote the nicht.' So all four voted.[1]

The Labour leaders sometimes allowed themselves the luxury of free voting in opposition, and not only on questions of conscience. In 1923 Mr. Henderson, Mr. Clynes and Mr. Alexander voted for the Rating of Machinery Bill, Mr. MacDonald, Mr. W. Adamson and most of the other leaders against it.[2] This was a case, however, in which it did not matter very much how the voting went, as the Minister had already promised to set up a committee to examine the questions raised, and it was clear that the Bill would not pass before the committee made its report.

Among the Conservatives in their rare periods in opposition, we find an instance of division among the leaders in 1924 over a watering-down clause in a Legitimacy Bill; Mr. Baldwin and some other Conservative leaders were in the (wholly Conservative) minority favouring the clause, while Mr. Neville Chamberlain, a seasoned campaigner against the harshness of society towards the illegitimate, voted to leave the Bill as it was.[3] On another occasion Mr. Chamberlain abstained on a bill on which his views were apparently to the left of those of his colleagues. On 27th November 1929, a meeting of the Association of Municipal Corporations, held under his chairmanship, unanimously passed a resolution in favour of a proposal, which had often been put before the House, to empower Local Authorities to run their own transport services without the need to come to Parliament with Private bills.[4] When the Omnibuses Bill came up for second reading three months later, however, Mr. Chamberlain did not

[1] Thomas Johnston, *Memories* (Collins, 1952), p. 102.
[2] H.C. Debs., 11th May 1923, vol. 163, col. 2840.
[3] Ibid., 27th June 1924, vol. 175, col. 876. Mr. Chamberlain had already brought in a Bastardy Bill under the ballot himself in 1920, and had been active in support of later proposals in this field. Cf. K. Feiling, *The Life of Neville Chamberlain* (Macmillan, 1946), p. 85.
[4] Mr. Scurr, the proposer of the Bill, referred to this in his second reading speech (H.C. Debs., 7th February 1930, vol. 234, col. 2254).

THE RÔLE OF THE OPPOSITION LEADERS

vote, although Mr. Baldwin and many of the Opposition leaders voted against the Bill.[1]

It would be unwise to infer, from the fact that since the war Opposition leaders have not voted against one another in divisions on balloted bills, that any instance of cross-voting would necessarily be regarded as a breach in their ranks. On bills introduced under the Ten Minutes Rule there have been many instances of disagreement among the Opposition leaders finding expression in the division lobbies. In 1951, for example, Mr. Churchill voted for the motion for leave to introduce a bill to make effective the stabilization of the date of Easter, while Mr. Crookshank, Mr. Macmillan, and other front bench Conservatives voted against it.[2] In 1953, Labour leaders voted against one another on three Ten Minute bills, the Death of the Speaker Bill,[3] the Peers Bill[4] and the Barristers (Licensing) Bill.[5]

It still remains true that when party leaders are in opposition they are rather more ready to vote according to their personal inclinations, against one another if necessary, than they can be when they are in power. Thus in 1948, when a proposal was brought forward (not as a private Member's bill, but as a private Member's amendment to a Government bill) to suspend the operation of the death penalty for five years, no office-holder of the Labour Government of the day voted in its favour, and many office-holders voted against it.[6] (There is indeed some evidence to suggest that although there was supposed to be a free vote on that occasion, the holders of office in the Government were instructed not to vote in favour of the proposal.)[7] Yet six years later, when the same private Member, Mr. Silverman, brought forward once again his proposal to suspend the death penalty

---

[1] H.C. Debs., 7th February 1930, vol. 234, col. 2334.

[2] Ibid., 20th March 1951, vol. 485, col. 2320. (The Easter Act, already on the Statute Book, provided that it should come into force only by an Order in Council after specified bodies had given their consent. The new Bill proposed to bring the old Act into operation forthwith.)

[3] Ibid., 25th February 1953, vol. 511, col. 2098.

[4] Ibid., 11th February 1953, vol. 511, col. 426.

[5] Ibid., 6th May 1953, vol. 515, col. 404.

[6] Ibid., 14th April 1948, vol. 449, col. 1094.

[7] Ibid., 15th April 1948, vol. 449, col. 1171. Cf. P. A. Bromhead, *Free Votes in the House of Commons*, Durham University Journal, June 1953, p. 105.

for five years, with a Conservative Government in office, many Labour Party leaders and former office-holders voted for the proposal, but none against it.[1] The same thing happened again at a full-dress debate on the subject which took place early in 1955.[2]

The two main trends that we have observed in the behaviour of Opposition leaders, on the one hand towards diminished participation and on the other hand towards greater solidarity of action when they do participate in debates and votes on private Members' bills, are in full agreement both with the trends in the behaviour of Ministers and with recent developments in the character of government as a whole.

[1] H.C. Debs., 1st July 1953, vol. 517, col. 414. On this occasion Mr. Silverman made use of the Ten Minutes Rule. Eleven Labour back-bench Members voted against the proposal.

[2] *Weekly Hansard*, 10th February 1955, col. 2186. The debate of 1953 was on a.Ten Minute bill to suspend the death penalty, that of 1955 on an amendment, moved by Mr. Silverman, to a Government motion to 'take note of the Report of the Royal Commission on Capital Punishment'.

Chapter V

THE RÔLE OF ASSOCIATIONS AND OF ROYAL COMMISSIONS

1. ASSOCIATIONS IN THE COMMUNITY

MANY private Members' bills deal with intricate and technical questions. On such matters, as we have seen, it is often felt that the Government ought to advise the House. Alternatively it may be argued that the House of Commons should decide freely, but only on the basis of some agreement reached, after exhaustive discussion outside Parliament, by the interested parties. Thus on a Slaughter of Animals Bill in 1930, Mr. Greenwood, the Labour Minister of Health, thought that the House should make no decision until full agreement had been achieved between the bodies whom the Bill directly concerned.[1] In 1939 the Parliamentary Secretary to the Ministry of Labour opposed the second reading of a Shops Bill on the ground that the matter ought to be dealt with on the basis of discussion between the employers' and the employees' organizations, so as 'to hammer out a solution which could be presented to the Ministry of Labour for serious examination'.[2]

This brings us to the study of the rôle of private organizations in general in relation to private Members' bills—a rôle of the first importance.

Among the general public there is an immense fertility of ideas

[1] H.C. Debs., 12th December 1930, vol. 246, col 748.
[2] Ibid., 24th February 1939, vol. 344, col. 851.

about ways of making the world a better place, most of which require an increase in the repressive mechanism of the state. Almost every scheme for betterment unites a number of people, and there is usually at least one society for every idea. Meetings are held, resolutions are passed, many of which, however laudable, get no further for years. Thus at a recent meeting of a county branch of the Council for the Preservation of Rural England one of the Council's Officers is reported to have said that he thought 'legislation should be introduced to allow policemen to fine on the spot people who left litter about or defaced the countryside in any way'.[1]

There are many ways in which the House of Commons may be said to 'represent' the electorate, and one of these many ways is linked with the heterogeneity of the membership of the House. Each Member is indeed elected because he is his party's candidate, having been chosen to be candidate, as a rule, because he has satisfied the dominant element in the constituency party that he will serve them well as candidate and as Member. Yet there is no all-embracing uniformity among Members of Parliament; the variety of their personal predilections seems to be infinite. Every society that deserves consideration is likely to find some Member of Parliament who is (or is prepared to become) actively sympathetic to its objectives, although it was not because of that sympathy, but for other reasons, that he was first chosen as a candidate and then elected to Parliament.

2. ASSOCIATIONS AND MEMBERS OF PARLIAMENT

Associations having objects of their own to pursue do indeed regularly try to extract pledges from Members of Parliament at the time when they are most vulnerable—that is, during election campaigns, when candidates are often approached with requests that they should undertake, if elected, to support this or that proposal. It seems somewhat unlikely, however, that pressure on candidates at election time is really a factor that needs to be taken into account in relation to the results of elections, except in so far as such pressure is concerned with questions of national policy on a large scale, which are not likely to be dealt with in private Members' bills. Matters brought up in this way at election time

[1] *Manchester Guardian*, 26th September 1953.

ASSOCIATIONS AND MEMBERS OF PARLIAMENT

generally have nothing to do with the party programmes, but are sometimes introduced, at a local level, into the election struggle, as in 1923 when Lady Astor made the proposal to restrict the sale of liquor to persons under 18 an issue of her campaign.[1]

Almost every private Member's bill has an organization of some kind interested in it. Its principles have probably been approved by meetings of local branches as well as by a national conference of the organization concerned, and the organization may have devoted much energy to the gathering of factual information, to the dissemination of propaganda to educate public opinion, and to attempts to influence Members of Parliament. In the United States the direct approach by associations to Congressmen is on a huge scale, and in the context of the character of American Parties such 'lobbying' is of immense importance in the whole legislative process.[2] In this country associations recognize that it is not much use trying to influence votes of the House of Commons on issues connected with Government bills, and they direct their main attentions rather to the Government itself. But with proposals brought in as private Members' bills there is a good deal more in the way of direct pressure on private Members in general, and a Member in charge of a bill will usually be acting in close touch with the group or groups behind it. Often there will be a group no less bent on trying to secure the bill's defeat, and again there may be several different groups all more or less in agreement in general but at loggerheads with the main group over particular points.

One of the most obvious and crudest ways by which interested groups may try to influence the passage of legislation in a direction which they desire is by sending circular letters to all Members of Parliament. Another method is to encourage individuals or local associations to write to their own Members. Of the two methods, there is little doubt that the second is the more likely to be effective, provided that the letters appear to be spontaneous. Circulated printed matter is rarely read and more rarely heeded, and may do more harm than good to the cause of those who

[1] Cf. H.C. Debs., 9th March 1923, vol. 161, col. 915.

[2] The paramount importance of private organizations in the legislative process in the United States has been amply recognized by recent American commentators, e.g. V. O. Key, *Parties, Politics and Pressure Groups*, Bailey and Samuel, *Congress at Work*, Bertram Gross, *The Legislative Struggle*, etc.

ASSOCIATIONS AND ROYAL COMMISSIONS

distribute it. Similarly letters to Members are much more effective if they appear to have been sent spontaneously, than if they appear too evidently to be coming in as the result of an organized campaign.

A comment of Sir Alan Herbert is worth quoting on this point. In February and March 1937, between the committee and the report stages of the Matrimonial Causes Bill, there was 'a massive postal bombardment of Members . . . chiefly the work of the Mothers' Union, who claimed that their 500,000 members were united against us'. The promoters of the bill were worried at first, recognizing that 'such a bombardment, in the past, is said to have caused a stampede of Members', but in retrospect, Herbert's assessment is thus: 'In fact, I think, it caused little but annoyance. It was too early, too violent, and too evidently organized. Members pay due attention to the views of their constituents; but they are never much impressed by those who unite only because somebody tells them to.'[1]

It would be unwise to suggest that Members of Parliament are wholly impervious to pressure from their constituencies, though they are probably affected less by fear of damaging their electoral chances through the loss of votes, than by fear of falling into disfavour with important elements in the local party organization. A study of the voting behaviour of Labour Members on the Sunday Observance Bill of 1953 would appear to support this view. This Bill, which aimed to make the British Sunday 'brighter' by allowing certain entertainments which are now forbidden, produced a great deal of activity on the part of Sabbatarian associations. When we analyse the voting we find that 22 of the 54 Labour Members for London and its suburbs voted for the second reading, as compared with only two of the 116 Labour Members for constituencies in Scotland, Wales, Lancashire and County Durham. On the other hand, there is no evidence to suggest that Labour Members with small majorities were peculiarly slow to support the Bill. Twelve of the 54 who voted for the second reading had majorities of under 3000, and three had majorities of under 1000.[2]

---

[1] A. P. Herbert, *The Ayes Have it*, op. cit., p. 147.
[2] H.C. Debs., 30th January 1953, vol. 510, col. 1438. Among all Labour Members the proportions with small majorities were about the same. Of the 295 elected in 1951, 62 had majorities of under 3000, 21 of under 1000.

It is notorious that Sabbatarianism is very strong, particularly among the people who dominate the local Labour Party organizations, in those areas whose Labour Members had so little enthusiasm for the Bill. It is hard to avoid the conclusion that the notorious strength of sabbatarian feeling among Scottish, Welsh and Northern Socialists had some effect on the voting behaviour of the Labour Members from those areas. With most Members, specific pressure or actual instruction would not be needed.

In this instance, there was a very widespread agreement among the leaders and adherents of a particular party, but with the more usual type of private Member's bill, where feeling is less concentrated, pressures from constituencies are less likely to produce results in the division lists.

Another device occasionally used by associations is to get up public petitions with the greatest possible number of signatures, asking the House to vote for or against a bill that is about to come forward. Thus the introduction of the Sunday Observance Bill, which we have just examined, led interested bodies to get up a petition for its rejection. The petition, signed by over half a million people, was presented the day before the Bill was due to come up for second reading.[1]

Organizations do not limit their activities to attempts to influence votes. They try also to find Members of Parliament to speak on their behalf in the House, and they may also devote much energy, if it seems worth while, to stating their own case directly to the promoters of bills and to the Government.

Any organization that has its points to make will try to get an M.P. to be prepared to state its case, above all at the committee stage, but the discussion between the spokesmen of the divergent points of view does not take place only in the parliamentary stages proper. The different organizations concerned may send their representatives to take part in informal conferences in the House of Commons and elsewhere, where as far as possible they will try to strike bargains and to make compromises with one another by direct negotiation. Thus in 1921, when a Criminal Law Amendment Bill was before Parliament, there was a meeting in the Palace of Westminster where, in Lady Astor's words, 'practically every organization interested was represented', and where it was agreed that these bodies should work together to secure the

[1] H.C. Debs., 29th January 1953, vol. 510, col. 1163.

passing of the Bill by abstaining from introducing controversial amendments.[1]

3. THE IMPORTANCE OF CONSULTATION WITH ASSOCIATIONS

A Member who brings forward a bill without having previously discussed its contents with as many as possible of the interested bodies, including the hostile ones, jeopardizes his chances of success. The need for full consultation with the organizations concerned is well illustrated by the fate of Miss Irene Ward's bill of the 1938-9 session, proposing to bring miners' nystagmus within the scope of workmen's compensation. Miss Ward had won the fourth place in the ballot and her Bill had had its first reading, along with the other balloted bills, on 11th November 1938. It came up for second reading on 9th December. But it had been drawn up without the collaboration of the Miners' Union, whose representative only saw the text of the Bill on 6th December. The two intervening days had been spent in hurried discussion between Miss Ward, the Miners' representatives and the Home Office, but insuperable difficulties still remained unresolved. On the 9th Mr. Gordon Macdonald, speaking for the miners, moved the rejection of the bill, saying, 'Miss Ward ought to have had one or two months to discuss this in advance with the interests concerned'.[2] In the circumstances it was clearly useless to press the bill, and the second reading motion was negatived without a division.

It is possible to argue that the increasing necessity for consulting outside bodies in the preparation of all legislation is a factor tending to reduce the suitability of private Members' bills as a method of bringing in legislation. When the consultations are carried on under the aegis of a Government Department it is generally clear to all concerned that the Minister is the effective arbiter, and he is well placed for persuading the different interests concerned to agree to a reasonable compromise. When a mere private Member of Parliament is in charge of the discussions, however, he has not this authority behind him, and the interests

---

[1] Cf. Lady Astor's Question, asking for facilities for the Bill, H.C. Debs., 15th June 1921, vol. 143, col. 409.

[2] H.C. Debs., 9th December 1938, vol. 342, cols. 1501-7.

may be unready to accept the ultimate verdict of a parliamentary Standing Committee, or even of the majority of the House at the report stage. For this reason the appropriate Minister himself may conceivably step in and take a part in the discussions, but his position is then often less satisfactory than it would be if he had full responsibility, in terms clearly understood by everyone concerned, for the measure under discussion. On occasion, however, it may be better for the Minister to appear to be in a detached position than in a position of direct responsibility.

4. ROYAL COMMISSIONS

We have now recognized that the House of Commons, conscious of the need for adequate knowledge of the problems and for a responsible attitude in decision-making, does not make its decisions, even on wholly 'non-political' matters, like a debating society. The importance of the private discussions between the promoters of a bill and the various interested bodies, with the Government sometimes taking part, has been noticed. But apart from these discussions there are often other important preliminaries to be gone through before a private Member's Bill is likely to have a successful passage through its parliamentary stages. The debates and votes, even when entirely free, on bills of any substance at all, are generally preceded by enquiries held outside Parliament, by Royal Commissions or Departmental Committees or other ad hoc groups set up by the Government of the day for the purpose of obtaining as much relevant information as possible and of providing the House with reports and recommendations which can be regarded as the result of the informed deliberation of fair-minded and well-qualified people. A glance through Professor and Mrs. Ford's *Breviate of Parliamentary Papers*[1] is enough to show how extensively such committees have enquired into every aspect of British life.

The first time a substantial or complicated proposal for reform is brought before Parliament as a private Member's bill, the most that can be expected in the way of concrete results is generally a promise by the Government to set up a Committee to enquire into the matter. The eventual success of the proposal will in all

[1] P. & G. Ford, *A Breviate of Parliamentary Papers*, 1917–39 (Blackwell, 1951).

probability only follow a favourable recommendation by the Committee, and the Committee's proposals are likely to be followed fairly closely in the bill that is finally brought before Parliament.

Indeed, committees of this sort play a very important part in the legislative process. The fact that a Royal Commission or a Committee is set up and makes a report is, however, no guarantee that action will arise out of its report. As a rule no Government feels itself under any obligation to implement a Royal Commission's proposals; indeed there is a widespread, and not wholly erroneous, opinion among the general public, that the establishment of such Commissions is a device whereby Governments try to consign awkward proposals to a decent oblivion.[1] A proposal for a Royal Commission may therefore meet with opposition in the House of Commons.

Thus in 1951, when Mrs. White brought forward her Matrimonial Causes Bill, the Attorney-General said: 'These are all grave social problems. They require great study and consideration before legislation is passed in regard to them.' The solution which he offered was the appointment of a Royal Commission, and it appears that he did his best to encourage Members to vote against the Bill.[2] The House rejected his advice by voting for the second reading by 131 votes to 60,[3] but later the sponsors accepted the Government's offer. When the Bill reached the Standing Committee Mrs. White at once advised the Committee to make no attempt to proceed with it.[4] The Committee agreed with her proposal by 20 votes to 8, the eight rebels all being Labour Members.[5]

Once a Committee has been appointed it would evidently be undesirable for Parliament to pass a bill before the Committee has completed its work. If a bill should happen to be introduced while its subject-matter is under deliberation in a Committee, the object is usually either to draw public attention to the Committee's work, or, more constructively, to leave time for the ultimate passing of the bill during the current session, with

---

[1] Sir Alan Herbert, in *Independent Member*, p. 102, cites the Royal Commission on Betting of 1932 as an instance of a body which made recommendations which long went unheeded.   [2] Cf. above, pp. 62 and 104.
[3] H.C. Debs., 9th March 1951, vol. 485, cols. 999 ff.
[4] Official Report, Standing Committee 'B', 1950–1, col. 881.
[5] Ibid., col. 902.

the Committee's recommendations incorporated during the later parliamentary stages.

To take an example at random, the passing of legislation allowing people legally to adopt children, and to be secure against any claims from the natural parents, followed the introduction of private Members' bills on the subject and the reports of committees. A Home Office Committee was set up in 1921 and reported in favour of legislation on the matter,[1] but nothing concrete was done for the time being. Meanwhile the stream of private Members' bills continued. The Committee on Child Adoption, under the chairmanship of Mr. Tomlin, was set up in 1924 and presented three reports, of which the first was a general survey of the problems involved and of the measures needed to deal with the problems,[2] and the second made certain recommendations and actually contained a draft bill embodying these recommendations.[3] Meanwhile, yet another bill (the sixth on the subject since 1918) was introduced in 1925, but was dropped at the request of the Government in order that the full report of the Tomlin Committee should be available before Parliament took action. The bill eventually became law in 1926.[4]

The great merit of Royal Commissions is that they provide Parliament, the Government and the public with the background of balanced information and expert opinion without which it is hard to approach some types of decision in a responsible way. Their importance is all the greater because the British Parliament makes no use of Standing Committees of the American type, with powers to hear witnesses. It is worth remembering that much of the great reform legislation of the nineteenth century was based on the reports of Royal Commissions; in these cases it was the Government above all that relied on their reports. Nowadays, with all the opportunities that the Government has for consulting informally with appropriate bodies on matters related to the major problems of the day, the rôle of Royal Commissions is perhaps a little less important in relation to major questions than it was in the past, but in relation to questions of the type that form the subject-matter of most private Members' bills it remains of the first importance.

[1] Cmd. 1254 of 1921.   [2] Cmd. 2401 of 1924–5.
[3] Cmd. 2469 of 1924–5.
[4] The Adoption of Children Act, 16 & 17 Geo. 5, ch. 29.

Chapter VI

THE CRITERIA OF SUITABILITY FOR TREATMENT IN PRIVATE MEMBERS' BILLS

1. THE PRESENT POSITION: GENERAL

IN previous chapters an attempt has been made to trace historically the developments and changes in the practice of Parliament and of the Government in dealing with private Members' bills. The present chapter will seek to describe the position as it is in the middle of the twentieth century, and to define principles according to which particular classes of subjects may be regarded as suitable or unsuitable for treatment in private Members' bills.

2. SOME FACTORS MAKING FOR UNSUITABILITY

It is by now fairly widely agreed that private Members' bills should in general avoid large political issues although there is still room for an Opposition bill from time to time. When we examine the debates we find that one of the arguments most commonly put forward is that the matter under discussion ought to be dealt with by a bill for which the Government of the day would take full responsibility. The rule that private Members of Parliament may not propose money bills imposes a serious limitation on the scope of private Members' bills, and makes it unnecessary for us to discuss the undesirability of pork-barrel proposals.

SOME FACTORS MAKING FOR UNSUITABILITY

A. *Proposals for Constitutional Change*

A proposal for constitutional change, even if it does not raise controversial political issues, is likely to be regarded as outside the province of private Members' legislation. Thus in 1932, when a Conservative Member brought in a proposal to amend the Parliament Act by inserting into it a safeguard against 'tacking', other Conservatives were very lukewarm in their attitude, and Mr. Crookshank (who then held no office) said that this was a matter which could only be dealt with in a Government bill.[1] Just after one o'clock the House was counted out, and the debate came to an ignominious end.[2]

There have been instances of proposals for constitutional change being successfully brought in by private Members, with ministerial approval. The old constitutional rule that a Member of the House of Commons, on being appointed to ministerial office, should resign his seat and seek re-election, was finally abolished by an Act of 1926[3] which began its career as a private Member's bill.[4] Although the first step towards this change had been taken by means of a Government bill seven years earlier, the Government was probably loath to take the final step itself. The value of this precedent for the successful introduction of constitutional change by a private Member's bill is rather doubtful, because the habits of 1926 with regard to fit subjects for Friday debates were not at all the same as the habits of today. It is noteworthy too that in that debate not only the Prime Minister, but also Mr. Arthur Henderson and Sir John Simon, took part. The proposal was certainly recognized as having substantial importance as a constitutional amendment, but the Government no doubt preferred at that time not to bring it forward as a Government bill, both because its passing would give the Government, as opposed to Parliament and the people, specific advantage, and because there was some very vigorous opposition to this measure from the Conservative back benches, where there were several staunch defenders of the established order. In modern conditions, a bill of this type would probably be brought in by the Government after consultations with the Opposition.

[1] H.C. Debs., 16th December 1932, vol. 273, col. 692.
[2] Ibid., col. 718.
[3] Re-election of Ministers Act (1919) Amendment Act, 1926, 16 & 17 Geo. 5, ch. 19.   [4] H.C. Debs., 12th February 1926, vol. 191, cols. 1417 ff.

THE CRITERIA OF SUITABILITY

A special class of proposals for constitutional change is that concerned with demands for administrative devolution, or more particularly for some form of 'home rule' for Scotland or Wales. Several bills of this kind were brought in by private Members both before and after the war of 1914–18, and some of them passed their second reading stages, without making any further progress. Even now, enthusiasts for Scottish or Welsh home rule are not likely to be damped by any notion that great questions should be avoided on Fridays. There has indeed been no Scottish home rule bill since 1945, but it will not be very surprising if one is brought forward before very long. Mr. S. O. Davies' Government of Wales Bill of 1954–5, supported entirely by Scottish and Welsh Labour Members,[1] has revived the old tradition. It is noteworthy, however, that only 62 Members voted on the closure motion at the second reading debate, 48 of them against it.[2]

Attempts to regulate by private Members' bills the organization of and conditions of employment within the Civil Service have been considered as incursions by Parliament into a field which belongs properly to the Government's prerogative powers. In 1927, when a bill was introduced with the aim of forbidding the current practice of dismissing women civil servants on the ground that they had married, the Financial Secretary to the Treasury expressed his opposition in unusually uncompromising terms, although the bill had been introduced by a back-bencher of his own side. 'The House of Commons', he said, 'cannot take away from the Executive Government the responsibility for carrying on the administration of the country. . . . Is it conceivable that such a far-reaching change as this will be made by the House of Commons on the motion of Private Members, who have no responsibility and . . . most of whom are without any experience of administration?'[3]

In 1953, when some Conservative Members put forward a bill concerned with the organization of the Civil Service, the Government spokesman claimed not merely that the matter was unsuitable for a private Member's bill, but that it was unsuitable for legislation at all.[4]

---

[1] *Weekly Hansard*, 15th December 1954, col. 1776.
[2] Ibid., 4th March 1955, col. 2534. Cf. above, p. 70.
[3] H.C. Debs., 29th April 1927, vol. 205, col. 1221.
[4] Ibid., 24th April 1953, vol. 514, cols. 1710 ff.

SOME FACTORS MAKING FOR UNSUITABILITY

B. *Subjects requiring Special Negotiations*

A measure does not need to involve constitutional change or major party controversy before it is said to be too large or complicated for treatment by a private Member's bill. Since the 1920s, and particularly in the 1930s, the complaint that 'this matter ought to have been dealt with in a Government bill, because it is complicated, and because a settlement ought to be based on consultation and agreement', seems to run like a refrain through the Friday debates. A good illustration is provided by the terms of Captain Hudson's reasoned amendment to Mr. Ernest Winterton's Annual Holiday Bill in 1929: 'That this House declines to proceed with a Bill which materially affects every phase of industry, agriculture and commerce, which interferes with a long-established custom of employers and employed to settle conditions in their own industries, and which is consequently of so far-reaching a character that this House should not entertain it unless it is presented by a Government which is in a position, after full consultation with the interests concerned, to give the House authoritative information on the cost and effects of the proposal and the measure of agreement thereon throughout the industries affected.'[1] Captain Hudson added that if the Bill was given a second reading he hoped that it would go to a Select Committee, so that the interests affected would be able to come to state their case.

A matter may be said to be inappropriate for treatment in a private Member's bill on the ground that it is an inseparable part of a whole which is so large and complicated that only the Government is competent to take the responsibility of bringing in reforms. When Sir Hilton Young, a Conservative, brought forward a Rural Amenities Bill, Mr. Ede moved a reasoned amendment to suggest that the matter should be dealt with ultimately as part of a comprehensive planning measure.[2] The Minister of Health, Mr. Greenwood, also stressed the necessity for full and authoritative discussion before the introduction of far-reaching reforms concerning the powers of Local Authorities.[3] The Bill was given a second reading, but was later withdrawn. When a bill was brought in to assimilate the system of rating in London with

---
[1] H.C. Debs., 15th November 1929, vol. 231, col. 2435.
[2] Ibid., 21st February 1930, vol. 235, col. 1760.
[3] Ibid., col. 1827.

the system operating in the rest of the country, in accordance with the terms of a report of the Central Valuation Committee, it was said by the Government of the day to be in itself a perfectly appropriate bill for a private Member to introduce. Nevertheless the Government hoped that Parliament would make no such particular change in the law in advance of the more comprehensive changes it was itself intending ultimately to propose. This type of argument is heard very frequently indeed with reference to private Members' bills.

Very complex or technical questions would by now probably be regarded as generally unsuitable for treatment in private Members' bills, even if party issues were not involved. This does not mean that such subjects are never brought forward; they are, however, less common than in the past. Until comparatively recently the rating of machinery was a subject which came forward almost every year, although in 1922 there was a committee of the Cabinet trying to find a way through the maze of technical difficulties involved.[1] The problem has been brought forward again by Mr. Pargiter's Industrial and Agricultural Rates Bill, brought in on a low place in the ballot in the session of 1954-5, and talked out at second reading after a one-minute hearing.[2] Nowadays, on the introduction of a bill involving technicalities—and this term generally includes everything to do with the necessity for consulting Trade Unions and employers' organizations—it is at once complained that the questions concerned should be dealt with only by a Government bill.

Two complex and technical questions which have been the subject of some post-war private Members' bills are the closely allied topics of precautions against accidents at work and workmen's compensation. A brief study of the history of legislation on this subject will indicate the interplay of official proposals and private Members' proposals. The first Workmen's Compensation Act was passed in 1880, and it was followed by others in 1897, 1906 and 1917. In 1893 Asquith brought in a bill which Chamber-

---

[1] Cf. the speech of the Minister of Health, Sir Alfred Mond, on the second reading of the bill brought in in 1922 (H.C. Debs., 28th April 1922, vol. 153, col. 883). On this occasion the Government expressed neutrality and the bill was given a second reading by a large majority. (col. 928). There were officeholders on each side in the division.

[2] *Weekly Hansard*, 4th February 1955, col. 1515.

lain criticized because it did not go far enough, but it was defeated in the House of Lords. In 1918 both sides were dissatisfied with the existing system, and the Government set up a Departmental Committee, which made its report in 1920.[1] The Committee's work was in the main abortive, however. Seven of its twelve members made reservations on points of substance, and it was left for the Labour Party to go ahead with the promotion of its own measure. The Labour bill was introduced under the ballot by Labour Members who had won good places in 1922 (when the sitting on the Friday chosen was lost owing to the prolongation of the previous day's debate), in 1923, 1925 and then finally in every session except one from 1932 until the outbreak of war.

Since 1945 there have been a Safety of Employment Bill in 1949, a National Insurance (Industrial Injuries) Bill in 1952, a Safety in Employment Bill in 1954. The first two were both withdrawn at second reading, but on the third there was a division which ran, as in pre-war days, on party lines. It is probably fair to say that the main object of these recent bills has been little more than to prod the Government of the day to take action more quickly than it would otherwise have done in remedying admitted defects in existing legislation, brought about by changing conditions.

3. SUBJECTS WHICH APPEAR TO BE SUITABLE

It has been said that, in a general way, private Members' bills 'should be serious attempts at legislation in fields with which the political parties, as such, are not concerned'.[2] The modern tendency is undoubtedly towards concentration on constructive bills, which have a reasonable hope of being passed into law without the necessity for the Government to take over responsibility for them. Nevertheless, it is still quite legitimate to bring in a bill on a difficult and complicated subject, even if it is unlikely to pass, for the sake of educating public opinion and of pressing the Government to act on its own account. A very good example of such a bill is provided by Mr. Nabarro's Clean Air Bill of February 1955. Mr. Nabarro had for years been most zealous in urging state action for the promotion of more economical and cleaner use of fuel, and had seized many opportunities for bringing the subject

[1] Cmd. 816 and 909 of 1920.
[2] *The Economist*, 11th November 1950, p. 727.

forward on various occasions in Parliament.[1] He won a good place in the ballot in the session of 1954–5 and used it for the introduction of his Clean Air Bill,[2] a large and complicated measure of the kind which should normally be brought in by the Government. Mr. Nabarro's bill was based on the report, then recently published, of a Committee on air pollution under the chairmanship of Sir Hugh Beaver. The Government had already accepted the Committee's recommendations in principle.[3] In his second reading speech Mr. Nabarro said that his purpose in bringing the Bill forward would be achieved if the Government would undertake to bring in a bill of its own during the current session. The Minister gave this undertaking, and Mr. Nabarro withdrew his Bill. His reward came in the next session.[4]

Having suggested some general principles we may usefully attempt a more exact and detailed classification of the types of subject which, if we are to judge from recent experience, seem to be most often dealt with by private Members' bills. There seem to be three main classes, and some sub-divisions. In the first place we have proposals for social improvement, generally idealistic rather than selfish, in accordance with the aspirations of some group or other; secondly there are proposals for legal reform prompted by a dissatisfaction with some obscurity or mechanical defect in the state of the existing law, or by a feeling that the law is out of tune with current opinions and needs; lastly there are proposals for the legal definition of the status of particular bodies or professions. Some of these proposals are really analogous to private bills.

A. *Proposals for Moral and Social Betterment*

The first main class, that of the proposals which aspire to make the country a better place, probably includes the most interesting bills which are put forward, and bills of this type often arouse sectional opposition in so far as, for the sake of one group or for the general improvement of the community, they may propose to restrict the liberty of some persons or to make certain permitted practices illegal.

[1] In particular, he had made a long speech in seconding a private Member's motion on coal utilization, on 7th March 1952.
[2] *Weekly Hansard*, 4th February 1955, cols. 1426–1514. Cf. above, pp. 72 f.
[3] *The Times*, 27th January 1955.   [4] Cf. above, p. 75.

SUBJECTS WHICH APPEAR TO BE SUITABLE

The most important class of proposals under this main heading is the reform of the law relating to questions of personal behaviour in matters about which people have strong conscientious or 'moral' or religious feelings. Among these are the control of drinking, gambling and Sabbath-breaking. There are large and powerful societies dedicated to the reduction or prevention of 'vices', and they have been very active in attempting to sway Parliament. At election time candidates are regularly pressed by these bodies to give undertakings that if elected they will do their best to further proposals for restriction of drinking, etc., and many Members are not disinclined to be active for these objectives. Even in this field the argument that the matter in question ought to be dealt with in a Government bill is sometimes put forward, and indeed there have been many Government bills on licensing.

The legislative control of the sale of alcoholic liquor has a very long history, and, paradoxically enough, it is only recently that the subject has come to be regarded as belonging mainly to the class of matters suitable for treatment in private Members' bills. It has been estimated that at least 400 Acts have been passed, from that of 1552, whose preamble complained of the 'intollerable hurtes and trobles to the Comon Wealthe of this Realme' derived from drunkenness, to our modern Acts. About the beginning of the twentieth century the subject of drink control was a first-class political issue. Many private Members' bills on it were indeed introduced each year, but there was so much political feeling on the matter and so great a need to consider various established interests that only the Government of the day could aspire to bring in measures of substance with any real hope of passing. The Licensing Bill of 1908 was brought in as a Government measure and treated as a first-class political issue. As late as 1921, a private Member's bill was withdrawn after being opposed in the House on the ground that only the Government was competent to introduce legislation on the matter,[1] and the Government did itself bring in a bill giving effect to the proposals of a Round Table conference. The Bill eventually received the Royal Assent,[2] having passed through its main stages in the House of Commons without a single division, except on a proposal, put forward by Mr.

[1] H.C. Debs., 22nd April 1921, vol. 140, col. 2297.
[2] As the Licensing Act, 1921, 11 & 12 Geo. 5, ch. 42.

Horatio Bottomley, that it should go to a Committee of the whole House instead of a Standing Committee. Mr. Bottomley got only six Members into the lobby in favour of his proposal.[1]

The last occasion on which a proposal for total prohibition was discussed in the House of Commons was in 1931, just before the repeal of prohibition in the United States. The Home Secretary pointed out that the Royal Commission on Licensing would be making its report before very long, and suggested that Parliament could not usefully make new decisions about the drinking laws until the Commission had reported. The supporters of the Bill, unimpressed with this argument, divided the House, and were defeated by 137 votes to 18.[2]

Since 1948 a bill to exempt refreshment rooms at airports from certain licensing restrictions has twice been brought in under the Ten Minutes Rule. In 1952 there was a tie at the division (173 votes on each side), and the Speaker gave his casting vote in favour of the motion; in 1955 there was a favourable vote of 234 to 137.[3] The same bill was brought in under the ballot in the session 1953–4, but its introducer had a low place, and the bill was talked out three times.

Sabbatarians' proposals have been designed mainly to forbid or to restrict the Sunday opening of shops, places of entertainment, etc. There was a fairly steady stream of private Members' bills for the repression of 'Sabbath-breaking' in the early years of the present century, but few of them were introduced under the ballot. In 1931 a bill to forbid butchers' shops to open on Sundays was counted out before a word had been said on it.[4] A bill of more general intent, the Shops (Sunday Trading) (Scotland) Bill, promoted by the Lord's Day Observance Society, was put forward in 1934, but after a debate lasting the whole of a Friday's sitting its supporters were not numerous enough to be able to force the

[1] H.C. Debs., 7th July 1921, vol. 144, col. 2674.
[2] Ibid., 13th February 1931, vol. 248, cols. 759–844. The Royal Commission eventually made a report, at enormous length, and published the Minutes of Evidence of the seventy days of hearings. The detailed proposals of the Royal Commission were far removed from total prohibition, and there were many reservations by individual members (Cmd. 3988 of 1931–2).
[3] H.C. Debs., 24th June 1952, vol. 502, col. 2056, and 9th February 1955, *Weekly Hansard*, col. 1924.
[4] H.C. Debs., 24th April 1931, vol. 251, col. 1344.

closure. Although with 61 votes they outnumbered the 42 who voted against the closure, they fell far short of the hundred stipulated by the Standing Order.[1]

Legislation about the opening of cinemas on Sundays has been passed on the basis of Government bills. In 1931 a ruling of the courts, to the effect that Sunday cinemas were illegal under the law of 1780, made it imperative that the law should be either enforced or promptly amended. So the Labour Government brought in a Bill which proposed to make it legal for Local Authorities to allow or to forbid Sunday cinemas at their discretion. On a free vote the second reading was approved by 258 votes to 210,[2] but after being sent to Standing Committee the Bill was abandoned.[3]

In the new Parliament of 1931, the National Government brought in a Bill similar to that of their predecessors. This was given a second reading on a free vote by the narrow majority of 235 votes to 217,[4] but was dropped after the Standing Committee had passed an amendment confining its operation to the County of London.[5] Another Bill was brought forward, again by the Government, with clauses to placate as far as possible the enemies of Sunday opening, and passed through all its stages by large majorities (237 to 61 at the second reading[6] and 146 to 56 at the third reading).[7] By now the Government Whips had been put on,

---

[1] H.C. Debs., 9th March 1934, vol. 286, col. 2254.

[2] Ibid., 20th April 1931, vol. 251, col. 758. Mr. Clynes, then Home Secretary, in introducing the Bill, claimed to be 'an individual advocate', although in no sense committing (his) colleagues either officially or personally (col. 633).

[3] It was discussed in Standing Committee 'B' at nine meetings (30th June to 30th July 1931). The House was then adjourned for the Summer recess, during which the Government fell.

[4] H.C. Debs., 13th April 1932, vol. 264, cols. 833–962. Several Ministers, both National Liberal and Conservative, voted against the Bill although it was a Government measure.

[5] Standing Committee 'B', proceedings, 10th May 1932, p. 5. The majority was 27 to 23.

[6] H.C. Debs., 27th May 1932, vol. 266, col. 798. Sir H. Samuel, the Home Secretary, said in introducing the Bill that the Government was obliged to try to get some decision which Parliament could accept, and was putting the Whips on in support of the most acceptable compromise that it could find (col. 715).

[7] Ibid., 29th June 1932, vol. 267, col. 1982.

and they were largely, though by no means entirely, obeyed by Government supporters.

The most recent proposal regarding Sunday observance, that brought forward by Mr. John Parker in 1953, had an intention somewhat analogous to the bills on Sunday opening of cinemas, but went much further. It proposed that most of the old Sunday Observance Acts should be repealed, and that many forms of entertainment forbidden by the existing law should be permitted. The vote on this measure has already been mentioned above;[1] in relation to the present discussion the chief point of interest is that the House so decisively refused the Bill a second reading (by 281 votes to 57), but then very nearly approved the amendment proposing that there should be an enquiry into the matter by a Royal Commission or similar body. Over 100 of the Members who voted against the second reading voted in favour of the enquiry, and by so doing showed that they thought that the possibility of reform should be considered, but only on the basis of the sort of information that a Royal Commission's report would provide.

Even questions concerning the regulation of gambling are not entirely agreed to be the proper province of private Members' bills. Thus in 1922 Sir Edmund Bartley-Denniss, in the third reading debate on a very minor Gaming Bill (which had originated in the Lords, and aimed at giving some protection to bookmakers) said, 'The subject is one of general policy, and it is not, to my mind, a fitting subject for a private Member's bill.'[2] Nevertheless this Bill eventually passed and received the Royal Assent.

The session of 1934-5, although it allowed for no private Members' time, produced the Betting and Lotteries Act, a large and comprehensive measure introduced by the Government. But there have been several more private Members' bills on gambling since that time, in particular the successful Pool Betting Bill of 1954.

Another somewhat analogous question is that which relates to censorship of publications on moral grounds, and sometimes on other grounds too. The law has for a long time repressed and punished the publication of matter held to be seditious or blas-

[1] Pp. 66 f. and 120.
[2] H.C. Debs., 23rd June 1922, vol. 155, col. 1549.

phemous or obscene, and as people's opinions about the import of these words have changed, so the law has had to be changed from time to time. Two contrary influences have been at work, on the one hand the liberal tradition of modern times, and on the other hand an increasing concern with the duty of the state to protect the young from harmful influences. Private Members' bills in this field have generally had the objective of reducing the rigour of the law. In the present century many private Members' bills have been brought in with the intention of narrowing the definition of blasphemy, which was formerly very wide indeed. On the other hand, the 1920s and 1930s produced a succession of measures designed to repress seditious and blasphemous teaching to children, such as was said to be carried on at that time in certain youth classes run by political organizations. A Seditious and Blasphemous Teaching of Children Bill was given a second reading in 1933,[1] after being approved at a division which followed party lines, but it was not enacted.

Private Members' bills have concerned themselves with the censorship of plays, etc., and are probably the most suitable medium for the proposal of changes in the law in this sphere.[2]

In 1954 and 1955 the question of the repression of morally undesirable publications received much prominence. On the one hand, there were several prosecutions and attempts to order the destruction of books on the ground of obscene libel, in such conditions as to create apprehension in some quarters lest the reasonable rights of authors and publishers should be endangered; on the other hand there was anxiety about the harm which might be done to the minds of young people by so-called 'horror comics', which were being sold with complete impunity. On the matter of the horror comics, agitation became vigorous in the autumn of 1954, and the Home Secretary undertook to prepare legislation to deal with the matter.[3] His Children and Young Persons (Harmful Publications) Bill was duly brought in, and was given a second reading in February 1955.[4] The Government had

[1] H.C. Debs., 7th April 1933, vol. 276, cols. 2071–146.
[2] Mr. E. P. Smith's Censorship of Plays (Repeal) Bill was given a second reading by a majority of 76 to 37 in 1949 (H.C. Debs., 25th March 1949, vol. 463, col. 796).
[3] Cf. H.C. Debs., 21st October 1954, vol. 531, cols. 1376 f.
[4] *Weekly Hansard*, 22nd February 1955, cols. 1074–188.

decided that it had a duty to take responsibility itself for legislation in this field. The Bill was given a second reading without a division, and received the Royal Assent on the day Parliament was prorogued before the dissolution.[1]

Meanwhile, the Society of Authors had set up an unofficial committee to enquire into the desirability of reform of the law in relation to obscene publications in the wider sense. The committee produced a bill, the text of which was published in February 1955.[2] Leave to bring in the Bill under the Ten Minutes Rule was given shortly afterwards.[3]

It is interesting that in these two closely related matters the Government took upon itself the task of bringing in the bill to deal with the horror comics, but left untouched the broader question of the need to prevent court proceedings such as those which attacked Boccacio's *Decameron* on the ground of obscenity. The Government was indeed criticized, during the second reading debate on its Harmful Publications Bill, for not dealing with the whole business of obscene publications at the same time.

Another class of bills which aim at the general improvement of personal behaviour is that large group of projects which aim at the promotion of the welfare of animals, regarded as an end in itself (as distinct from animal welfare considered as a part of general agricultural policy, etc.). Bills of this type, always numerous, have tended to become even more numerous since 1948.

From the earliest times Governments have felt loath to make themselves responsible for the introduction of legislation for the protection of animals, probably for two main reasons. In the first place the main task of the Government is to govern the human beings within the community, and to promote their welfare. To expend its energy for the sake of animals, who are not members of this community, would probably be a diversion of limited governmental resources away from their proper objects. In the second place, animals have no votes. Laws for the protection of animals must nearly always impose restrictions on the activities of some human beings, and a party which identifies itself with the imposition of such restrictions may alienate voters—not many, but a few

[1] *Weekly Hansard*, 6th May 1955, col. 2053.
[2] *The Times*, 3rd February 1955.
[3] *Weekly Hansard*, 15th March 1955, col. 1136.

SUBJECTS WHICH APPEAR TO BE SUITABLE

here and there, perhaps in evenly-balanced constituencies. Nevertheless, the Government is often ready to treat animal welfare bills sympathetically, and to help the promoters in various positive ways. It can do this by taking part in or even arranging discussions between the promoters and representatives of the groups who are opposed to the bill, and by trying to find ways of satisfying the legitimate interests of the two parties. The resources of Government Departments, with their extensive experience of this sort of activity, are very valuable here.

It is sometimes said that too much of the energy of Parliament on private Members' days is devoted to the affairs of animals, and it is indeed remarkable that in the session of 1948-9, when private Members' time was provided for the first time for ten years, no less than seven out of the twenty bills introduced under the ballot were concerned with the welfare of animals in one form or another. Nine out of the 38 balloted bills to receive the Royal Assent during the period 1948-54 dealt with the welfare and comfort of animals, considered as ends in themselves.[1] Among the 64 unsuccessful balloted bills another nine were animal bills, though some of these were enacted in later sessions, in which they have been counted among the bills passed.

Animal protection bills are very varied in type and aim, and have a peculiar interest in that although they are essentially very far removed from party politics, some classes of them tend to arouse feelings, hostile and friendly, which correspond fairly nearly with party alignments. Proposals for the prohibition of hunting, which have been brought forward several times in the past fifty years, provide us with the most obvious example.

Other bills for the protection of animals have been brought forward, often with success, in a great variety of fields. Bills passed in the last few years have dealt with conditions in pet shops, with the control of slaughtering and related matters in various forms, with the regulation of the treatment of performing animals, with the repression of cockfighting, with the docking of horses' tails. Finally, there has been the central problem of the definition of cruelty to animals and the prescription of sanctions for acts of cruelty. In all these spheres, although the Government has been

[1] This figure does not include the Dogs (Protection of Livestock) Bill, which was not purely an animal welfare measure. In addition, one of the seven Ten Minute bills to be enacted dealt with the slaughter of animals.

concerned to see that the Acts when passed are sound and workable, and that they do not unduly injure human interests which may be regarded as legitimate, the initiative has almost always been taken by private Members of Parliament, and if there had been no private Members' bills most of this code would probably never have been enacted.

Some devices and schemes for making the world a better place are essentially rational rather than 'moral' in character. The atmosphere of England is not very favourable to proposals of this kind. The most conspicuous success in this direction has probably been the Act, introduced as a private Member's bill, which finally made Summer Time a regular institution of British life. But this institution had originally found its way in by the back door, as it were, as a wartime expedient with a limited purpose. The idea of saving an hour of daylight on summer evenings became current in the early years of the twentieth century, and in Great Britain a campaign in favour of the scheme was launched by a private individual (Mr. Willett) in 1907. The next year a private Member's bill was introduced in the House of Commons and sent to a Select Committee,[1] but made no further progress. After the beginning of the war of 1914 the Government received advice from an expert committee on fuel economy, to the effect that the introduction of daylight saving would help the war effort, and in May the Government provided a day[2] for a debate on a motion moved by a private Member in favour of the principle of daylight saving.

After the House had approved the motion, the Government brought in daylight saving under its special powers, which lapsed when the war was over. In 1922, however, the Government brought in a bill to make Summer Time permanent, and the bill was passed by a large majority. The definitive statutory adoption of Summer Time was left, however, to be dealt with by private Members' bills with wholly free votes, and although the Government provided facilities for the eventual enactment of the Bill of 1925,[3] it was influenced in its decision to do so by the size of the

---

[1] The Committee, which held fourteen meetings and heard 45 witnesses, reported in favour of the adoption of Summer Time. (Cf. Report of the Select Committee on the Daylight Saving Bill, H.C. 204 of 1908.)

[2] Monday, 8th May 1916; H.C. Debs., 5s., vol. 82, cols. 301-70.

[3] The Summer Time Act, 1925, 15 & 16 Geo. 5, ch. 64.

SUBJECTS WHICH APPEAR TO BE SUITABLE

favourable majority (289 to 63), and it still asked that the actual period should be determined by a vote of the House.

Soon after this another bill of rather similar type was enacted,[1] providing that the date of Easter should be stabilized as the first Sunday after the second Saturday in April. But the second section of the Act provided that it should come into force only by an Order in Council which might be made, subject to certain conditions, at some unspecified date in the future. There has been no such Order in Council, but with the Act on the statute book the Government at least has power to fix the date of Easter. In 1951 the House approved, by the large majority of 279 to 105, a motion under the Ten Minutes Rule for leave to introduce a bill to bring the provisions of the Easter Act into operation forthwith.[2] No further progress was made.

Among proposals which have so far not succeeded are that for the adoption of the metric system and that for the reform by legislation of the spelling of the English language. Attempts to persuade the British Parliament to pass legislation for the adoption of the metric system have a long history. There was a strong movement in this direction about the turn of the century. A Select Committee of 1895 reported favourably. The Lords passed a bill in 1904, and many public bodies, including the L.C.C., gave their support. A bill was introduced under the ballot in the Commons in 1907, but even in the early days of the 1906 Parliament, with an atmosphere probably more favourable to this sort of reform than ever before or since, the Bill was defeated on second reading by 150 votes to 118.[3] The subject has appeared again recently. Mr. Follick, after coming near to success with spelling reform,[4] brought in a Decimal Coinage Bill under the Ten Minutes Rule in 1955.[5] There was no opposing speech, and leave to introduce the Bill was given without a division, although Mr. Follick had expressed a hope that the proposal would be divided against.

Private Members' bills have from time to time dealt successfully

[1] The Easter Act, 1928, 18 & 19 Geo. 5, ch. 35. International and national chambers of commerce had been passing repeated resolutions in favour of stabilization since 1900, and in 1923 a conference, called by the League of Nations, reached general agreement on the subject.
[2] H.C. Debs., 20th March 1951, vol. 485, col. 2336.
[3] Ibid., 22nd March 1907, 4s., vol. 171, cols. 1311–64.
[4] Cf. above, p. 60.
[5] *Weekly Hansard*, 2nd February 1955, col. 1117.

with various subjects which do not apparently belong to the classes suitable for them. Some important contributions to our road traffic laws have been made by Acts of Parliament originally brought in by private Members. The original basic statute relating to the lighting of road vehicles was Mr. Lougher's Road Transport Lighting Act,[1] which only just survived a count during the second reading debate, but passed through its later stages in Government time.[2] Two private Members' bills in this field were enacted in 1953. Colonel Harrison's bill [3] received its second reading without debate,[4] and passed after comparatively little discussion. Most of the amendments accepted in the Standing Committee were put down by Colonel Harrison himself,[5] on the advice of the Ministry of Transport, which had fully performed its evident duty of making the bill as sound as possible, so that in the event the bill might almost as well have been a Government bill. In the same session Mr. Powell's bill on the same subject was also enacted,[6] having occupied no time at all in the House and only ten minutes in the Standing Committee, where a bare quorum assembled in order to hear Mr. Powell's brief explanation of four amendments which he proposed.[7]

There is one minor function which Parliament often performs very badly, because in some cases the difficulties involved in passing a private Member's bill are too great. The procedure is ill-adapted for making alterations to existing Acts by simple amendments whose desirability may well be suggested by the existence of the legislation already in force. Thus if Parliament in one year passes a bill laying down say £100 as the limit of compensation to certain classes of injured persons, it seems that if, twenty years later, the value of money has been halved, the limit should without serious obstacle be increased to £200. Yet, unless it can secure passage as an unopposed bill, with not a single objection being raised at any stage, the amending bill has in such a case to contend with the same difficulties as has any bill which is breaking fresh ground.

[1] 17 & 18 Geo. 5, ch. 37.
[2] H.C. Debs., 1st April, 28th July and 8th November 1927.
[3] The Road Transport Lighting Act, 1 & 2 Eliz. 2, ch. 21.
[4] H.C. Debs., 30th January 1953, vol. 510, col. 1435.
[5] Official Report, Standing Committee 'B', 1952–3, cols. 662–87.
[6] The Road Transport Lighting (No. 2) Act, 1953, 1 & 2 Eliz. 2, ch. 22.
[7] Official Report, Standing Committee 'B', 1952–3, cols. 703–6.

SUBJECTS WHICH APPEAR TO BE SUITABLE

In 1905 an Act was passed setting at £100 the limit of compensation that might be awarded to a farmer whose crops were destroyed by sparks from railway engines, but fifteen years later the proposal to increase the limit to £200 was for some time unable to make any headway, although in 1922, when a Railway Fires Bill was given a second reading by 134 votes to 27, the Government raised no obstacles. The Bill was brought in again under the ballot in 1923 and allowed to pass its second reading without a division after a debate of a few minutes, but at the report stage its opponents proposed an amendment to reduce the figure to £125. This proposal was debated at some length before the closure was moved by the Minister of Agriculture and carried by 179 votes to 40, and the amendment defeated by 213 votes to 13. At the third reading stage, however, the Speaker, in view of all the previous discussion, consented to the putting of the question on the closure almost at once.[1] It was carried easily and the bill was eventually passed.

Similarly, after a bill had been passed in 1895 authorizing magistrates' courts to order husbands to pay a maximum of £2 a week by way of maintenance allowance to wives from whom they were separated, it was not until 1949 that an amending bill was passed to allow magistrates to order the payment of maintenance allowances of more than £2 weekly.[2] Yet the fall in the value of money before 1949 had evidently made the bill's maximum provisions out of date long before.

Another type of private Member's bill which perhaps deserves to have its passage facilitated is the type which aims to remedy an admitted defect in an Act already in force. Thus in 1937 Sir Assheton Pownall used his place in the ballot for the introduction of a Road Traffic Bill which aimed to abolish the rule, created by the Road Traffic Act of 1934, forbidding people to share taxis. The Bill did eventually become law, but not before the House had spent almost the whole of a Friday in debating the third reading.[3]

[1] Cf. above, p. 41.
[2] H.C. Debs., 15th February 1949, vol. 461, cols. 1534–58. Even so, the second reading debate took almost an hour and a half.
[3] H.C. Debs., 30th April 1937, vol. 323, cols. 698–760.

B. *Legal Reforms*

Private Members often make themselves responsible for proposing reforms of the law, civil or criminal, particularly regarding family relationships. Such matters are often unsuitable for treatment by Government bills, because the decisions of principle to be made often involve people's personal convictions, and are at the same time divorced from general problems of administration. Nevertheless, it is evidently of importance to the Government that measures of this kind should be passed in a workable form, so, while leaving the decisions at the main stages to free votes of the House, the Government often collaborates very closely indeed in the work of considering details at the committee stage, taking part in and sometimes actually arranging discussions with interested bodies, suggesting amendments, both informally and formally, and giving its opinion on the amendments that are proposed by other Members. Even so, there is sometimes some complaint in the House and in the Press about the piecemeal character of legal reform introduced in this way, based apparently on an idea that some more far-sighted legislator out of the pages of Aristotle or Rousseau should preside over all reforms of this kind.

The modifications that have been made in the law relating to prohibited degrees of relationship in marriage provide some interesting examples. In 1907 the Deceased Wife's Sister Act[1] was passed, having been brought in as a private Member's bill. The defenders of the measure insisted that this was not the thin end of the wedge. Nevertheless, in 1921 a new private Member's bill[2] was brought in and enacted, making it legal for a woman to marry her deceased husband's brother, and the enemies of the marriage taboos were already advocating further changes.

Yet there has not been universal agreement that even modest proposals of reform in this sphere are suitable for treatment in private Members' bills. In 1927,[3] a new bill to allow a man to marry his deceased wife's niece was attacked by several Members on the ground that the subject was too important and far-reaching

[1] 7 Edw. 7, ch. 47.
[2] The Deceased Brother's Widow's Marriage Act, 1921, 11 & 12 Geo. 5, ch. 24.
[3] H.C. Debs., 4th March 1927, vol. 203, cols. 794 ff.

SUBJECTS WHICH APPEAR TO BE SUITABLE

for treatment in a private Member's bill, and at one point in the debate the Government's spokesman was taken to task for not giving the House a clearer lead on the matter.[1] The bill was talked out, but, rather surprisingly in view of the vehemence with which objections were raised, it was later given a second reading as an unopposed measure.[2] It did not get beyond the report stage on this occasion, and when it again came forward in 1929 it was passed by the Commons but defeated at third reading in the Lords, by 26 votes to 25. The bill finally passed in 1931, but only after Lord Eustace Percy had stigmatized the whole proceedings as 'nibbling' . . . 'living from hand to mouth' and 'an example of that type of legislation which brings Parliament into contempt'.[3]

Legislation regarding wills, and the protection of the interests of spouses and offspring, has resulted from a number of private Members' proposals. A Wills and Intestacies (Family Maintenance) Bill was brought in in 1931,[4] to provide that a surviving spouse must be entitled to receive at least half the effects of the deceased, half the estate or £1000, whichever was the less, and half the income. Two more bills on the same subject were introduced in the session of 1935-6, both of them by Members who won rather low places in the ballot. Eleanor Rathbone's bill got a nine-minute hearing before the close of business one day.[5] In the next session another bill, which aimed to give protection to the rights of children as well as widows, was more successful, being given a second reading after a debate of ninety minutes,[6] in the course of which the Solicitor-General said that the Government was neutral in its attitude. This bill did not get its later stages taken in private Members' time, and when the backers tried to bring the bill forward at the close of ordinary business at 9.43 p.m. on a day late in June, the Government insisted on adjourning the House instead, and put the Whips on to ensure that it got its way.[7]

Eventually the Inheritance (Family Provision) Act was passed in 1938, having been hotly contested. The second reading was

[1] H.C. Debs., 4th March 1927, vol. 203, col. 805.
[2] Ibid., 1st April 1927, vol. 204, col. 1658.
[3] Ibid., 1st May 1931, vol. 251, cols. 1935 f. The Bill passed as 21 & 22 Geo. 5, ch. 31.
[4] H.C. Debs., 20th February 1931, vol. 248, col. 1641.
[5] Ibid., 20th March 1936, vol. 310, cols. 849-52.
[6] Ibid., 22nd January 1937, vol. 319, cols. 512-37.
[7] Ibid., Monday, 28th June 1937, vol. 325, cols. 1757-62.

debated for the whole of a sitting and carried without a division after the closure had been approved by 159 votes to 29.[1]

The regulation of marriage and divorce has also been dealt with by private Members' bills. Here no Government has been inclined to take any responsibility in relation to the fundamental question. It seems that the question is one which, in the absence of any ecclesiastical authority with special powers, ought to be decided by the general feeling of the community about what is right and proper, and in this sense the House of Commons may be said fully to 'represent' the community and its opinions. The Summary Procedure (Domestic Proceedings) Bill passed with practically no trouble in 1937,[2] the year of Sir Alan Herbert's bill.

The law regarding the adoption of children, to which reference has been made in connection with Royal Commissions, is another field in which private Members' bills have made a valuable contribution.[3] Private Members have also made a substantial contribution to the reform of the law of libel in the direction of protecting authors and publishers from the dangers to which their trade is subject. Here again that energetic Independent Member, Sir A. Herbert, played a substantial part, though the consummation came only after he had ceased to be a Member of the House. He was concerned in the first printing of a bill in 1937, and the bill was actually introduced under the ballot by Sir Stanley Reed in the next session.[4] It was withdrawn after the Attorney-General had promised that a Committee would be set up to look into the matter. The Committee, whose chairman was Lord Porter, eventually made its report in 1945, and a new bill, based on the Committee's Report,[5] was brought in by Mr. Lever and enacted, with substantial assistance from the Government, in 1952.[6]

Reform of the penalties exacted by the criminal law has always been a relatively fertile subject for private Members' proposals. Proposals of this kind have a very long history. Before the beginning of the nineteenth century, the brutalities of the old criminal

[1] H.C. Debs., 5th November 1937, vol. 328, cols. 1291-1374.
[2] It had its second reading on 5th February 1937. (H.C. Debs., vol. 319, cols. 1939-82.)
[3] Cf. above, p. 125.
[4] H.C. Debs., 3rd February 1939, vol. 343, col. 576. Cf. A. P. Herbert, *Independent Member*, pp. 124 ff.
[5] Cmd. 7536 of 1945.
[6] Cf. above, pp. 63 ff.

law began to be whittled away bit by bit, generally by statutes which began their parliamentary career as private Members' bills. In more recent times there were many private Members' bills for the abolition of corporal punishment—an end which was ultimately secured by the inclusion of this provision in a comprehensive Government bill passed in 1948.[1] More recently there has been an unsuccessful bill for the restoration of corporal punishment.[2]

There have been many bills aiming to abolish the death penalty, but (apart from a bill under the Ten Minutes Rule) the last legislative proposal of this kind, which was passed by the House of Commons but defeated in the Lords, was in fact in the form of a proposed new clause moved by a private Member for insertion in a Government bill.[3]

By now, however, the whole apparatus of the penal system, with the intricate inter-relationships of the objectives of deterrence and reform, has become so much a single whole that the subject is probably scarcely suitable for treatment in private Members' bills. Reforms in this field have recently been made by Government bills, which have been brought in from time to time, each in its day embodying the current ideas of police and Home Office and of the experts on whom the Home Office rely. As we have seen, Mr. Silverman's amendment to the bill of 1948, in which he proposed that the death penalty should be abolished, was treated almost as though it were an independent bill, but the Government's decision to allow a free vote on this affair caused it so much embarrassment that a 'casual majority' of the House of Commons, as Mr. Churchill then called it, is unlikely in the future to be considered competent to make the final decisions in this field.[4]

C. *Regulation of Professions*

The last of the three main classes of subjects, that of bills concerned with the legal definition of the status of particular bodies

---

[1] The Criminal Justice Act, 11 & 12 Geo. 6, ch. 58.
[2] H.C. Debs., 13th February 1953, vol. 511, cols. 758–846. Cf. above, p. 67.
[3] H.C. Debs., 14th April 1948, vol. 449, cols. 979–1098.
[4] The free vote of February 1955 was not quite of the same kind as that of 1948, because the question before the House was merely whether to agree or to disagree with an opinion.

or professions, can be disposed of very briefly.[1] The public interest requires that many occupations or professions, such as those of doctors, dentists, nurses, solicitors, etc., should be subject to special regulations. The right to exercise these professions must be granted only to persons who have successfully undergone appropriate tests of competence, or at least there must be some mark which will enable would-be clients to recognize those who have passed such tests. Qualified practitioners must be registered, and there must be provision for removal from the registers, subject to adequate safeguards, of individuals who have failed to observe certain standards of conduct. The task of devising the standards and so on must be performed by some recognized body or other in each case, unless the state undertakes the task itself. In this country we have preferred to leave this task to private bodies, but the status and powers of these bodies must be regulated by law. Bills must therefore be brought in from time to time, and it is generally not convenient for the Government itself to promote the bills. Although the bills have some of the characteristics of Private bills (as opposed to private Members' bills, which are Public bills) it is for various reasons not suitable to have them subject to the rules which normally apply to Private bills. It is therefore left to private Members to bring in the necessary bills, but they do this, really, only in default of some special machinery to govern such legislation.

It may very well be argued that the present system is unsatisfactory. If the leading members of some profession think that a bill needs to be passed with reference to the status of that profession, it seems undesirable that the bill can only be effectively brought in if some Member of Parliament who has won a good place in the ballot is prepared to use his place for the purpose. It is true that if full agreement has been reached outside Parliament it may be possible for a bill to be brought in and passed as an unopposed measure, but it often happens that differences of opinion have arisen between groups within the profession or between different registration societies, and that these differences are brought into the parliamentary proceedings; in such cases there is no chance of a measure going through without opposition.

It seems that in this field there is something to be said for the

[1] Cf. Sir A. M. Carr-Saunders and P. A. Wilson, *The Professions* (1933), Roy Lewis and Angus Maude, *Professional People* (Phoenix House, 1952), etc.

SUBJECTS WHICH APPEAR TO BE SUITABLE

establishment of a special type of procedure, akin to the procedure for Private bills, but with special features to answer the needs of bills of this type. The device of the Select Committee, which hears evidence from the bodies concerned, has sometimes been used.[1]

Another class of bills even more akin to Private bills is that of measures regulating the affairs of particular charities. Bills of this type are fairly numerous, but they need not concern us here at all, because they are almost always allowed to pass through all their stages without discussion in the House, and are therefore not introduced under the ballot.

This disposes of the general classification of subjects which seem to be suitable for treatment by private Members' bills. It must be emphasized that no list or classification could claim to be exhaustive, or to do more than suggest the broad outlines of classes of subjects which seem to be suitable. The criteria of suitability are clearly liable to considerable changes in the long run, and even in the short run they cannot be rigid. A subject may become suitable for treatment in a Government bill simply by virtue of having once been the subject of a private Member's bill which has led to an enlightening debate. Nevertheless, our attempts at a rough classification do suggest that there are, at any time, many fields in which private Members may perform a useful service by bringing measures forward for discussion in Parliament.

[1] Cf. Jennings, *Parliament*, op. cit., p. 186.

Chapter VII

ALTERNATIVE METHODS OF
PROPOSING LEGISLATION

BEFORE we embark on our final evaluation of the whole system of private Members' bills, it is necessary to go back and examine briefly the use which Members make of their opportunities for introducing legislative proposals outside the balloted time on Fridays. We must concern ourselves with four main types of business: bills introduced in the ordinary way under S.O. No. 35, but not under the ballot; bills under the Ten Minutes Rule (S.O. No. 12); motions brought in under the ballot on alternate Fridays; and finally other opportunities which may arise in the course of various kinds of debates.[1] The last two categories are, in a sense, outside the scope of our study of private Members' bills, but in so far as we can only pass judgment on the main topic if we have taken into account the alternative methods of bringing ideas forward indirectly, we must say something about these possibilities.

1. NON-BALLOTED BILLS BROUGHT IN WITHOUT
PRELIMINARIES

The first class of proposals to be considered consists of the bills which private Members introduce by virtue of the exercise of the unrestricted right which they possess, under S.O. No. 35, to put

[1] Cf. above, pp. 13 f.

down bills for automatic first reading. When a bill is brought in and read a first time in this way it is ordered to be printed, and a day is named for its second reading. But this naming of a day is generally a fictitious procedure; the bill may be put down on the order paper, but that does not mean that it will be dealt with. It is in fact unlikely to get a second reading unless the House is prepared to let it go through without debate, as an unopposed bill.

The main rules of procedure with unopposed bills have been mentioned above. Such bills can be taken through their second reading stages on Fridays after four o'clock,[1] provided that there is no objection from any Member. As they do not take any parliamentary time, their passage is free from difficulties connected with the parliamentary time-table.[2] But there still remains the great difficulty of ensuring that there will be no objection, and this difficulty seems to be rather more formidable now than it was in the past. With bills of this type the whole of the discussion on the principles, if there is any, takes place privately, outside the formal sittings of Parliament, between the different interested bodies and persons who must all be satisfied before the measure can go forward in Parliament without opposition. The participants in such discussions may well include Members of Parliament and representatives of Government Departments as well as of the organizations concerned. Parliament will only be prepared to act as a rubber stamp for a private Member's bill if it is quite certain that there is full agreement on the measure outside.

When we consider the increasing importance of organized interest groups in modern communities, it is perhaps surprising that the number of unopposed bills has not increased. We might have expected to see more measures dealt with outside Parliament and presented to Parliament in some finally agreed form. That there has been no increase in this direction is perhaps due to the fact that, although organized interest groups become more

[1] The Fridays given up to motions may be used for this purpose. Sometimes unopposed private Members' bills are allowed to proceed on Government days. This happened seven times in 1948–53. Cf. above, pp. 17 f.

[2] Bills which have been read a second time in this way usually go through Standing Committee, and take their place in the queue of balloted bills going through the private Members' bills Committee. If there is such general agreement on the principles of a measure that it had an unopposed second reading, it is not likely to take very long in Standing Committee.

ALTERNATIVE METHODS OF PROPOSING LEGISLATION

important, they do not become any readier finally to agree to compromises not wholly acceptable to themselves.

It must not be forgotten that, although we do not devote much attention to unopposed bills in our general consideration of private Members' bills, about half of the private Members' bills passed over the years have in fact been introduced and passed through Parliament under this procedure.

It is when we come to examine the figures relating to the bills brought in, neither under the ballot nor with a hope of being allowed to proceed as unopposed bills, that we find revolutionary changes during the past half century. Fifty years ago, if a Member had an idea that it would be a good plan to change the law of the land in some way, he had little hesitation about writing down a bill to effect his purpose and introducing it into Parliament. The number of bills brought in, though never as great as the number brought in in the United States Congress, nevertheless bore comparison with the number brought in in France. The practice in this matter resembled the still-surviving practice with regard to motions. Even now there is a steady stream of motions put down on the Order Paper by private Members, without any real prospect that they will ever be discussed. The only practical purpose served by the putting down of a motion in this way is that it gives the Member who has put it down the chance of asking the Leader of the House on Thursday if time will be found for a debate on it. He knows quite well that the answer will be in the negative, but at least he has the satisfaction of drawing some public attention to the matter in question. Just so, fifty years ago, a Member with an idea for a bill would introduce it without being deterred by the fact that it would probably never be debated.

In the early years of the twentieth century, bills were introduced on all manner of subjects, large and small. The days of the less rigid time-tables of the mid-Victorian era were not so very far away, and the habits formed in those easier conditions did not die out for some time after the conditions had changed. In many cases, the same bill was brought forward year after year, in the hope that by some piece of good fortune it would come up for debate, and also perhaps with the idea that, if at some future time the sponsor happened to win a good place in the ballot himself, he could strengthen his arguments by referring to the bill's long parliamentary pedigree. Between 1900 and 1906 there was at least one bill each year on Church discipline, on Sunday closing, and on the proposal that Local Authorities in Scotland should have the right to institute Prohibition on a local basis.

Many of the bills brought forward dealt with questions which would now be regarded as unsuitable for treatment in private Members' bills. Constitutional questions were popular. There were many bills on women's suffrage and on other reforms of the franchise, including Proportional Representation. In 1906 there were eight different franchise bills; in 1912 there were twelve different education bills.

The annual tally of private Members' bills introduced has in the long run declined fairly steadily since the beginning of the present century, though with considerable fluctuations in the short run. From a fairly steady average of about 160 a year until 1906, it rose to almost 200 a year during the years of the Liberal Government of Campbell-Bannerman and Asquith. After 1919, from under 70 a year during the 1918 Parliament, the figure rose once more to a fairly steady average of just under 100 a year from 1923 to 1931, with never less than 82 or more than 122 in any single full session. In the changed conditions of the 1930s the number fell off very steeply, to about sixty a year until the beginning of the war. Since 1948 the total has been more like thirty a year.[1]

It must be remembered that these figures include all classes of private Members' bills. If we eliminate balloted bills, Ten Minute bills and bills which pass unopposed, we find that the total of 'other' bills has fallen from over 100 a year before 1914 to almost nothing at all in the past few years.

This decline is significant of a change in the general conception of the function of Parliament. At the beginning of the twentieth century people still thought of Parliament as though part of its essence as the forum of the nation was to be a law-making body in its own right, and it seemed natural and proper that if a Member had an idea for a bill he should use his right to introduce it. By now people have become accustomed to the notion that the Government is the normal initiator of legislation, and they have come to recognize that the scope of private Members' bills had better be kept within certain bounds, recognized though not necessarily very well defined. Little useful purpose is served by

[1] Cf. Appendix C.

the exercise of the right to introduce a bill neither under the ballot nor under the Ten Minutes Rule nor with a hope of passing unopposed, and so Members now rarely introduce bills this way. In much the same way the citizens outside Parliament have come to use sparingly their right of presenting public petitions, except when the petition is part of a larger campaign.[1] The reason is that the British public, like its representatives in the House of Commons, has come to have a more sophisticated view of the working of parliamentary democracy. It is realized, inside Parliament and outside it, that it is not much use making gestures. Actions in support of ideas are judged by their effectiveness, and plans of action are judged by their likely effectiveness.

If a man has an idea that he would like to promote some reform or other, he generally writes to the newspapers about it or uses other devices of publicity to canvass his idea. He finds others like-minded with himself. If he and the other enthusiasts are in earnest, they first form a society, with officers and a constitution; then they raise money by one means or another, so that they can pay for the advice of legal experts who will help them to put their proposal into a form in which it will be workable and legally acceptable; then they approach the Government and try to persuade it to adopt their proposal. Only after they have failed to do this do they turn to private Members of Parliament and try to get them to introduce bills that have a fair prospect of passing, or at least of being debated. To have the proposal adopted by the Government as the result of a direct approach is the best possible thing. If this cannot be achieved, then a debate in Parliament is the next best, because it may contribute towards the education of public opinion in favour of the proposal. If a Member wishes to bring in a bill and fails to win a place in the ballot, the Ten Minutes Rule gives him an opportunity to draw public attention to his proposal far more effectively than would his exercising of

[1] Cf. the public petitions in favour of 'equal pay' for women employees of the state and teachers, presented on 9th March 1953. On the same day, Parliamentary Questions on this subject were asked, and a bill was presented under the Ten Minutes Rule. The whole business created quite a stir, and received the Press publicity that was desired (H.C. Debs., 9th March 1954, vol. 524, cols. 1903 ff, 1938). Similarly, on 4th December 1952, Mr. P. Freeman both presented a petition and asked a Question relating to the desire of the R.S.P.C.A. to make illegal the use of gin-traps for killing rabbits (H.C. Debs., vol. 508, cols. 1727 and 1736).

BILLS UNDER THE TEN MINUTES RULE

the right simply to bring in the bill for an automatic first reading. The latter procedure has one advantage; it ensures that the House will order the bill to be printed and if it is a fairly original measure the printing itself may be useful. The bill is likely to be noticed, and perhaps discussed, in the Press, and some Members of Parliament may become interested.[1] In this sense, then, the automatic introduction, while less useful than successful introduction under the Ten Minutes Rule, may be more useful than an unsuccessful Ten Minute motion. In recent years, however, the value of the publicity obtained under the Ten Minutes Rule has clearly been found to outweigh the danger that the House may refuse leave to introduce.

2. BILLS UNDER THE TEN MINUTES RULE

The Ten Minutes Rule was not in operation during the period 1939–50, but it was revived, by a decision in which the House, by 235 votes to 229, rejected the advice of Mr. Herbert Morrison, then Leader of the House, for the session of 1950–1. It has continued in operation since then. It is the device which allows a Member to move a motion, on a Tuesday or Wednesday at the commencement of public Business (that is, at about 3.30 or 3.45 p.m.), that leave be given to bring in a bill. He may make a short speech, limited by convention, but not by written rule, to ten minutes in duration. (The average length is in fact about seven minutes.) One member may make an opposing speech of similar length, after which the question must be put. If the decision is unfavourable, the matter is closed; if it is favourable, all that has happened is that the House has given leave to do something which could have been done without leave in any case.

At first sight the whole procedure seems to be irrational and useless, and it has often been under attack.[2] It has evident advantages, however. A very uncontroversial measure may stand a better chance of being given a second reading unopposed if it has been first introduced under the Ten Minutes Rule than if it

[1] Sir A. P. Herbert, in *Independent Member*, op. cit., p. 124, suggests that the printing of his bill on the law of libel in the session of 1937–8 was useful.
[2] For example, Mr. Crookshank, in his memorandum to the Select Committee on Procedure of 1931, suggested that Ten Minute bills should be abolished (H.C. 161 of 1931, Q. 2909, p. 285).

ALTERNATIVE METHODS OF PROPOSING LEGISLATION

has been brought in as an unballoted bill under S.O. No. 35.[1] Six Ten Minute bills in the four sessions 1950–4 went on to receive the Royal Assent in this way.[2] On the other hand, if a Member wishes to bring in a controversial measure, and fails to win a place in the ballot, he gets admirable publicity for his proposal by bringing it in under the Ten Minutes Rule. During the four sessions 1950–4, 14 of the 35 Ten Minute proposals were decided by divisions, and in these divisions the number of Members voting was never less than 321.[3] The greatest number was 465, and the average 396—nearly twice the average number voting in the rare divisions on second readings of balloted bills during the same period. The reason why the Ten Minutes Rule gives such good publicity is that it enables measures to be brought forward at a time when the House is at its fullest, instead of, as with the ballot for bills or motions on the adjournment, at the end of a period of sitting, when all except those who are specially interested have gone home. It is also useful as a means of bringing forward proposals in relation to problems which present themselves suddenly during the course of a session.

An interesting point is that the custom of restricting the subject-matter of private Members' bills to subjects which do not involve violent controversy, or deal with questions of far-reaching importance, does not seem to have been followed with regard to Ten Minute bills. It may be that because the question before the House relates to nothing more than the permission to bring in a bill, Members feel that they have a little more latitude than on Fridays in bringing forward large questions. This would apparently not be universally agreed, however. In some cases the opposing speaker has based his opposition mainly on the argument that the matter under consideration is too large to be dealt with at all in such a hurried and casual manner. Thus in 1953, when Mr. Paget brought forward his interesting and simple proposal that peers

---

[1] Cf. Lord Hemingford, *What Parliament is and does* (Cambridge U.P., 2nd ed., 1948), p. 40.

[2] Cf. below, Appendix E. In addition, one Ten Minutes Rule bill was enacted after being debated on second reading on one of the private Members' days. None of the five bills approved on division at the introduction stage made any progress.

[3] In one of the two divisions of the short session of 1954–5, however, only 192 Members voted (*Weekly Hansard*, 8th March 1955, col. 176). The bill in question, the Treason Bill, dealt with an important question.

should be allowed to continue to sit in the House of Commons if they did not take the oath in the House of Lords,[1] Colonel Elliot argued that 'this was not a matter for perfunctory discussion and decision of the House, nor should even the principle be discussed in that way'.

Another constitutional question was brought up as a Ten Minute bill a fortnight later, when Sir Edward Keeling proposed the Death of the Speaker Bill.[2] His object was to provide that in the event of the Speaker's death the Chairman of Ways and Means should automatically take over the functions of the Speaker for the time being, in order that the business of the House should not be interrupted for the period that would be consumed by the appointment of a new Speaker. With this Bill the Member opposing suggested that this 'summary manner' was ill-adapted for a proposal for constitutional change.

Some interesting considerations related to party discipline, both in general and as it applies in particular to Ministers and to Opposition leaders, arise in relation to Ten Minute bills. The Whips are normally not put on, the parties have little time to discuss in advance what their attitude is to be, and the decision when made is really quite inconclusive. The freedom of the vote seems to extend further, as a rule, than on other types of business.

The voting on both the constitutional proposals mentioned above was across party lines, although the Peers Bill was much more popular among Labour Members than among Conservatives. Of the 145 in favour of it, only 20 were Conservatives (including at least six who seemed to be potential beneficiaries), and of the 238 against it, only 44 were Socialists. On the Death of the Speaker Bill, which received a favourable vote of 172 to 149 (the smallest total vote on any Ten Minute bill in the session), the parties were about evenly divided; the 172 in favour included 85 Conservatives. In both cases the Government was hostile, though on the Death of the Speaker Bill Mr. Crookshank was the only Cabinet Minister to go into the lobby, while on the Peers Bill five Cabinet Ministers voted. On both bills the Labour leaders were divided. Mr. Attlee and Mr. Morrison joined with the Government in opposing the bills, while some of their Labour frontbench colleagues were in favour. Another Labour Member's bill

[1] H.C. Debs., 11th February 1953, vol. 511, col. 424.
[2] Ibid., 25th February 1953, vol. 511, col. 2095.

ALTERNATIVE METHODS OF PROPOSING LEGISLATION

of 1953, Mr. Donnelly's proposal to give to the Bar Council disciplinary power over barristers,[1] produced a similar result. Three of the Ten Minute bills of the session of 1950-1 produced divisions on party lines. One of these, aiming to restrict the rent of garages in London,[2] was supported by the Labour Party, with twelve Cabinet Ministers, including Mr. Attlee himself, voting for it. The motion was carried by 269 votes to 196. The other two were backed by Conservatives, and were defeated. The first was Sir Herbert Williams' proposal to give the House the power of praying against all Statutory Instruments which have to be laid before Parliament,[3] and the second was Mr. Hutchinson's proposal to improve the basis of compensation paid to owners of property requisitioned by public authorities for demolition.[4] This was a subject to which Conservatives had frequently returned in the past few years, at Question time and on the Adjournment. On both these bills many party leaders voted, and Mr. Hutchinson's supporters in the lobby included Mr. Churchill, Mr. Eden and Mr. Butler.

Some recent balloted bills had already made previous appearances on the parliamentary scene as Ten Minute bills. The bill to compel football pool promoters to publish their accounts, which was passed into law in 1953, made its first appearance when it was brought in under the Ten Minutes Rule in 1950.[5] In view of the considerable discussion and difficulty that arose in 1954, it is interesting that the first stage in 1950 was passed without a division, although it is true that Mrs. Braddock, who as a Member from Liverpool felt particularly interested in football pools, made a speech in mild opposition on the ground that the Royal Commission on gambling had not yet completed its labours. The bill to allow the parking of motor-cars without lights in lighted streets was also brought in in 1950 without any more opposition than a speech expressing doubt whether it would be wise to create so obvious a loophole for abuse as this.[6]

In so far as a bill introduced under the Ten Minutes Rule, even

---

[1] H.C. Debs., 6th May 1953, vol. 515, col. 396.
[2] Ibid., 27th February 1951, vol. 484, cols. 1924-30.
[3] Ibid., 21st February 1951, vol. 484, cols. 1291-300.
[4] Ibid., 28th February 1951, vol. 484, cols. 2097-104.
[5] Ibid., 28th November 1950, vol. 481, col. 953.
[6] Ibid., 5th December 1950, vol. 482, col. 209.

BILLS UNDER THE TEN MINUTES RULE

if it is successful at that stage, is unlikely to have its second reading taken during the time allocated for private Members, the operation of the Ten Minutes Rule should probably be considered quite separately from the operation of normal private Members' time. Except with potential 'unopposed' bills, the time spent on Ten Minute bills should probably be regarded as time spent on the preliminary ventilation of legislative ideas and occasionally on matters not themselves connected with legislation. When we recognize that the usefulness of the device is limited to the giving of advance publicity, we can claim that it serves a useful purpose.

Seeing that at any given moment there are always many Members of Parliament with ideas and complaints of various kinds, about all sorts of topics, that they would like to have ventilated, it is perhaps surprising that the Ten Minutes Rule has not been used to excess. A Member who has asked a Parliamentary Question and received an unsatisfactory answer, or who is dissatisfied with the way some Government Department has acted in some sphere, often finds that the procedure of the House provides him with no adequate opportunity for bringing his complaint into the open. He may ballot for the half-hour's adjournment at the end of each day, but there is strong competition for this, and he may well fail to get his half-hour. Even if he gets his half-hour, he will speak to an almost empty House. There must then be a temptation for him to invent some bill related to his grievance, and propose a motion for permission to bring in his bill under the Ten Minutes Rule. Seeing that the motion only relates to permission to bring in a bill, there does not need to be any actual ready-drafted bill in existence at the time when the motion is moved, and if the motion is defeated there will be no need to produce a bill. Mr. Crookshank did indeed complain in 1931 that Ten Minute bills were often used 'for giving publicity to some (generally ephemeral) grievance, which could be done better between 11 and 11.30'.[1] On the whole, however, private Members have since 1949 shown a reasonable amount of self-denial over their use of the Ten Minutes Rule.

It is of course quite legitimate to seize a specially suitable moment for the introduction of a bill, a moment when some striking instance of an abuse, real or imagined, attributable to the

[1] Memorandum to the Select Committee on Procedure, H.C. 161 of 1930–31, Minutes of Evidence, Q. 2909.

existing state of the law, is fresh in the public mind,[1] and so to attempt to enlist strong support for one's own proposals, but it would be unfortunate if Ten Minute bills were regularly introduced simply as a device for raising complaints and grievances which could not be raised by any other means under the existing procedure. It can probably be argued that private Members' bills should never be used as mere pegs on which to hang complaints. Ten Minute bills are particularly ill-adapted for this purpose, in so far as they give the Minister no opportunity to reply; the short opposing speech is normally made by a private Member, and when he has finished, the question must be put. Our conception of the function of Parliament requires that when a Government Department is attacked its representative ought to be able to reply to the attack. An attack in a vacuum, as it were, has no place in the normal relationships between Parliament and the Government.

The excessive use of the Ten Minutes Rule as a device for bringing forward current grievances would, then, apparently be undesirable both because it would soon obstruct normal business and because it would be out of tune with our normal conceptions of the proper functions of parliamentary give-and-take.

The self-denial of Members in this matter can perhaps be attributed to two factors. One, much the more important, is the strength of the respect for unwritten rules dictated by common sense and supported by the House's readiness to show its irritation and boredom with a tiresome proposal; the other is the recognition that if there were abuse, the whole device of the Ten Minutes Rule would probably be swept away. If a Member feels tempted to use the Ten Minutes Rule for the ventilation of some particular grievance, he must consider what will be the opinion of his party as a whole, and how his own reputation as a parliamentarian will be affected. Even a rebellious and highly independently-minded Member will not want to incur the displeasure of his party colleagues and of the House generally for some action contrary to the unwritten rules. So far, at any rate, the respect for these rules has generally been adequate to prevent abuse of the Ten Minutes Rule.

[1] Thus Mr. Silverman, an enthusiastic campaigner for the abolition of the death penalty, brought in a Ten Minute bill on that subject just after the murderer J. H. Christie had confessed to the murder of Mrs. Evans, whose death had hitherto been attributed to her husband.

PRIVATE MEMBERS' MOTIONS

It may be suggested that, if bills brought in under the Ten Minutes Rule are in the first place not to be regarded as private Members' bills in the same way as are balloted bills, and are in the second place not properly concerned with current grievances against the existing administration, there seems to be little scope left for them. Of what use then can they be? The answer cannot be given by the statement of any general principle, but only by reference to the uses to which the device has been put. Judging by the experiences of the last few years, it would probably be fair to say that on the balance these occasional little parliamentary excursions along the most varied by-ways have been good rather than bad. Nothing very constructive has been achieved, but at least some interesting ideas have been ventilated, and Members have had a few opportunities of exercising their own personal powers of decision in voting without instruction from party Whips.[1] It is probably salutary for Members to do this from time to time. The total time consumed each year has been a good deal less than the equivalent of a single ordinary day's business,[2] and so it is hardly possible to make any very serious complaint on the ground that too much of the time normally spent on essential business has been sacrificed.

3. PRIVATE MEMBERS' MOTIONS

We must now examine briefly the methods by which private Members can advocate legislation indirectly, without actually bringing in bills at all. At present ten Fridays every session, taken alternately with the Fridays which are available for private Members' bills, are reserved for motions introduced by private Members, the time being distributed among the various aspirants

[1] They have this opportunity on Fridays too, on those rare occasions when there is a division. But it must be remembered that a Ten Minute bill these days generally draws out two or three times more Members to vote than a Friday bill. If a free vote does Members good, a Ten Minute bill ensures that the benefits are widely diffused.

[2] During the first four sessions after the restoration of the Ten Minutes Rule the average time consumed on debates and divisions on motions under it came to about $2\frac{1}{2}$ hours a session. The time spent on the speeches was an average of about 13 minutes on each bill, with a minimum of five minutes and a maximum of 25 minutes. Fourteen of the 35 motions produced divisions, so the average time consumed on each bill, counting the time taken by the divisions, was about 17 minutes.

ALTERNATIVE METHODS OF PROPOSING LEGISLATION

by means of a ballot which is held, not at the beginning of the session, but from time to time. These Fridays are used for bringing forward motions, as in a debating society, which if they are passed become resolutions expressing opinions or intentions, such as 'that this House calls upon the Government' to take some action or other.

A Member who desires to advocate some reform, and fails to win a place in the ballot for private Members' bills, can often achieve the first part of his purpose, namely a discussion, by moving a motion embodying the principles of his bill. He can invite the House to express an opinion that the law on some subject or other should be changed, or more specifically that the Government ought to introduce a bill. Thus we have had a motion to the effect that a British woman should not lose her nationality on marrying a foreigner,[1] and more recently one calling upon the Government 'to consider at the earliest opportunity what amendments of the law are desirable and practicable in the licensing laws', on the ground of their irksomeness to foreign tourists.[2]

The abolition of the time for private Members' bills and the substitution for it of time only for balloted motions[3] would be regrettable, because there is an essential distinction between the two types of debate, and it is useful that there should be this distinction. When a Member wishes to propose a change in the law it is generally better that he should be able to do so by bringing in his own bill, rather than by introducing a motion, couched in general terms, calling on the Government to introduce a bill.

Furthermore, the debates on motions have a distinctive character and usefulness of their own, which would probably suffer if a lack of facilities for introducing bills led Members habitually to propose motions with legislative intent. Most debates on private Members' motions are on subjects which could not well be embodied in bills,[4] and the true and proper purpose of these

[1] H.C. Debs., 18th February 1925.
[2] Ibid., 4th July 1953, vol. 503, cols. 769–860.
[3] Harold Laski (*Parliamentary Government in England*, op. cit., p. 166) suggests that private Members' motions should be retained but not bills.
[4] During the period 1950–5 the subjects of the private Members' motions debated first on their several days have included the utilization of coal (7th March 1952), compensation for industrial injuries (2nd May 1952), Equal Pay (16th May 1952), licensing laws and the tourist trade (4th July

debates is probably best served when they are concerned with such general questions as 'the need for full utilization of scientific resources',[1] or 'the need for more attention to cleanliness in the handling of food in shops', etc.[2]

Private Members' motions have in general been used more often than bills for the introduction of debates desired by the party organizations. In describing the practice of the 1920s, Mr. Robert Morrison suggested that 'in 99 per cent. of cases the Members in all parts of the House whose names are read out as successful get up and read out a formula off a piece of paper which has been supplied to them by the Whips'. His 99 per cent. is perhaps an exaggeration, but Sir Archibald Sinclair agreed that the practice was very usual.[3] In 1946 Mr. Stuart, the Conservative Chief Whip, agreed with Sir Robert Young that the practice had been very common—and he had the experience of the 1930s freshest in his mind.[4]

Even when subjects for motions are supplied by the Whips, the Whips in recommending subjects tend to be guided by their knowledge of the feeling among their back-benchers, rather than by the prompting of the leaders. If the Whips find that there is a widespread desire among their Members for a debate on a particular subject, they may well try to have a debate on that subject by enlisting the collaboration of the winner of the ballot on a Friday. In this way the intervention of the Whips counteracts the capriciousness inherent in the operation of the ballot by itself.

Since 1948, although private Members' motions have often dealt with non-party questions, their range has on the whole been much wider than has that of the bills. There have been no motions on behalf of the welfare of animals, which is too narrow a subject to attract attention in a general discussion of principle. There has occasionally been a motion on a purely party matter, but such motions have been rare, particularly since 1950. In 1950 four of

1952), the colour bar (1st May 1953), and the compulsory acquisition of land and property (25th March 1955). Any of these six subjects might well have been incorporated into a bill. The other 43 motions all dealt with questions essentially unconcerned with changes in the law.

[1] Cf. H.C. Debs., 5th May 1950, vol. 474, cols. 2060-150.
[2] Cf. Ibid., 2nd February 1951, vol. 483, cols. 1213-90.
[3] H.C. 161 of 1930-1, Minutes of Evidence, Q. 1258.
[4] Select Committee on Procedure, H.C. 189-1 of 1945-6, Minutes of Evidence, Q. 3887.

ALTERNATIVE METHODS OF PROPOSING LEGISLATION

the five days produced party debates and party divisions. There were two forthright Opposition attacks on aspects of Government policy, in one case state trading in food and in the other case the continuance of petrol rationing.[1] In 1950–1, there was an Opposition Member's motion condemning the Government's failure to build up adequate stocks of raw materials, and advocating increased encouragement for private traders.[2]

Since 1950 divisions have become very rare on motion days. One of the two divisions of the session 1950–1 produced a minority of three, and in the four sessions 1951–5 there were only four divisions in all. In most cases the subject of the motion has been agreed to without a division, or withdrawn or talked out without the question being put. In such divisions as there have been the voting has tended to be on party lines, though the vote may not have been in the fullest sense a party vote. On these occasions there has been a debate on policy, in which the views of the parties as such have been involved, but in which the responsibility of the Government is not involved in the same way as it would be in a similar debate on a normal Government day. In 1952, for example, a Labour Member moved that there should be closer co-operation between the countries of the sterling area, and that the Government should take steps to promote such co-operation.[3] A Conservative moved an amendment to the effect that the closer co-operation, which was indeed desirable, should be left to private enterprise, and the debate proceeded along these lines, concerning itself with broad and fundamental economic policy in such a way that Parliament could well be said to be performing Bagehot's 'educative' function. There was a division on party lines, in which the amendment was defeated by 113 votes to 66.

4. INCIDENTAL OPPORTUNITIES FOR ADVOCATING LEGISLATION

The general procedure of the House provides several other types of opportunity in the course of the year for making general

[1] H.C. Debs., 12th and 19th May 1950.
[2] Ibid., 2nd March 1951. On this matter the vote went against the Government by 167 votes to 163.
[3] Ibid., 22nd February 1952, vol. 496, cols. 567–664.

ADVOCATING LEGISLATION

proposals for changes in the law. The most important of these opportunities is the six-day debate on the Speech from the Throne, with which each session of Parliament begins. But here again there is only an opportunity to make general suggestions, and there is the serious objection that the pattern of the debates makes it quite unlikely that a Member who has advocated some new legislation will receive even an answer; the next man to speak in the debate may well talk about some other subject altogether.

It is again always possible to ask an ordinary Parliamentary Question whose effect is to recommend that a bill with some intention or other should be introduced, but this device is of practically no value, because it provides no opportunity for bringing forward, even very shortly, arguments in favour of the proposed bill. To attempt to do so would be to misuse Question time.

Finally, it is sometimes possible for an ingenious Member to advocate legislation without going out of order by using one of the other procedures of the House for this purpose. We have already noticed the ingenuity of Mr. Follick, who used a debate in Committee of Supply on the Navy Estimates to suggest that naval signalling could be made more effective if messages were sent out in the revised spelling.[1] But, while one may find some satisfaction in the contemplation of such ingenuity, it is in general desirable that the different forms of debate should be used for the purposes for which they are intended, and conversely that every worthwhile purpose should have a form of debate available to suit it.

This brief study of the alternative methods whereby private Members may advocate legislation by other means than the straightforward proposal of bills has served to show that, while there are indeed such methods, it is on the whole undesirable that they should be used. The institution of time for private Members to bring in their own bills must be judged, then, on its own merits and demerits. In the last resort, when we look at the list of bills introduced, when we consider the debates, fruitful and unfruitful, and finally when we consider the bills that have eventually been passed, we can hardly fail to recognize that there have been many interesting and educative discussions, some of which could hardly have been achieved by any other means.

[1] Cf. above, p. 14n.

Chapter VIII
CONCLUSION

IN finally assessing the part played by private Members' bills in the contemporary British Parliament, we shall look at the subject not only from the point of view of the immediate problems of modern Britain, but also with reference to the question how far the system satisfies the general requirements of what we assume to be 'democratic' government. We shall, then, be to some extent concerned with references to processes in other countries of the modern world, as well as with the immediate problems arising out of British experience.

On one side it may be argued that in a democratic legislature every Member ought to have the right not only to introduce bills without limit, but also to have his bills effectively discussed and voted upon. On the other side it may be claimed that in the conditions of the modern world governmental responsibility is so all-embracing that it is not really suitable for individual Members to propose bills at all.

The first point of view would find few exponents in Britain or in the countries of the Commonwealth which have adopted the British form of parliamentary government. Yet the restrictions which are accepted in Britain are apparently out of tune with the theories of such men as Locke, to whom our system owes so much, and certainly at variance with the practice which is current in France, in the United States, and in many other democratic countries, where restrictions such as are found in Britain would be considered intolerable. Indeed, in France, although the deputies bring in about 1000 bills and 1000 motions a year, every one of which is at least committed to a Standing Committee and handed over to a Rapporteur for preliminary examination, there is still some dissatisfaction that the facilities and scope are not even better.[1]

Judged by the standards of French or American democracy, the severe restriction on the effective right of our Members of Parliament to bring forward their own bills vitiates the democratic character of our form of government. On the other hand, this self-evident fact does not appear to have caused much concern in Britain or much reprobation abroad. Many British writers, from Lord Hewart twenty years ago to Mr. Christopher Hollis in 1949 and Professor G. W. Keeton and the contributors to *Parliament: A Survey* in 1952, have recently expressed anxiety over the domination of Parliament by the Executive. But their complaints are directed mainly at other things than the limitation of the effective capacity of private Members to bring in bills.[2] They are more concerned with the excesses of party discipline in general, and also with the increase of delegated legislation and of executive supremacy in judicial or quasi-judicial matters. Yet, although they do not concern themselves primarily over the comparative decline of the private Member as legislator, they nevertheless seem sometimes to be speaking language such as we might hear from Frenchmen or from Americans when they complain in their general terms of the excessive power of the Executive. In so far as they think like this, they might be expected to demand a greater

---

[1] Cf. Journal officiel, documents de l'Assemblée Nationale, 1951, No. 240, Exposé des motifs (explanatory memorandum) to the bill of M. Lecourt (M.R.P.). Mr. Lecourt and his M.R.P. colleagues complained that the procedure was so much encumbered with texts awaiting discussion that private Members' bills got inadequate opportunity for debate on the floor of the Assembly. He proposed a delegation of full legislative power to two Committees sitting jointly. The Italian Parliament already delegates extensive powers to its Standing Committees. (Cf. Franco Pierandrei, *Les Commissions législatives du Parlement italien*, in *Revue française de Science politique*, vol. II (1952), pp. 557–80.

[2] Professor Keeton, in *The Passing of Parliament* (Benn, 1952), devotes a few sentences on p. 62 to the restriction of private Members' time, and Mr. Hollis, in *Can Parliament Survive?* (Hollis and Carter, 1949), a much smaller space (p. 66). The twelve distinguished contributors to the symposium *Parliament: A Survey* (Allen & Unwin) say between them nothing whatever about private Members' bills.

CONCLUSION

initiative for Members to introduce their own bills. The fact that they do not do so seems to require some explanation.

The root of the matter seems to lie in the fact that the British Parliament is not above all a law-making body, but a place where things are discussed. However much this fact may have been observed and repeated, by Bagehot and others, the very use of the terms 'Legislature' and 'Executive', in juxtaposition with one another, in relation to the British system of government, is misleading, because these terms inevitably lead one to think of Parliament as the Legislature and of the Government as the Executive. If we would describe the effective parts of the British constitution, we would do much better to say that the Government of the day is the effective doer of things, both legislative and executive. The activities and the decisions of the state machine, both general and particular, in both these spheres, are all part of a single whole, for all of which the Government is collectively responsible. Parliament is the body which discusses what the Government has done, is doing and intends to do, and in the process of discussion it not only forces the Government publicly to justify its decisions, but often succeeds in persuading the Government to modify its actions or its intentions. Its power and effectiveness in this sphere are in reality greater than they seem to be, but it can only have this power and effectiveness as a partner of a Government enjoying adequate authority to decide and to act. Conservatively-minded commentators recognize these facts, and it is for this reason that they can accept the restricted rôle of private Members as proposers of bills.

Most Frenchmen and Americans, accustomed to the idea of the sacrosanctity of the legislative rights of the people's representatives, would find it hard to accept such a restricted rôle for the National Assembly or for Congress. The sacrosanctity of these rights is derived from the revolutionary theory which in both countries is an integral part of the tradition of government. It may be true that the conditions of the modern world make it impossible for these rights to have the same meaning in fact as they have in theory, but nevertheless the rights have to be maintained formally intact. The British system, lacking a theoretical foundation, has allowed the rights of the representatives to be fundamentally modified by changes which have come about without any deliberate intent. On the one hand there has been the

CONCLUSION

progressive restriction of private Members' time, and on the other hand there has been the development of the idea that the scope of private Members' bills had better be kept within a restricted field.

It would probably be almost universally agreed that private Members of Parliament can make their most useful contribution to government by speaking in major debates on subjects about which they are qualified to speak, by asking Parliamentary Questions, by concerning themselves with matters of administration affecting their constituents, and in general by forcing the Government to justify or amend its decisions, great and small. The proposing of bills has only a secondary importance.

So far most observers would agree. But some would go further and say that these main functions are so much more useful than the function of introducing bills that it is not worth while for private Members to spend any time at all in introducing bills on their own account. It is really a matter of allocating priorities for the different functions, according to the value which one may set on them. The question regarding private Members' bills can be stated thus: 'Is the function of introducing bills worth while enough for us to be prepared to give ten Fridays a session to it? Ought we rather to give more time, or less time, or no time at all?' Or again, 'Ought we to devise some change in the machinery of Parliament so that a much greater number of bills might be not only introduced but examined, as in France or the United States?'

In attempting to answer these questions we must take into account the use that the House has made of private Members' time. We must form our judgments mainly with reference to the more modest constructive bills of recent years, though we must also pay attention to the other uses that were made of private Members' time in the past; we have already recognized the possibility that new conditions might produce a reversion to the old habit of bringing in party bills.

When private Members' Fridays are used for big questions of party controversy the debates may be useful and educative, not only for the benefit of the Government and the public at whom the bills are directed, but also for the benefit of the politicians and enthusiasts who bring them forward. Mr. Herbert Morrison may indeed have spoken scornfully, in 1946, of the efforts made by his own Party in the 1920s and 1930s, but it is probably fair to say that the Labour Party itself gained in stature and maturity of outlook through the very fact of having to defend its projects and to listen to the strictures which were pronounced against them. Certainly, when the Party came into power, the debates on the old bills were valuable experience, and the Party and the House as a whole were probably the better able to deal with the new official bills for having looked at the unofficial bills in the past.

We must now examine Mr. Morrison's further argument that the time spent on his Party's bills was wasted because anything really worth discussing can be brought up under the other forms of procedure. There are indeed several other types of occasion on which the Opposition may bring forward proposals obliquely. The twenty-six days which are allotted each year for 'Supply' do indeed belong to the Opposition, in so far as the Opposition chooses the subjects for debate on those days, but after all, the rules of procedure do not permit advocacy of legislation during Supply debates.[1] There are the debates on the Address and censure debates and others which may be specially arranged by agreement between the Whips through the usual channels. But in none of the debates of these kinds does the Opposition have to bring forward any specific proposal. If there are to be opportunities for the Opposition to advocate legislation it seems well that it should be allowed to bring in a specific, drafted bill, and to have to defend the terms of that bill before the House.

We may now go on to look at the less important and controversial measures which have been the usual type since 1948. Has the time spent on these been worth while, we may ask. Would it not have been better, seeing that the Government itself is always short of time for the bills which it knows to be essential, if the whole of the time for legislation had been allocated by the Government? If that had been done, it may be argued, all the worthwhile and necessary measures that were in fact brought in by private Members and passed would probably have been brought in by the Government, and having been brought it would have been dealt with much more expeditiously. It cannot be denied that the debates on some minor measures of the past few

[1] This rule has often been criticized, though its effects could be weakened by an increased use of the device of having Supply debates on the motion 'that Mr. Speaker do now leave the chair'.

CONCLUSION

years have been inordinately long, sometimes because of factors directly connected with the system of allocating time. We have noticed the day that was lost through the prolongation of the debate on the Intestates' Estates Bill in order to prevent discussion on the bill to prevent the sale of council houses in Scotland. On that occasion, not only was a worthwhile and uncontroversial measure nearly lost, but a whole day of parliamentary time was lost too. If the Government had had control of that day, it might itself have brought in the Intestates' Estates Bill, and in that case the second reading might well have been disposed of in an hour or less, leaving more time for discussion of other deserving and uncontroversial but hardly 'essential' measures which the Government could also have brought in.

This argument deserves a good deal of attention, particularly in so far as we judge private Members' Fridays by their fruits. If we look back over the list of private Members' bills that have been passed, in relation to the length of time spent, not on them only, but on all private Members' bills, we must admit that all the bills passed have been acceptable to the Government of the day, in principle and in detail, and could therefore appropriately have been brought in as Government bills. If they had been so brought in, it is likely that in general the proceedings on each bill would have been shorter than they were in fact. The same results might well have been achieved with a much smaller expenditure of parlimentary time.

Against this argument it can be pointed out that Governments have in fact not been very forward in bringing in proposals to achieve the ends which have been achieved in private Members' time. This may be true, but on the other hand, each session has either provided time for private Members or been exceptionally encumbered with Government business. In the normal sessions the Government has felt that it need not bring these proposals forward, because private Members can look after them on the private Members' days.

In the long run, then, if we evaluate private Members' time with reference only to its productivity of additions to the statute book, we shall probably be bound to admit that the same results could have been achieved more expeditiously if the Government had had a little more time, in which it could have brought in all the worthwhile private Members' bills as Government bills. On

CONCLUSION

the other hand, if we contented ourselves with evaluating private Members' time in this way we should be leaving at least two very important points out of the account. The first of these is that the Government could hardly be expected to bring forward a bill actually objectionable to itself. Many bills which are introduced and lead to worthwhile discussions, but fail to pass, would have no chance of being introduced at all, except by the various oblique means which we have described above. The debates on bills which have no hope of passing may well be educative[1] and useful in other ways. Also, although the right of Members to introduce bills is, as we have suggested, no longer fundamental to our conception of democracy, a complete withdrawal of that right would slightly injure the balance of our system by removing what can at least be called a safety-valve.

The second point is that even among private Members' bills which are introduced with a good chance of passing—even among those which actually do pass—there are some which it would be impolitic for the Government to introduce on its own account. It must be remembered that although a Government may be very concerned, and even primarily concerned, with the fulfilment of its duties and its responsibilities, it must have some thought about the next election. No Government wants to risk losing votes unnecessarily. It may and it should be prepared to take unpopular action which it believes to be necessary for the preservation of the state, but there is no reason why it should risk the disfavour of certain sections of the population, such as Sabbatarians, or opponents of divorce, by proposing a bill in a field concerned with Sunday-observance or divorce; for the state of the law in fields such as these has little relationship with the material well-being and permanence of the state as a whole. It would be hard to defend the thesis that changes in the law in subjects of this kind are never desirable, yet in view of the position of the Government it seems that private Members' bills are the only

[1] A parliamentary debate may well have a direct and immediate educative effect. On the Fireguards Bill of 1952 Mr. G. Williams said that he hoped that the debate would be useful as impressing on the public the danger of unguarded fires and radiators (H.C. Debs., 14th March 1952, vol. 497, col. 1823), and a fortnight later Mr. Gough expressed a hope that the holding of a debate on the Intestates' Estates Bill would contribute to a reduction in the number of people dying intestate (H.C. Debs., 28th March 1952, vol. 498, col. 1134).

CONCLUSION

means whereby changes are likely to be initiated. We have seen that in some bills of this type the Government has made itself responsible for giving advice with regard to matters of detail and technical questions, and has acted as an intermediary between interested groups, but in general it has done these things only after the House of Commons has pronounced a favourable decision on the principles. For the Government to help to make a bill, once through its second reading, as good, as workable and as generally acceptable as possible, is not the same thing as for the Government to take the responsibility for initiating the bill.

The recent tendency towards concentration on uncontroversial bills has produced a very interesting result in the form of an increased independence of Parliament from the discipline of Party on private Members' days. Already in the 1920s there was a widespread desire that private Members' bills, once through their second reading stages, should be released from their former excessive dependence on the provision of facilities by the Government for their later stages. This desire bore fruit in the appointment of the Select Committee on Procedure of 1927 and in the resultant redistribution of private Members' time in favour of the later stages of bills. We have also noticed the further redistribution in 1950.

No longer depending almost entirely on the Government for time for the later stages of their bills, private Members have come to develop a greater independence on these occasions, which contrasts strikingly with the decline of their independence on normal occasions. In 1939 Sir Ivor Jennings was able to write that the Government remained in control on Fridays and always got its way without much difficulty, that the Whips would be put on if the Government did not want a bill to pass, and that no bill of which the Government disapproved could possibly avoid defeat.[1] This interpretation is amply supported by the evidence up to that time. But since 1948 the House has tended to show a more independent spirit on Fridays. The increased power of the party machines on ordinary occasions seems now to be counterbalanced by an increased insistence on the right of Members to judge independently on matters which are outside the scope of the parties.

The new development is due in the first place to the general

[1] Jennings, *Parliament*, op. cit., p. 354.

attitude of many Labour Members. For various reasons socialists care deeply for their right, under their standing orders, to judge independently on matters of conscience, and they are probably all the more inclined to be jealous in guarding their rights for the fact that their Party's rules explicitly require them to observe strict discipline on normal occasions.[1] Just as it was the Conservative Members who led the way towards the concentration on uncontroversial subjects for Friday bills, so it seems that it is the Labour Members who are now leading the way towards a somewhat greater autonomy for the House of Commons in bringing these proposals forward, and in passing judgment on them.

This new independence does not seem likely to be carried to the point of irresponsibility, and so long as it remains within reasonable bounds it is a healthy tendency, and one which should help to preserve the vitality of Parliament.

The fact that Fridays are private Members' days gives a special interest to them, which is reflected, if not by large attendances of Members, at least by a great readiness on the part of the Press to report very extensively the debates which take place on Fridays.[2] The reason for this is easy to see, however, and it has only a little to do with the fact that proposals have been brought in by private Members and not by the Government. The reason is essentially that many of the private Members' proposals are News, in the journalist's sense; they often deal with rather novel subjects which are easy to understand and about which it is easy to form an opinion. Again they often deal with subjects about which there are strong feelings abroad, or with subjects which excite a special sentimental or morbid interest.

Spelling reform, daylight saving and the like are, or were when first proposed, novel and attractive ideas, easy subjects for everyday gossip and argument. Proposals for the protection of animals can be sure of a ready audience among a people notorious for the strength of their sentiments about all kinds of quadrupeds and

---

[1] It is not suggested that Labour discipline is in fact stricter than Conservative discipline. Labour discipline tends to draw more attention to itself. Perhaps this is because to many people of Conservative temperament, leadership, authority and so on are part of the accepted order of things.

[2] In the Select Committee on Procedure of 1945-6 Mr. Crookshank suggested that Friday was the best day of the week for the Press (H.C. 189-1, op. cit., Minutes of Evidence, Q. 3665).

CONCLUSION

birds. A very large number of people either like to drink alcoholic liquor themselves or have a violent antipathy to alcohol, for others no less than for themselves, and much the same can be said of gambling. Given the interest of the public in everything to do with crime, discussions in Parliament about proposals to reform criminal law can be expected to be widely reported in the newspapers. The same aspect of the public taste can be expected to find a peculiar attraction in matters to do with divorce, though here the religious attitudes on the subject lend spice to these arguments. The very strength and extent of this popular interest, not all of it praiseworthy, in many of the topics which are often brought forward by private Members, makes it understandable that the popular Press should give much space to its reports on bills dealing with these matters.

It does seem that there is merit in a topic which arouses public interest in the transactions of Parliament, if only for the reason that, as is so often piously said, the greatest possible contact between Parliament and electorate is essential for the health of a parliamentary democracy. It is probably no bad thing that the subjects which are widely discussed and thought about by ordinary people should sometimes be discussed in Parliament, on the basis of unofficial Members' proposals.

The machinery for dealing with private Members' bills has some evident imperfections, on paper at least. The ballot is inescapably irrational, and it remains true that some proposals which really do deserve to be brought forward and discussed have to wait for an unduly long time before they get a hearing. Yet the various possible remedies which we examined in Chapter 1 are all rather unsatisfying, in that they concentrate on attempts to remove the irrational elements of the existing system, rather than on trying to create a system that will really work.

The best solution to this problem seems to lie in the development of a habit of voluntarily curtailing speeches and debates on relatively uncontroversial private Members' bills, and particularly on the second reading stage. There must always be many bills which are too important to be allowed to pass under the 'unopposed' procedure, and yet which do not really require to be debated for three or four or five hours on second reading. Various proposals have been made for ways of making easier the passage of such bills, but all of these involve the creation of new apparatus

CONCLUSION

of the kind to which the House of Commons does not take kindly. These proposals must be recognized as being less desirable than the growth of a spontaneous habit of brevity, fostered perhaps by a greater readiness of the Speaker to grant the closure. After all, in the French National Assembly it is very usual for a private Member's bill to be allowed to pass after two or three speeches, lasting in all ten or fifteen minutes. It is true that these bills have been dealt with in advance by the appropriate Standing Committee, and that they are introduced to the Assembly, not by their original proposers, but by their Rapporteurs, who have the advantage of being detached persons.[1] The British House of Lords has shown itself adept at economical debate. Of the 36 private Members' bills enacted in 1948–53, 22 occupied the Lords on second reading for between ten minutes and an hour each, as compared with two in the House of Commons.

On this point, a study of the proceedings on Fridays since 1948 suggests that there may be a contemporary trend in the direction of an increased readiness to allow uncontroversial bills to pass after debates of moderate length. Certainly the number of bills disposed of each day in the sessions 1952–3 and 1953–4 was unprecedentedly high. If the House becomes accustomed to giving a second reading to six or seven bills on a single Friday our complaints about excessively long debates will no longer be applicable. It is interesting to observe this trend, because it appears to have been produced by the separate and spontaneous decisions of individual Members.[2] It is as though each of many Members had argued, said to himself, one on one day, another on another day, 'I am interested in this subject, I should like to see the bill pass, and I have something to say about it; but the best service that I can perform is to keep silent or to make my points

---

[1] It should be mentioned, however, that if the proposer of a bill himself belongs to the Committee to which it is sent, he may well be appointed for his own bill.

[2] The intensity of the indignation directed (mainly by his colleagues of the Labour Party) against Captain Hewitson for preventing the Pool Betting Bill from getting a second reading seems to have arisen from a widespread agreement that the measure should be allowed to pass. Yet it was a proposal involving a good deal of controversy, and sought to impose unpalatable duties on wealthy and influential corporations. It seems that in the situation of twenty years previously, Captain Hewitson's action would have seemed so normal that it would have excited no comment. Cf. above, p. 30.

CONCLUSION

very briefly indeed, and in so far as I wish to achieve concrete results in the form of the acceptance of amendments, my best plan will be to put these points privately to the promoters before the committee stage.'

If it is indeed true that the House is becoming readier to abstain from superfluous oratory, the old arguments about the inadequacy of private Members' time for its purposes will tend to disappear. It is not likely to disappear altogether, but such a development would seem to follow quite logically from the more general development towards a habit of normally concentrating on constructive and uncontroversial proposals for Friday debates. The genius of the English Parliament resides partly in its ability to adapt itself unobtrusively, spontaneously and almost unconsciously to changes in the situation with which it has to deal. A growing economy of words on private Members' bills should therefore cause us little surprise; it would be a modification of practice such as has often been seen before, and it would seem also to match the more substantial change that there has been in relation to the general character of private Members' bills.

In conclusion, then, it may be said that changes in the machinery seem scarcely to be required; provided that the House is left to develop its own usages with regard to private Members' bills, it seems likely that it will continue to adapt its habits to the changing situation.

Perhaps the most important aspect of the value of private Members' bills in the contemporary situation is related to the increased and increasing authority of the Government as such in the House. Party discipline has long been established, but it becomes with each year more strongly entrenched. The continued provision of opportunities for the introduction of private Members' bills, and for debate on such bills without the normal operation of party discipline, provides a valuable counter-weight to the increase in the Government's authority on all normal occasions. It does much to preserve the variety of types of activity which is so good for the general vitality of Parliament. Finally, it must be admitted that the concrete achievements of the system of private Members' bills, in the way of proposals discussed, opinions formed, and Acts of Parliament put into the statute book, are by no means negligible, and that these would by themselves provide substantial justification for the continuance of the system.

APPENDIX A

THE RULES OF THE HOUSE REGARDING THE ALLOCATION OF TIME OF PRIVATE MEMBERS' BUSINESS

1. *Standing Orders Nos. 4 and 5.*

4. (1) (*a*) Subject to the provisions of paragraph (2) of this order, government business shall, until Easter, have precedence at every sitting except at the sittings of Wednesdays and Fridays, at which sittings unofficial Members' business shall have precedence; and on Wednesdays notices of motions shall have precedence of orders of the day, and on Fridays public bills shall have precedence of motions.

(*b*) After Easter government business shall have precedence at all sittings, except the sittings on the first, second, third and fourth Fridays after Easter Day and the sittings on the third, fourth, fifth and sixth Fridays after Whit-Sunday.

(*c*) At the sittings on Wednesday, when government business has not precedence Mr. Speaker shall at seven of the clock, if the first motion (other than a motion for the adjournment of the House made after the commencement of public business) has not been disposed of, proceed to interrupt the proceedings thereon and such business shall be disposed of as if it were business interrupted at ten of the clock under Standing Order No. 1. (Sittings of the House.)

(2) In the case of a session beginning between Easter and Christmas the following modifications of paragraph (1) of this order shall have effect:

(*a*) Government business shall have precedence on as many Wednesdays immediately before Good Friday as the number of Wednesdays before Christmas on which it has not had precedence, and on as many Fridays immediately before Good Friday

APPENDIX A

as the number of Fridays (reduced by three) on which it had not precedence before Christmas.

(b) After Easter government business shall have precedence at all sittings except the sittings on the second, third, fourth and fifth Fridays after Easter Day.

5. After Whitsuntide (or, in the case of a session beginning between Easter and Christmas, after Easter) public bills other than government bills shall be arranged in the following order: considerations of lords amendments, third readings, considerations of report not already entered upon, adjourned proceedings on consideration, bills in progress in committee, bills appointed for committee, and second readings.

Note: These Standing Orders still remain in force in 1955, but have not been complied with in any session since 1939. In each session a sessional order has been passed, either, as in 1939–48, giving precedence to government business for the whole of the session, or making temporary provision for the allocation of private Members' time for the session concerned. These sessional orders have followed the same general pattern for each session since 1950.

2. *A Typical Recent Sessional Order.*

The sessional order for the Session of 1954–5, passed on 1st December 1954 (*Weekly Hansard*, cols. 156–7) reads as follows:

(1) Save as provided in paragraphs (2) and (5) of this Order, Government Business shall have precedence at every sitting for the remainder of the Session;

(2) Public Bills, other than Government Bills, shall have precedence over Government Business on the following Fridays, namely, 4th and 18th February, 4th and 18th March, 1st and 29th April, 13th May, 10th and 24th June and 8th July;

(3) On and after Friday 13th May, Public Bills other than Government Bills shall be arranged on the Order Paper in the following order:—Consideration of Lords Amendments, Third Readings, Considerations of Reports not already entered upon, adjourned Proceedings on Consideration, Bills in progress in Committee, Bills appointed for Committee and Second Readings;

(4) The ballot for unofficial Members' Bills shall be held on Thursday, 9th December under arrangements to be made by Mr.

APPENDIX A

Speaker, and the Bills shall be presented at the commencement of Public business on Wednesday, 15th December;

(5) Unofficial Members' notices of Motions and unofficial Members' Bills shall have precedence over Government Business in that order on the following Fridays, namely 28th January, 11th and 25th February, 11th and 25th March, 22nd April, 6th and 20th May, 17th June and 1st July; and no Notices of Motions shall be handed in for any of these Fridays in anticipation of the ballot under paragraph (6) of this Order;

(6) Ballots for precedence of unofficial Members' notices of Motions shall be held after Questions on the following Wednesdays, namely 15th December, 26th January, 9th and 23rd February, 9th March, 6th and 20th April, 4th and 25th May and 15th June; and

(7) Until after Wednesday, 15th December, no unofficial Member shall give notice of Motion for leave to bring in a Bill under Standing Order No. 12 (Motions for leave to bring in Bills and nomination of Select Committees at commencement of Public Business) or for presenting a Bill under Standing Order No. 35 (Presentation or Introduction and first reading).

3. An example of a new order superseding an existing one for a particular session is provided by the Order of 20th April 1955, viz.: 'Resolved, that during the remainder of the present session, government business shall have precedence on Fridays' (*Weekly Hansard*, 20th April 1955, col. 317). The last five private Members' Fridays of the session were thus swept away by the arrangements for the dissolution of Parliament on 6th May.

APPENDIX B

TWO BILLS OF 1949

The Hairdressers' (Registration) Bill of 1949 was a very good example of a bill defeated with great difficulty by the Government of the day, and because of their many interesting features the proceedings will be looked at in some detail.

The object of the Bill, which was presented by one Labour Member and supported by eleven others, but by no Conservatives, was to set up a professional body, the British Hairdressing Board, which was to have the power of registering hairdressers and of deciding the terms on which they were to be registered and on which their registration might be cancelled. It was to be an offence to practice the trade of hairdressing without being registered.

The main justification for the Bill, the proposers said, was that under the existing law a barber could keep a dirty shop or be untrained in cutting hair or in the use of electrical and other equipment, and even though he should cause injury to his customers through his professional inadequacy could not be prevented from continuing to practise his trade to the public detriment. The proposed new Board would protect the public against incompetent and unsuitable barbers.

The Bill had a good pedigree. It had been introduced but never debated in 1936, and in 1939 it had been introduced under the Ten Minutes Rule. It had, according to Mr. Sparks, who introduced it, the support of the majority of hairdressers, of the National Union of Distributive and Allied Workers, and of the Joint Industrial Council.[1] It passed its second reading without a division after a debate of an hour and twenty-five minutes, in which the only private Member to raise serious objections was Mr.

[1] H.C. Debs., 11th February 1949, vol. 461, cols. 719 ff.

APPENDIX B

Beverley Baxter, the only Conservative who spoke. His strictures were directed, however, at the pretentiousness of the Bill, and not at its general objects.

The only really hostile speech during the second reading debate was that of Mr. Younger, the Under-Secretary of State at the Home Office. He did not believe that the Bill was the right way to achieve the legitimate objective of protecting the customer. He was not aware of any demand for the Bill either from the public at large or from the public health authorities; furthermore, he thought that there were serious administrative objections to the proposed measure. The legitimate object of the Bill was to protect customers of hairdressing shops against infection and against injury through misuse of appliances. Such protection could best be given, not by the proposed Hairdressing Board, but by the public health authorities using the powers they alread y had under existing laws. Again, he doubted whether, in a trade like this, it was possible to arrive at a satisfactory minimum standard of training which would be suitable for all kinds of hairdressing establishments. In view of all these considerations the Government could not recommend the House to give the Bill a second reading.[1] When the Question on the second reading was put, however, the Government did not carry its opposition to the point even of demanding a division. In order to defeat the second reading the Government would probably have had to rely on Conservative votes, and in any case it seems that the general Conservative attitude was one of 'lack of interest', as Mr. Baxter put it,[2] rather than of active opposition.

The Bill duly went to Standing Committee 'E', where the Government did its best to kill it. Mr. T. Fraser, Joint Under-Secretary of State for Scotland, read out a statement which was like a second reading speech, rather than Committee point.[3] His justification for treating the Committee in this way was his view that the Bill was so fundamentally wrong in its approach to the problem of the control of hairdressing establishments that there

[1] H.C. Debs., 11th February 1949, vol. 461, cols. 737–42.
[2] Ibid., col. 735.
[3] The Government received bitter criticism for this action from both sides of the House, e.g. Mr. Viant (Labour) (Official Report, Standing Committee 'E', 22nd March 1949, Hairdressers' Bill, col. 235), and Sir Thomas Moore, Conservative (H.C. Debs., 1st July 1949, vol. 466, col. 1711).

APPENDIX B

was no purpose in the Government's taking up any of its time in the examination of individual proposals for improvement. The Government, he said, 'do not believe that any amendments could remove the objections which they see to the Bill. Their view is that whatever need there may be for controlling the hairdressing craft, the form of control proposed in the Bill is fundamentally wrong.'

The main objection was, he said, that the Bill, however it might be amended, proposed to establish control by the craft itself, and this the Government believed to be wrong. The proposed Board (or Council) 'would have effective means in the long run of controlling the numbers in the trade. The Government do not think that such wide restrictive powers should be placed in the hands of any trade, and they have no reason to suppose that they could be entrusted to the hairdressing trade more safely than to other trades.' He repeated the view, stated by Mr. Younger at the second reading debate, that such control as was needed in the interest of health and safety could best be exercised by the Local Authorities. The only measure of encouragement that he gave was by saying 'if on further examination it appears that there is any widespread need and demand for some additional measure of control, the Government would be prepared to regard this as a suitable subject for inclusion in public health legislation at the next convenient opportunity'.[1]

There seems to be some suggestion, in this statement of the official viewpoint, that this was not the kind of subject that could be adequately dealt with by a private Member's bill, and that a responsible decision on the proper form of control could only be made by the professionals at the Home Office, who would alone be capable of gathering together all the relevant information and of deciding, as it were in a judicial way, how to use the information once gathered. So, in the opinion of the Government, the control of hairdressers was a subject which amateurs had better leave alone.

---

[1] H.C. Debs., 1st July 1949, vol. 466, col. 21. The opinion seems to have been current among barbers, if one is to trust casual conversations in the chair, that the real reason why the Government killed the Bill was that they wanted to protect the ex-servicemen who had taken short courses of training at special schools opened by the Government after the war. The Bill was indeed not easy to fit in with the Ministry of Labour's training scheme.

APPENDIX B

The governmental statement threw the Committee into some confusion. If this was the attitude of the Government there seemed to be no purpose in continuing with the discussion of amendments. What was the use of the Committee's members spending a great deal of time on the Bill when they knew in advance that their time would be wasted?[1] On the other hand, the House, without a dissentient vote, had imposed on the Committee the task of going through this Bill in detail, and of making improvements in it. What right had the Committee to renounce its duty—even if it wanted to—just because the Government had shown its opposition to the Bill as a whole?

The general attitude in the face of Mr. Fraser's statement was one of bitter indignation that the Government should treat private Members with so little respect.[2] Eventually the suggestion that the Bill should now be laid down was defiantly repudiated by both Labour and Conservative Members. The Committee adjourned for a week in order that its members and the promoters of the Bill might have time to think what should be done.

During the next week the promoters of the Bill worked very hard in an attempt to make it acceptable to the Government. They prepared amendments which would completely reconstruct the Bill, making it much shorter and more modest in its pretensions, and greatly reducing the authority of the body that it proposed to create. The British Hairdressing Board of the original bill, 'with perpetual succession and a common seal and with powers to acquire and hold lands without licence in mortmain'[3] now gave way to a 'representative council for the hairdressing craft', to include 'representatives of employers, employees and

[1] Cf. (Mr. Lennox-Boyd) H. C. Debs., 1st July 1949, vol 466, col. 21 and col. 29: 'We are all busy people and an absolutely fruitless discussion of something which can obviously never become law is a waste of time.'

[2] Cf. (Mr. Charles Williams) ibid., col. 26: 'The House of Commons has unanimously approved of this Bill, and although the Government on that occasion disapproved, they could not get a single hon. Member or right hon. Member to support them in the Lobby. It is monstrous that we should now be dictated to by the Government and told that the first private Member's Bill after ten years is to be thrown out in this way. It is an act of sabotage against the Committee, and I very strongly protest...' and Mr. Kinley, a Labour Member: 'If private Members' Bills have any value at all, it must arise from the fact that as members of the House we discuss a Bill without any Government interference one way or the other' (col. 27).

[3] Clause 1 (1).

APPENDIX B

members of the public, together with an independent chairman to be nominated by the Secretary of State'.[1]

The Committee met for its second sitting on March 8th, and again Mr. Fraser came along to represent the Government. He lost little time in taking the floor.[2] He began by recognizing that the promoters of the Bill had gone a long way towards meeting the criticisms that had been made, but said that nevertheless the Government's attitude remained the same as before. Even now the Bill would have the effect of giving the trade the power of controlling the entry of new recruits, and the Government had already indicated that this was a fundamental defect. The Home Secretary did not want the responsibility of appointing the chairman of the Council.

With regard to the future solution of the problem of control of hairdressing, however, Mr. Fraser was now somewhat more conciliatory and less dogmatic than he had been a week earlier. The appointment of a council for registration, such as the Bill now proposed, would indeed be a leap in the dark which the Government must steadfastly oppose, but discussion on the general question of control need not end now. 'There is so much yet to be said about the hairdressing trade. There is so much worthwhile discussion that can yet take place. It is not as if this really must be done within the lifetime of the present Parliament.'[3] He hoped that the promoters of the Bill would not proceed any further with it now, but leave the matter to be looked at from every angle by the professionals.

This expression of the Government's position was so similar to that which had been given a week earlier that the Committee might again have decided to adjourn to discuss its policy; but it was now determined to go on without any further interruptions, and after some hard things had been said about Mr. Fraser's new intervention,[4] the Committee proceeded with the discussion of the amendments which the sponsors now proposed. Mr. Sparks still hoped that, in spite of Mr. Fraser's statement, the Government would eventually be won over to the support of an amended

[1] Official Report, Standing Committee 'E', 8th March 1949, col. 52.
[2] Ibid., cols. 54 ff.
[3] Ibid., col. 55.
[4] Cf. Mr. Lennox-Boyd (Conservative) and Mr. Turner-Samuels (Labour), who followed Mr. Fraser (ibid., cols. 56 ff.).

APPENDIX B

Bill: 'I had a very long talk yesterday evening with the Home Secretary on this Bill, and I think that, despite what has been said here, much will depend on the form in which the Bill emerges from the Committee as to whether my right hon. Friend will see fit to waive his objections.'[1] The discussion of the rest of the amendments took the rest of the second sitting, and four more sittings.[2]

The new Bill went back to the House for the report stage on 1st July. This stage took just under an hour and a half, and discussion was mostly directed at the position under the Bill of people such as physiotherapists.

The third reading debate followed immediately, and here Mr. Irvine, a Labour Member, moved that the Bill 'be read on this day three months'. Perhaps the most important point that he made was that the Bill as it stood would give no protection at all to the public, at least for a very long time, because 'all present practising hairdressers would become registered by the mere fact that they were practising now'.[3] The Bill did not even contain any express provision for the removal from the register of any barber, once registered, on the ground that he failed to observe the proper standards of cleanliness and hygiene. He made other objections too. Sir Thomas Moore, a Conservative who had taken a very active and helpful part in the deliberations of the Standing Committee, announced that he would not support the third reading but would abstain. During his speech he gave several indications to suggest that, while he was not the spokesman of the Conservative Party as such, he was nevertheless speaking on behalf of many of the Conservatives who had interested themselves in the Bill. 'My hon. friends and I', he said, 'do not like this Bill as it stands. . . . Speaking for myself and many of my colleagues, we cannot lend our support to the Bill in the Lobby.'[4]

The Government, whose voice had not been heard since Mr. Fraser withdrew from the debate after the second sitting of the Standing Committee, once again expressed uncompromising hos-

---

[1] Official Report, Standing Committee 'E', 8th March 1949.
[2] The days of sitting were 1st, 8th, 10th, 15th, 17th and 22nd March.
[3] H.C. Debs., 1st July 1949, vol. 466, col. 1707.
[4] Ibid., col. 1711. In fact only eleven Conservatives voted in the division, eight for the Bill and three against it.

tility to the Bill. This time it was the Home Secretary himself who delivered the official opinion.[1]

In the division the Bill was defeated by 67 votes to 53. The Government on this occasion did not put the Whips on against the Bill—indeed, they could not, as the supporters of the Bill were all Labour Members—but they went down and voted against it themselves in a body. The majority included 19 Ministers, among them 13 of the 14 members of the Cabinet with seats in the House of Commons, nine junior Ministers and six Whips—a total of 34 office-holders.[2] Thus this division was remarkable for bringing out to vote what was probably the largest number of Cabinet Ministers to have voted in a division for many years. Of the unofficial Members who voted, both Conservative and Labour Members showed majorities in favour of the Bill.

A fortnight after the Hairdressers' Bill had had its second reading, the Government had to cope with a proposal put forward by some of its own back-benchers, which involved much more serious controversy, and in which people's feelings were deeply involved. The Protection of Animals (Hunting and Coursing) Bill came up for its second reading debate on 25th February, and at the time its fate was regarded as an indication of what might be expected with an even more controversial proposal, the Prohibition of Foxhunting Bill. The Hunting and Coursing Bill did not refer to the difficult topic of foxhunting, but only, more modestly, to the hunting of deer, otter, or badger, and the coursing of hare or rabbit. In fact, as the more modest bill, which came up first, was defeated, the second, and more ambitious, bill was withdrawn without ever being discussed at all.

Mr. Cocks, the proposer of the Hunting and Coursing Bill, claimed that it was not a party measure,[3] and he did indeed have a Conservative to second him in the debate.[4] The validity of his claim is scarcely borne out by the division list, however. The Bill was eventually defeated by 214 votes to 101. The 101 Members who voted in favour included only two Conservatives, one of

[1] H.C. Debs., 1st July 1949, vol. 466, cols. 1728-34.
[2] Ibid., col. 1739.
[3] Ibid., 25th February 1949, vol. 461, col. 2175.
[4] Ibid., cols. 2189 ff. We may also mention that all eleven of Mr. Cocks' original supporters were Labour Members. (Cf. H.C. Debs., vol. 460, col. 1243.)

APPENDIX B

whom was the seconder, and when we analyse the votes which constituted the majority, we find that, if we leave aside the holders of ministerial offices, five-sixths of the opponents of the Bill were Conservatives. Here, as with the Hairdressers' Bill, the Government was faced with a large body of its own supporters who wanted something which it, as a Government, did not want.

The Minister of Agriculture, Mr. Williams, spoke very strongly against the Bill during the second reading debate, and his speech was particularly interesting because he had to justify the fact that now, as Minister, he was expressing an opinion on this subject which was the opposite of the opinion which he had expressed on a similar bill 24 years before. In the 24 years since that speech was made in a committee room in this Palace of Westminster, he said, he had learned a good deal, not only about hunting, but ... about governing people. He had made a very patient and meticulous examination of this question, and he was convinced that if the Bill were passed the methods that would have to be used for killing these animals (whose numbers had of necessity to be restricted) would almost certainly cause them not less but more suffering than was involved by the methods that were impugned in the Bill. His words are worth quoting:

'After very careful consideration by the Government of the whole situation, we have reached the conclusion that this Bill cannot have the Government's support, and I advise the House to refuse it a Second Reading on the following major grounds: first, that it is based on the false premises that its provisions would lessen cruelty; second, that the suppression of these sports without effective and efficient alternatives would lead to much less satisfactory activities, and third, and this is of some importance, it would alienate the support of the rural population to our food-production programme, which is vital in the national interest.'[1]

There is an almost ironical ambiguity in Mr. Williams' remark about the undesirability of alienating the rural population. If it is taken literally, it seems to mean that 'we' in the sense of 'Parliament', or 'the authorities', or 'that anonymous entity which the public regards as "they"' must not alienate the rural population, damage their morale, and cause them to produce less food. Alternatively, 'we' can be taken to mean 'the Labour Party'. There is probably some truth in both these interpretations. A factor which

[1] H.C. Debs., 25th February 1949, vol. 461, col. 2235.

APPENDIX B

undoubtedly contributed to the Government's feelings on the Bill was the recognition that dislike of hunting is in fact usually associated with people of the Left; and the analysis of the voting in the division bears this out. Thus if the Bill had been passed, the Labour Party might have lost some votes, because the Government would have incurred a public odium that did not rightly belong to it, and because the public would have associated the Labour Party with the Bill in a general way.

APPENDIX C

PRIVATE MEMBERS' BILLS AND GOVERNMENT BILLS INTRODUCED AND PASSED

	Public Bills which received the Royal Assent.		Public Bills introduced into but not passed by the House of Commons.		Sessional average for each Parliament.† Private Members' Bills.	
	Introduced by		Introduced by		Introduced but not passed.	Passed.
	Government	Private* Members.	Government	Private Members.		
1902	30	14	18	153	} 149·5	10·25
3	38	11	11	151		
4	29	10	26	135		
5	17	6	36	159		
6	55	5	23	183	} 183·75	10·4
7		13		155		
8	53	18	15	207		
9	41	10	14	189		
10	32	8	10	168		
11	49	11	15	209	} 197·75	7·5
12–13	29	4	15	224		
13	35	4	24	169		
14	80	11	17	189		
19	107	5	15	28	} 51·75	7·75
20	82	5	14	54		
21	54	14	8	59		
22	56	7	13	66		
23	35	10	8	82	82	10
24	40	3	19	119	119	3
24–5	83	14	11	83	} 71·2 (79·25)	13·2 (14·25)
26	51	17	3	65		
27	36	10	4	93		
28	36	16	4	76		
28–9	33	9	1	39		
29–30	48	5	12	91	} 84·75	6·0
30–1	48	7	9	88		
31–2	48	5	1	48		
32–3	41	13	2	48	} 30·75 (48·7)	7·75 (11·5)
33–4	50	10	4	50		
34–5	44	3	5	7		
35–6	42	11	2	33	} 43·25	14·5
36–7	59	11	1	38		
37–8	54	20	3	58		
38–9	105	16	6	44		
45–6	83	0	0	0		
46–7	55	0	0	0		
47–8	68	0	0	0		
48–9	101	5	2	18		
50	39	0	0	0		
50–1	58	8	1	22	} 17·7	11·0
51–2	56	12	3	19		
52–3	41	11	1	15		
53–4	61	13	2	15		

Source: House of Commons Annual Returns.

* The figures for private Members' bills which received the Royal Assent exclude charity bills.

† Counting the two sessions of 1921 and the two sessions of 1922 as one session for each year. The figures in brackets for the Parliaments of 1924–9 and 1931–5 are the averages obtained by omitting from the calculation those sessions in which there was no private Members' time.

APPENDIX D

A LIST OF THE PRIVATE MEMBERS' BILLS ENACTED IN 1948-53, WITH INDICATION OF THE SCOPE OF EACH BILL

1948-9 (12, 13 & 14 Geo. VI)

Chapter No.

98 ADOPTION OF CHILDREN. Makes provisions regarding the legal arrangements concerning adoption.

70 DOCKING AND NICKING OF HORSES. Restricts the practices of docking and nicking.

100 LAW REFORM. Amends the law relating to divorce and other matrimonial proceedings, the admissibility of evidence as to access, etc.

99 MARRIED WOMEN (MAINTENANCE). Increases the allowance that a court of summary jurisdiction may order a man to pay to his wife who is living apart from him. The increase merely adjusts the sum to the change in the cost of living since the original Act was passed.

52 SLAUGHTER OF ANIMALS (Scotland). Extends the provisions of the 1928 Act so as to cover swine.

1950-1 (14 & 15 Geo. VI)

58 FIREWORKS. Confers powers of seizure where dangerous fireworks are found, and makes provisions regarding licences for firework factories and the marking of fireworks.

57 NATIONAL ASSISTANCE (AMENDMENT). Authorizes the removal from home of persons in need of care, by a process

APPENDIX D

Chapter
No.

    involving less delay than that provided for by the Act of 1948.

33 FRAUDULENT MEDIUMS. Repeals the Witchcraft Act of 1735 and makes new provisions for the punishment of persons who fraudulently purport to act as spiritualistic mediums or to exercise powers of telepathy, clairvoyance, etc.

35 PET ANIMALS. Regulates conditions in pet shops and the sale of pet animals.

36 CRIMINAL LAW. Gives some protection against 'white slavers' to women who are already prostitutes, etc.

39 COMMON INFORMERS. Abolishes the common informer procedure.

40 NEW STREETS. An Act to secure the satisfactory construction, lighting, sewage, furnishing and completion of streets adjacent to new buildings, and to oblige and empower Local Authorities to adopt such streets.

49 SLAUGHTER OF ANIMALS. Extends provisions of the Act of 1933, and implements certain recommendations of the departmental committee on the export and slaughter of horses.

1952 (15 & 16 Geo. VI and 1 Eliz. II)

41 AFFILIATION ORDERS. Increases to 30/- the maximum weekly payment in respect of a child under an affiliation order, and extends the period of operation, so that if a child is receiving schooling or training the parents may be obliged to provide aliment until the child reaches the age of 21.

50 CHILDREN AND YOUNG PERSONS (AMENDMENT). Makes new provision for dealing with children who are ill-treated or in need of care and protection.

51 COCKFIGHTING. Makes it unlawful to have possession of any instrument or appliance designed or adapted for use in connection with the fighting of a domestic fowl.

APPENDIX D

Chapter No.	No. of pages of statute book.	
28	1	CORNEAL GRAFTING. Makes provision with respect to the use of the eyes of deceased persons for therapeutic purposes.
31	1	CREMATION. Provides for the regulation of crematoria.
40	4	CROWN LESSEES (PROTECTION OF SUBTENANTS). Abolishes exemptions from the Rent and Mortgage Interest Restriction Acts, etc., which arise by reason of the subsistence of a superior interest belonging to the Crown, the Duchy of Lancaster or the Duchy of Cornwall.
66	9	DEFAMATION. Amends the law relating to libel and slander and other malicious falsehoods.
43	7	DISPOSAL OF UNCOLLECTED GOODS. Authorizes the disposal of goods accepted in the course of a business for repair or other treatment but not re-delivered.
42	3	HEATING APPLIANCES (FIREGUARDS). Prohibits the sale or letting of certain heating appliances without an effective fireguard.
46	2	HYPNOTISM. Regulates the demonstration of hypnotic phenomena for public entertainment.
64	26	INTESTATES' ESTATES. Amends the law of England and Wales about the property of persons dying intestate.
49	1	COURT OF CHANCERY OF LANCASTER.

1953 (1 & 2 Eliz. II)

Place in ballot.	Chapter No.	No. of pages of statute book.	
8	28	2	DOGS. Provides for the punishment of persons whose dogs worry livestock on agricultural land; and for purposes connected with the matter aforesaid.

APPENDIX D

Place in ballot.	Chapter No.	No. of pages of statute book.	
19	7	½	LAW REFORM (PERSONAL INJURIES). Amends section two of the Law Reform (Personal Injuries) Act of 1948, in relation to the assessment in Scotland of damages for death.
6	26	13	LOCAL GOVERNMENT (MISCELLANEOUS PROVISIONS). Empowers Local Authorities to establish capital funds and repairs and renewal funds, to provide omnibus shelters, to increase their annual charges for the maintenance of dustbins.[1]
16	24	1	NAVY AND MARINES (WILLS). Provides that men of the Navy and Marines may effectively make wills by methods previously not available to them.
9	19	9	PHARMACY. Provides for the examination and registration of chemists and druggists.
13	21	5	ROAD TRANSPORT LIGHTING. Provides that every motor-car, lorry, etc., must carry two rear lights at night, that overhanging loads must be lit, etc. Much of the detail regarding the rules is left to be dealt with by the Minister in regulations. Some such regulations have in fact been made (the Lighting (Reversing Lights) Regulation, S.I. 1546 of 1953 (22nd October 1953), the Lighting Regulations of 19th August 1954 (S.I. 1954, No. 1105), the Road Vehicles Lighting (Special Exemption and Amendment) Regulations of 24th September 1954 (S.I. 1281 of 1954).)
14	22	1	ROAD TRANSPORT LIGHTING (NO. 2) ACT. Provides that regulations may be made to extend the conditions under which

[1] *The Local Government Journal* (vol. 61, 1953, p. 2272) complains that the Act confuses the dustbin issue even more than before. Cf. also, p. 424.

APPENDIX D

Chapter No.	No. of pages of statute book.	
		vehicles may be parked at night without lights. S.O. No. 12
23	1	ACCOMMODATION AGENCIES. Prohibits the taking of certain commissions in dealing with persons seeking houses or flats and the unauthorized advertisement for letting of houses and flats.
27	1	SLAUGHTER OF ANIMALS (PIGS). Provides for the humane slaughter of pigs in places other than slaughterhouses or knackers' yards. S.O. No. 35
10	2	AGRICULTURAL LAND. An Act to make it an offence to remove surface soil from land in certain circumstances.
11	½	HARBOURS, PIERS AND FERRIES. Extends the power of the Secretary of State under the Act of 1937, to authorize the undertaking by certain Local and Harbour Authorities of operations in connection with marine works.

APPENDIX E

SUMMARY OF APPENDIX E

Of the 49 bills enacted, not one was the subject of a division on second or third reading. 16[1] were brought in on 'good' places in the ballot, but two of these owed their success in the first place to having their second readings taken unopposed. 22[2] were brought in on 'low' places in the ballot; of these, 9 received their second readings unopposed and without having been debated, one was talked out but later allowed to pass unopposed, and one was counted out but later allowed to pass unopposed. The other 11 were approved at second reading after debate.

Of the remaining 11 bills enacted, 7 were first brought in under the Ten Minutes Rule and 4 under S.O. No. 35. All of these, with the exception of one Ten Minute bill and one other bill, received their second readings unopposed.

Of the 49, 8 were complicated enough to occupy the Standing Committee for more than one sitting each. Two of these 8 had originally been brought in on low places in the ballot.

[1] Of a total of 31 on good places.
[2] Of a total of 71 on low places.

APPENDIX E

PRIVATE MEMBERS' BILLS WHICH WERE ENACTED
1948-49

Place in ballot.	Member introducing.	Party.	Title of Bill.	Commons debates.			Standing Committee.		Lords debates.			Lords amendments.	
				Stage.	Day & order.	Time h.m.	Date.	Order.	Stage.	Date.	Time h.m.	Day & Order.	Time h.m.
(1)	(2)	(3)	(4)	(5)	(6)	(7)	(8)	(9)	(10)	(11)	(12)	(13)	(14)
2	Nield	C	Adoption	2 R. Rep.	2:1 8:2	3.30 2.25	29 Mar.– 5 Apr. (3 stgs).	2nd	2 R. Ctee. Rep.	11 July 21 July 28 July	1.42 1.21 0.45	Govt. time 5 Dec.	1.20
10	Monslow	L	Married Women (Maintenance)	2 R. Rep.	2:2 8:3	1.22 0.40	3 to 12 May (3 stgs.)	4th	2 R. Ctee.	7 July 21 July	1.13 0.34	Govt. time 5 Dec.	0.55
16	Sir D. Whyte	C	Docking and Nicking of Horses	2 R. Rep.	4:3 10:2	1.30 0.15	5 July	7th	2 R.	20 July	0.20		
18	Sir P. Macdonald	C	Law Reform (Misc. Provs.)	2 R. Rep. 3 R.	1:3 10:1 ,, ,,	0.1 0.30 1.25	12 Apr.	3rd	2 R. Ctee. Rep.	28 July 27 Oct. 23 Nov.	0.44 1.9 0.15	Govt. time 5 Dec.	1.50
21	Major Ramsay	C	Slaughter of Animals (Scotland)	2 R. Rep. 3 R.	6 : unopposed 8:1 ,, ,,	0.1 0.6	8 Mar.	Scot. S.C.	2 R.	14 July	0.1		

The days allotted for Private Members' Bills in this session were:
1st: 11 Feb, 2nd: 18 Feb. 3rd: 25 Feb. 4th: 4 Mar. 5th: 11 Mar. 6th: 18 Mar. 7th: 25 Mar.
The days allotted for the later stages were : 8th: 24 June. 9th: 1 July. 10th: 8 July.

PRIVATE MEMBERS' BILLS WHICH WERE ENACTED
1950–51

Place in ballot.	Member introducing.	Party.	Title of Bill.	Commons debates.			Standing Committee.		Lords debates.			Lords amendments.	
				Stage.	Day & order.	Time h.m.	Date.	Order.	Stage.	Date.	Time h.m.	Day & order.	Time h.m.
(1)	(2)	(3)	(4)	(5)	(6)	(7)	(8)	(9)	(10)	(11)	(12)	(13)	(14)
1	Monslow	L	Fraudulent Mediums	2 R. Rep.	1:1 7:1	4.0 Nil	12 Dec.	1st	2 R.	3 May	0.42	9:1	0.4
2	Kinley	L	New Streets	3 R. 2 R. Rep. 3 R.	,, 2:1 7:2 ,,	0.20 1.45 0.40 2.40	13 to 22 Feb. (3 stgs.)	2nd	2 R. Ctee. Rep. 3 R.	3 May 7 June 14 June 21 June	0.30 1.20 0.26 0.4	10 : 2	0.8
3	Heald	C	Common Informers	2 R. Rep. 3 R.	3:1 8:2 ,,	4.30 0.2 0.10	14 Mar.	4th	2 R. Ctee.	5 June 12 June	0.24 0.1	10 : 1	0.4
6	Russell	C	Pet Animals	2 R. Rep. 3 R.	,, 6:1 8:3	4.55 0.7 0.40	24 Apr.	S.C. "C"	2 R.	7 June	0.36		
15	Colegate	C	Slaughter of Animals	2 R. Rep. 3 R.	,, 7 : unopposed 9:3	0.25 1.40	8 May	8th	2 R.	12 July	0.6		
18	Moyle	L	Fireworks	2 R. Rep. 3 R.	12 Mar. unopp. 8:4 ,,	0.45 0.10	26 Apr.	7th	2 R. Ctee. Rep. 2 R.	14 June 28 June 12 July 7 June	0.35 0.41 0.13 0.25	Govt. time 27 July	0.14
Ten min. Rule 13 Dec.	Mrs. Castle	L	Criminal Law	2 R.	21 Jan. unopp. at 4 p.m.		6 Mar.	3rd					
S.O.35 6 June	Dr. Broughton	L	National Assistance	3 R 2 R 3 R.	8:1 4 July unopp. after Ctee. unopp.	0.10	10 July Whole House Govt. time	Ctee.	2 R. Ctee.	23 July 26 July	0.11 0.1		

The days allotted for Private Members' Bills in this session were: 1st: 1 Dec. 2nd: 26 Jan. 3rd: 9 Feb. 4th: 23 Feb. 5th: 9 Mar. 6th: 6 Apr. Later stages had precedence on: 7th: 20 Apr. 8th: 4 May. 9th: 8 June. 10th: 22 June.

PRIVATE MEMBERS' BILLS WHICH WERE ENACTED
1951–52

Place in ballot.	Member introducing.	Party.	Title of Bill.	Commons debates.			Standing Committee.		Lords debates.			Lords amendments.	
				Stage.	Day & order.	Time h.m.	Date.	Order.	Stage.	Date.	Time h.m.	Day & order.	Time h.m.
(1)	(2)	(3)	(4)	(5)	(6)	(7)	(8)	(9)	(10)	(11)	(12)	(13)	(14)
1	H. Lever	L	Defamation	2 R. Rep.	1:1 7:1 9:7	3.35 All day 3.55	21 Feb. to 27 Mar.	1st (10 stgs.)	2 R. Ctee. Rep.	15 July 28 July 31 July	1.35 3.40 0.55	Govt. time 24 Oct.	1.20
2	Cole	C	Children and Young Persons	2 R. (a) (b) Rep.	2 : no sitting 3 : unopposed 8 : 3	Nil 2.0	29 Apr. 1 May (2 stgs.)	5th	2 R. Ctee.	1 July 15 July	0.6 0.25	Govt. time 28 July	0.3
3	Sir A. Hudson	C	Crown Lessees (Protection of Sub-Tenants)	2 R. Rep.	3:1 8:2	1.30 0.15	8 Apr.	3rd	2 R.	10 July	0.10		
4	Bullard	C	Heating Appliances (Fireguards)	2 R. Rep. 3 R.	4:1 9:3 ,, ,,	All day Nil 0.2	20 May	8th	2 R.	15 July	0.13		
5	Hylton-Foster	C	Intestates' Estates	2 R. (a) (b) Rep.	5:1 28 Apr. unopp. 5 July Nil	3.55 Nil	24 June	12th	None			Govt. time 28 Oct.	0.15

8	Crouch	C	Affiliation Orders	2 R. 3 R.	3:2 9:1	0.48 0.9	22 Apr.	4th	2 R.	14 July	0.8
14	Hastings	L	Hypnotism	2 R. 3 R.	6: unopposed 9:6	0.7	17 June	11th	2 R.	10 July	0.11
17	P. Bell	C	Lancaster Palatine Court	2 R. 3 R.	6: unopposed 9:4	0.3	29 May	9th	2 R. Ctee.	10 July 21 July	0.6 0.10
20	S. Marshall	C	Cockfighting	2 R. R.–3 R.	6: unopposed 9:5	Nil	12 June	10th	2 R. Ctee.	15 July 22 July	0.8 0.10
Ten min. R. 30 Jan.	Reeves	L	Cremation	2 R. Rep.	19 Feb. unopp. 8:1	0.30	1 Apr.	2nd	2 R.	10 June	0.4
Ten min. R. 20 Feb.	Miss E. Burton	L	Disposal of uncollected Goods	2 R. Rep.	12 Mar. unopp. 9:2	0.30	13 May	7th	2 R.	10 July	0.9
Ten min. R. 14 May	Sir H. Williams	C	Corneal Grafting	2 R. (Remaining stages all taken in succession unopposed after Second Reading)	21 May unopp.				2 R. Ctee.	27 May 10 June	0.13 0.6

The days alloted for Private Members' Bills in this session were:
1st: 1 Feb. 2nd: 15 Feb. 3rd: 29 Feb. 4th: 14 Mar. 5th: 28 Mar. 6th: 25 Apr.
Later stages had precedence on: 7th: 9 May. 8th: 23 May. 9th: 27 June. 10th: 11 June.
The second of the days, 15 February, was lost because the House then stood adjourned after the death of King George VI.

On the Intestates' Estates Bill the Second Reading stage had to be carried on to a second day because the House was counted out on the first day.

On the Defamation Bill, in addition to the ten sittings of the Standing Committee mentioned here, there was one other sitting of the Committee at which no quorum was present.

PRIVATE MEMBERS' BILLS WHICH WERE ENACTED
1952–53

Place in ballot.	Member introducing.	Party.	Title of Bill.	Commons debates.			Standing Committee.		Lords debates.			Lords amendments.	
				Stage.	Day & order.	Time h.m.	Date.	Order.	Stage.	Date.	Time h.m.	Day & order.	Time h.m.
(1)	(2)	(3)	(4)	(5)	(6)	(7)	(8)	(9)	(10)	(11)	(12)	(13)	(14)
6	Mitchison	L	Local Government (Misc. Provisions)	2 R. Recomm Rep. 3 R.	6 : 1 10 : 3 10 : 3 ,, ,,	3.30 0.55 1.20 0.17	21 Apr. to 7 May	6th (5 stgs.)	2 R. Ctee.	23 June 2 July	0.33 0.5		
8	Teeling	C	Dogs (Protection of Livestock)	2 R. (a) (b) Rep. 3 R.	6 : 2 9 May 10 : 5 ,, ,,	1.25 unopp. 0.46 0.37	19 May	8th	2 R. Ctee.	23 June 2 July	0.38 0.13		
9	Hall	L	Pharmacy	2 R. 3 R.	5 : 2 8 : 2	0.17 0.17	1 Apr.	5th	2 R.	5 May	0.13		
13	Col. Harrison	C	Road Transport Lighting (Rear Lights)	2 R. Rep. 3 R.	3 : unopposed 8 : 1 ,, ,,	1.36 0.40	24 Feb.	2nd	2 R. Ctee. Rep.	7 May 14 May 9 June	0.48 0.16 0.52	10 : 1	0.4
14	Powell	C	Road Transport Lighting (Amendment)	2 R. Rep.	4 : unopposed 10 : 2	0.9	17 Mar.	4th	2 R.	23 June	0.15		

16	Fleetwood-Hesketh	C	Navy and Marines (Wills)	2 R. Rep. 3 R.	3 : unopposed 9 : 1 Nil ,, ,, 0.6	10 Mar.	3rd	2 R.	11 June	0.5
19	Brooman-White	C	Law Reform (Personal Injuries) (Scotland)	2 R. (Remaining stages all taken in succession unopposed after Second Reading)				2 R.	20 Jan.	0.20
Ten min. R. 16 Dec.	Sir G. Hutchinson	C	Accommodation Agencies	2 R. 3 R.	23 Jan. unopp. 7 : 2 0.18	12 Feb.	1st	2 R. Ctee. 3 R.	14 May 11 June 17 June	0.24 0.38 0.23
Ten min. R. 15 Apr.	Brig. Rayner	C	Slaughter of Pigs	2 R. Rep. 3 R.	8 : 3 10 : 4 ,, ,,	14 May	7th	2 R. Ctee.	23 June 2 July	0.38 0.22
S.O. 35	Vaughan-Morgan	C	Agric. Land (Removal of Surface Soil)	2 R. (Remaining stages all taken in succession unopposed after Second Reading)	5th Dec. unopp. 1.14 0.6 0.8			2 R. Ctee.	20 Jan. 27 Jan.	0.15 0.20	7 : 1 0.8
S.O. 35	Grimond	Lib.	Harbours, Piers and Ferries (Scotland)	2 R.	23 Jan. unopp.	12 Feb.	Scot. S.C.	2 R. Ctee.	14 Apr. 28 Apr.	0.9 0.3

The days allotted for Private Members' Bills in this session were:

1st: 28 Nov. 2nd: 12 Dec. 3rd: 30 Jan. 4th: 13 Feb. 5th: 27 Feb. 6th: 13 Mar. Later stages had precedence on: 7th: 27 Mar. 8th: 24 Apr. 9th: 8 May. 10th: 12 June.

PRIVATE MEMBERS' BILLS WHICH WERE ENACTED

1953–54

Place in ballot.	Member introducing.	Party.	Title of Bill.	Commons debates.			Standing Committee.		Lords debates.			Lords amendments.	
				Stage.	Day & order.	Time h.m.	Date.	Order.	Stage.	Date.	Time h.m.	Day & order.	Time h.m.
(1)	(2)	(3)	(4)	(5)	(6)	(7)	(8)	(9)	(10)	(11)	(12)	(13)	(14)
1	Moyle	L	Slaughter of Animals	2 R. Rep. 3 R.	2 : 1 8 : 2 ,, ,,	3.35 0.51 0.28	17 Feb.	4th	2 R. Ctee.	22 June 15 July	0.37 0.8		
4	Lady Tweedsmuir	C	Protection of Birds	2 R. Rep. 3 R.	1 : 1 7 : 1 ,, ,,	3.20 2.15 1.50	15 to 26 Feb.	1st (4 stgs.)	2 R. Ctee. Rep. 3 R.	15 Apr. 29 Apr. 11 May 13 May	0.20 3.25 0.45 0.26	9 : 1	2.48
2	Lady Davidson	C	Protection of Animals (Anæsthetics)	2 R. Rep. 3 R.	3 : 1 9 : 3 ,, ,,	1.20 0.4 0.4	3 Mar.	6th	2 R.	22 June	0.42		
5	Watkins	L	Marriage Act (1949) (Amendment)	2 R. 3 R.	6 : 1 9 : 6	1.10 0.3	5 May	12th	2 R.	5 July	0.8		
6	Sir Wavell Wakefield	C	Hire-Purchase	2 R. 3 R.	19 Mar. 9 : 4	unopp. 0.5	7 Apr.	10th	2 R. Ctee.	15 June 5 July	0.50 0.32		

204

No.	Member	C/L	Bill	Stage	Date	Time		Date		Date	Time
8	Peyton	C	Law Reform (Limitation of Actions)	2 R. Rep. 3 R.	1 : 2 8 : 1 ,, ,,	1.20 0.10 0.48	2 Feb.	2nd	2 R. Ctee.	20 May 11 June	1.0 0.30
9	W. T. Williams	L	Industrial and Provident Societies	2 R. 3 R.	19 Mar. 9 : 5	unopp. 0.1	14 Apr.	11th	2 R.	17 June	0.20
11	Remnant	C	Protection of Animals (Amendment)	2 R. Rep.	3 : 2 9 : 2	1.0 0.3	24 Feb.	5th	2 R.	1 June	0.10
13	Mulley	L	Pool Betting	2 R. (a) (b) Rep. 3 R.	2 : 2 3 : 5 8 : 3 ,, ,,	1.18 1.24 2.18 0.4	17 to 31 Mar.	9th (3 stgs.)	2 R. Ctee.	19 May 1 June	0.12 0.27
14	F. Harris	C	Juries	2 R.	1 : 3	0.6	10 Feb.	2nd	2 R.	1 June	0.9
16	Nabarro	C	Coroners	2 R.	3 : 3	0.30	10 Mar.	7th	2 R.	11 May	0.13
S.O. 35 24 Nov.	Skeffington	L	Law Reform (Enforcement of Contracts)	2 R. Rep. 3 R.	3 : 4 7 : 3 ,, ,,	0.40 0.40 0.7	10 Mar.	8th	2 R.	19 May	0.33
Ten min. R. 2 Dec.	Miss Ward	C	Rights of Entry (Gas and Electricity Boards)	2 R. (Remaining stages all taken unopposed after Second Reading)	11 Dec.	unopp.			2 R.	24 Feb.	0.29

The days allotted for Private Members' Bills in this session were:
1st: 4 Dec. 2nd: 29 Jan. 3rd: 12 Feb. 4th: 26 Feb. 5th: 12 Mar. 6th: 26 Mar.
Later stages had precedence on: 7th: 9 Apr. 8:h: 7 May. 9th: 21 May. 10th: 25 June.
The fifth of the days, 12 March was in fact lost because the previous day's sitting went on for so long that the House could not sit on the Friday.
On 10th March the Standing Committee took two bills in succession.

APPENDIX F
PRIVATE MEMBERS' BALLOTED BILLS WHICH DID NOT PASS
1948–49

Place in ballot.	Member introducing.	Party.	Title of Bill.	Second Reading. Day & order.	Second Reading. Time taken h.m.	Result.
(1)	(2)	(3)	(4)	(5)	(6)	(7)
1	Piratin	Comm.	Safety in Employment	1 : 1	3.30	Withdrawn at 2 R.
3	Cocks	L	Protection of Animals (Hunting and Coursing)	3 : 1	All day	Defeated 101–214 at 2 R.
4	Sir W. Darling	C	Cockfighting	4 : 1	0.26	Passed all stages in H.C.
5	Follick	L	Spelling Reform	5 : 1	All day	Closure carried 127–46. 2 R. defeated 84–87
6	Brig. Peto	C	Pet Animals	6 : 1	1.40	Passed 2 R. and Committee; no time provided for later stages
7	E. P. Smith	C	Censorship of Plays (Repeal)	7 : 1	4.40	Passed 2 R., 76–37. Passed Committee too late (10th), 1 Dec.
8	Fairhurst	L	Prohibition of Foxhunting	None		Withdrawn before 2 R.
9	Morley	L	War Damage (Amendment)	6 : 2	3.0	Passed 2 R. Passed Committee too late (9th), 10 Nov.
11	Grimston	C	Public Bodies (Admission of Press)	7 : 2	0.15	Talked out
12	P. Thorneycroft	C	Analgesia in Childbirth	4 : 2	3.0	Passed 2 R. Defeated 44–108 on 3 R.
13	Sparks	L	Hairdressers' (Registration)	2 : 2	1.25	Passed 2 R. Defeated 53–67 on 3 R.
14	Bing	L	Licensing (Tied Houses)	Not debated		
15	Osborne	C	Coal Mines (Protection of Animals)	6 : 3	0.4	Withdrawn
17	Sir H. Morris-Jones	N. Lib.	Secretary of State for Wales	Not debated		
19	Guy	L	Loss of Employment	Not debated		
20	Sir W. Wakefield	C	Statutory Instruments (Parliamentary Control)	1 : 4 2 : 3 4 : 4	0.2 0.3 0.1	Talked out Talked out Talked out

The days allotted for Private Members' Bills for this session were:
1st: 11 Feb. 2nd: 18 Feb. 3rd: 25 Feb. 4th: 4 Mar. 5th: 11 Mar. 6th: 18 Mar. 7th: 25 Mar. Later stages had precedence on: 24 June, 1 and 8 July.

PRIVATE MEMBERS' BALLOTED BILLS WHICH DID NOT PASS

1950-51

Place in ballot.	Member introducing.	Party.	Title of Bill.	Second Reading.		Result.
				Day & order.	Time taken h.m.	
(1)	(2)	(3)	(4)	(5)	(6)	(7)
4	Bevins	C	Transport (Amendment)	4 : 1	All day	Passed 2 R., 242-234. Standing Committee voted against all the clauses
5	Mrs. White	L	Matrimonial Causes	5 : 1	All day	Closure, Div. 102-99. 2 R., Div. 131-60. S. Committee reported unfavourably
7	N. Davies	C	Trade Union	6 : 2	0.2	Talked out
8	Mrs. Hill	C	Deserted Wives	2 : 2	2.45	Closure motion defeated 44-51.
9	Major McCallum	C	Hill Farming	1 : 2	0.55	Talked out
10	Col. Hutchison	C	Gas Undertakings (Scotland)	9 : 4	2.30	Talked out
11	McKie	C	Rivers (Prevention of Pollution) (Scotland)	Not debated		
12	Marples	C	Representation of the People	3 : 2	0.2	Talked out
13	J. Rodgers	C	Security of Employment (Service Contracts)	7 : 3	1.5	Talked out
				Not debated		
14	M. Lindsay	C	Public Bodies (Admission of Press)	Not debated		
16	Sorensen	L	Colour Bar	Not debated		
17	Capt. Orr	U.U.	Representation of the People	Not debated		
19	Longden	L	National Insurance (Amendment)	8 : 5	0.10	Withdrawn
20	Col. Banks	C	Packaging and Handling Food	8 : 6	0.4	Withdrawn

The days allotted for Private Members' Bills in this session were:

1st: 1 Dec. 2nd: 26 Jan. 3rd: 9 Feb. 4th: 23 Feb. 5th: 9 Mar. 6th: 6 Apr.
Later stages had precedence on: 7th: 20 Apr. 8th: 4 May. 8th: 8 June. 9th: 22 June.

On the 8th day (4 May 1952) the House was adjourned at 1.20 p.m., after disposing of the later stages of four bills and the Second Reading stages of two others.

PRIVATE MEMBERS' BALLOTED BILLS WHICH DID NOT PASS

1951–52

Place in ballot.	Member introducing.	Party.	Title of Bill.	Second Reading. Day & order.	Second Reading. Time taken h.m.	Result.
(1)	(2)	(3)	(4)	(5)	(6)	(7)
6	Dr. Summerskill	L	Women's Disabilities	6 : 1	All day	Talked out. (Closure on 2 R. approved by 54–20, and therefore not carried)
7	Brig. Rayner	C	Representation of the People	Not debated		
9	Sir J. Barlow	C	Companies	3 : 3	2.40	Talked out
10	H. Hynd	L	Loss of Employment (Compensation)	Not debated		
11	Steele	L	Housing (Temporary Prohibition of Sale of Small Houses (Scotland)	Not debated		
12	Brockway	L	Declaration of Human Rights	8 : 4 9 : 7	1.0 0.3	Counted out Talked out
13	W. T. Williams	L	Industrial and Provident Societies (No. 2)	Not debated		
15	Bing	L	Licensing (Amendment) (Tied Houses)	Not debated		
16	Erroll	C	Directors, etc., Burden of Proof	10 Mar. (Govt. day)	Nil	Passed 2 R. unopposed. Debated for 3¾ hours on Report on last Private Members' day, and talked out (closure refused) on 3 R.
18	Keeling	C	Bank Holidays (Amendment)	Not debated		
19	G. Finlay	C	Riding Establishments	1 : 2	0.22	Talked out (closure refused)

The days allotted for Private Members' Bills in this session were:
1st: 1 Feb. 2nd: 15 Feb. 3rd: 28 Feb. 4th: 14 Mar. 5th: 28 Mar. 6th: 25 Apr.
Later stages of bills had precedence on: 7th: 9 May. 8th: 23 May. 9th: 27 June. 10th: 11 July.

On the second of these days, 15 February, the House did not sit, as it was then still adjourned owing to the death of King George VI.

PRIVATE MEMBERS' BALLOTED BILLS WHICH DID NOT PASS

1952–53

Place in ballot.	Member introducing.	Party.	Title of Bill.	Second Reading.		Result.
				Day & order.	Time taken h.m.	
(1)	(2)	(3)	(4)	(5)	(6)	(7)
1	Simmons	L	Press Council	1 : 1	All day	Closure defeated, 116–124 on 2 R.
				9 : 2	3.59	Withdrawn at 2 R.
2	Watkins	L	National Insurance (Industrial Injuries)	2 : 1	3.58	Withdrawn at 2 R.
3	Parker	L	Sunday Observance	3 : 1	All day	Defeated 57–281 on 2 R.
4	Wing-Cdr. Bullus	C	Criminal Justice	4 : 1	All day	Defeated 63–159 on 2 R.
5	Follick	L	Simplified Spelling	5 : 1	4.40	Passed 65–53; passed Standing Committee, but no further progress
7	Miss Herbison	L	Foundry Workers (Health and Safety)	2 : 2	1.4	Passed 2 R.; no further progress
10	D. Williams	C	Game (Duck and Geese)	Not debated		
11	Reeves	L	Abortion	5 : 3	0.1	Talked out
12	Dr. Summerskill	L	Women's Disabilities	9 : 3	1.48	Talked out
15	Viant	L	Toy Weapons	7 : 4	1.25	Counted out
17	Major Legge-Bourke	C	Civil Service Appointments Board	2 : 3	0.3	Talked out
				8 : 5	1.45	Talked out
18	Major Beamish	C	Protection of Animals	Not debated		
20	F. Harris	C	Protection of Animals	Not debated		

The days allotted for Private Members' Bills in this session were:
1st: 28 Nov. 2nd: 12 Dec. 3rd: 30 Jan. 4th: 13 Feb. 5th: 27 Feb. 6th: 13 Mar.
Later stages had precedence on: 7th: 27 Mar. 8th: 24 Apr. 9th: 8 May. 10th: 12 June.

PRIVATE MEMBERS' BALLOTED BILLS WHICH DID NOT PASS

1953-54

Place in ballot.	Member introducing.	Party.	Title of Bill.	Second Reading. Day & order.	Second Reading. Time taken h.m.	Result.
(1)	(2)	(3)	(4)	(5)	(6)	(7)
3	Wm. Paling	L	Safety in Employment (Inspection and Safety Organization)	4 : 1	All day	Closure motion defeated 75-82
7	Alport	C	National Insurance (Small Incomes)	6 : 2	0.38	Withdrawn
10	Spearman	C	Animals (Cruel Poisons)	Not debated		
12	D. Marshall	C	Ministers of the Crown (Fisheries)	10 : 1	3.38	No time for further progress
15	Ian Harvey	C	Licensing at Airports	5 Feb. 3 : 6 8 : 4	0.1 0.16	A P.M. motion day at 4 p.m. Objection made to passing unopposed Talked out Talked out
17	Grimston	C	Representation of the People (St. Albans)	6 : 3	0.12	Counted out (1.4 p.m.)
18	Col. Stoddart-Scott	C	Marriage (Certificates of Medical Inspection)	Not debated		
19	R. D. Scott	C	Salmon and Freshwater Fisheries (Protection)	Not debated		

The days allotted for Private Members' Bills in this session were:
1st: 4 Dec. 2nd: 29 Jan. 3rd: 12 Feb. 4th: 26 Feb. 5th: 12 Mar. 6th: 26 Mar.
Later stages had precedence on: 7th: 9 Apr. 8th: 7 May. 9th: 21 May. 10th: 25 June.

The 5th of the days, 12 March, was in fact lost because the previous day's sitting went on for so long that the House could not sit on the Friday.

BIBLIOGRAPHY

Most of the material for this study has been taken from the Official Report of the House of Commons Debates, House of Lords Debates and House of Commons Standing Committees. The Commons Journals have also been used. Newspapers, particularly *The Times* and the *Manchester Guardian*, are a further indispensable source.

Apart from these, the following sources have been used:

Report of the Select Committee on Procedure (Unofficial Members' Business), H.C. 102 of 1927.

Report of the Select Committee on Procedure on Public Business, H.C. 161 of 1930-1.

Third Report of the Select Committee on Procedure, H.C. 189-1 of 1945-6.

Sir Thomas Erskine May's *Treatise on the Law, Privileges, Proceedings and Usage of Parliament*, 15th ed., edited by Lord Campion and T. G. B. Cocks, Butterworth, 1950.

Sir Gilbert Campion, *Introduction to the Procedure of the House of Commons*, 2nd ed., Macmillan, 1947.

Eric Taylor, *The House of Commons at Work*, 1st ed., Penguin, 1951. (A second edition of this work was published in 1955.)

J. Redlich, *The Procedure of the House of Commons*, London, 1908.

A. L. Lowell, *The Government of England*, London, 1908.

W. I. Jennings, *Parliament*, Cambridge University Press, 1939.

A. P. Herbert, *The Ayes Have It*, Methuen, 1937.

S. Gordon, *Our Parliament*, Hansard Society, 4th ed., 1952.

A. P. Herbert, *Independent Member*, Methuen, 1950.

P. and G. Ford, *A Breviate of Parliamentary Papers, 1917-39*, Blackwell, 1951.

INDEX

Adamson, William, 53, 118
Addison, Dr. C., 96
Adoption of children, 57, 125, 146
Air pollution, 70, 72, 132
Alexander, A. V. (Lord), 114
Animal welfare, 58 f., 138 ff., 187
Ashley, Lt.-Col. W. W., 91
Asquith, H. H., 11, 101, 130
Astor, Lady, 119, 121
Atholl, Duchess of, 53*n*.
Attlee, C. R., 68, 113, 157, 158

Baldwin, Stanley, 47, 53 f., 89, 96 ff.
Balfour, A. J., 10, 101
Ballot, private Members', 20 f.
Banbury, Sir Frederick, 41*n*.
Barr, James, 24
Barristers, help with drafting, 26
Baxter, Beverley, 182
Beaver Committee, 132
Bevan, Aneurin, 68
Bevins, J. R., 39, 61, 113
Bills:
   Acquisition of Land (1912), 28
   Adoption (1948–9), 57
   Analgesia in Childbirth (1948–9), 38, 60
   Annual Holiday (1936–7), 90, 106, 129
   Clean Air (1954–5), 70, 72, 131
   Coal Mines (Protection of Animals), 58
   Cockfighting, 65
   Common Informers (1950–1), 23, 62
   Criminal Justice (1952–3), 66
   Criminal Law (1950–1), 63

Bills (*continued*):
   Death of the Speaker (1952–3), 157
   Deceased Wife's Sister (1907), 144
   Decimal Coinage (1954–5), 141
   Defamation (1951–2), 3, 22, 37, 41, 63 f., 146
   Deserted Wives (1950–1), 28, 63
   Docking and Nicking of Horses (1948–9), 56 f.
   Dog Racing (Local Option) (1932–3), 23
   Dogs (Protection of Livestock) (1952–3), 30, 67, 109
   Ecclesiastical Disorders (1908), 28
   Fireguards (1951–2), 65, 172*n*.
   Fireworks (1950–1), 62 f.
   Fraudulent Mediums (1950–1), 62
   Government of Wales (1954–5), 70, 128
   Hairdressers' (1948–9), 39, 61, 103, 181 ff.
   Hire-Purchase (1937–8), 47
   Hotels and Restaurants (1933–4), 98
   Housing (Temporary Prohibition of Sale) (Scotland) (1951–2), 30
   Industrial and Agricultural Rates (1954–5), 130
   Inheritance (Family Provision), 145
   Intestates' Estates (1951–2), 30, 104*n*.
   Leasehold Enfranchisement (1954–55), 70 f.
   Married Women (Maintenance) (1948–9), 57

INDEX

Bills (*continued*):
  Matrimonial Causes (1936-7), 3 f., 23, 108, 110
  Matrimonial Causes (1950-1), 39, 62, 103, 109, 124
  Methylated Spirits (1933-4), 28
  Mines and Quarries (1953-4), 72
  National Assistance (1950-1), 63
  Navy and Marines (Wills) (1952-53), 67
  New Streets (1950-1), 25, 62
  Non-Industrial Employment (1954-5), 71
  Omnibuses (1929-30), 114
  Peers (1952-3), 156
  Pet Animals (1951-2), 34, 61 f.
  Pool Betting (1953-4), 30, 68 f., 136
  Poor Prisoners' Defence (1930), 110
  Press Council (1952-3), 66
  Prevention of Unemployment (1919, etc.), 51, 112
  Prohibition of Foxhunting (1948-9), 187
  Proportional Representation (1921), 96
  Protection of Animals (Hunting and Coursing) (1948-9), 98, 102, 187 ff.
  Public Bodies (Admission of Press) (1948-9), 57
  Racecourse Betting (1928), 35, 40, 95
  Railway Fires (1922, etc.), 143
  Rating of Machinery (1923), 114
  Re-election of Ministers (1926), 89, 127
  Rent Restriction (1924), 57
  Representation of the People (1950-1), 62
  Representation of the People (1952-3), 68
  Road Transport Lighting (1927), 142
  Road Transport Lighting (1952-53), 67, 142, 158
  Roman Catholic Relief (1926), 97

Bills (*continued*):
  Safety of Employment (Employers' Liability) (1948-9), 60
  Seditious and Blasphemous Teaching of Children (1932-3, etc.), 137
  Shops (1908), 35, 105
  Shops (1938-9), 117
  Shops (Sunday Trading) (Scotland) (1933-4), 134 f.
  Slaughter of Animals (1930, etc.), 57, 62, 117
  Spelling Reform (1948-9, etc.), 59 f., 110
  Statutory Instruments (Control), (1948-9), 57
  Sunday Observance (1952-3), 66, 98, 102, 136
  Temperance (Wales) (1924), 95, 97
  Trade Union (1950-1), 61
  Trade Union (Political Fund) (1924-5), 47, 53 f., 99
  Transport (Amendment) (1950-1), 39, 55, 61, 93, 102, 113
  Treason (1954-5), 156
  Women's Disabilities (1951-2), 31
  Women's Emancipation (1919), 105
  Women's Enfranchisement (1908), 28
  Workmen's Compensation (1932, etc.), 51, 112
Bonar Law, Andrew, 106
Bottomley, Horatio, 134
Brabazon, Col. J. T. C. Moore- (Lord), 92
Braddock, Mrs., 158
Brown, W. J., 24
Butler, R. A., 158
Buxton, Noel, 97, 99

Campion, Lord, 24, 43
Castle, Mrs. Barbara, 61
Cautley, Sir Henry, 89
Cecil, Lord Hugh, 47, 53
Censorship of Publications, 136 ff.
Chamberlain, (Sir) Austen, 96
Chamberlain, Neville, 94 f., 114

INDEX

Church measures, 96
Churchill, (Sir) Winston, 95, 98, 115, 147, 158
Civil Service, bills for reform of, 128
Clifton Brown, Mr. Speaker, 43
Closure, 71, 104
  Frequency of closure motions, 32
  Practices with regard to private Members' bills, 28 ff.
Clynes, J. R., 89, 114
Cocks, F. S., 104, 187
Criminal Law, 14, 63, 107, 115 f., 121, 146 f.
Crookshank, H. F. C., 21, 115, 127, 155*n*., 157, 174*n*.

Davies, H., 71
Davies, N., 61
Davies, Rhys, 40, 95
Davies, S. O., 128
Daylight saving, 97, 99, 140
Death penalty, 14, 107, 115 f., 147
De Freitas, Geoffrey, 59
De la Bère, (Sir) Rupert, 23, 108
Dilke, Sir Charles, 35, 105
Divorce law, 3 f., 23, 39, 62, 108, 110 f., 146
Donnelly, Desmond, 158
Drink regulation, 49, 119, 133

Easter, date of, 141
Ede, Chuter, 35, 113, 129
Eden, (Sir) Anthony, 158
Elliot, Walter, 157
Errington, Sir Eric, 73
Eyres-Monsell, Sir Bolton (Lord), 27

Fireguards, 65
Fisher, H. A. L., 96
Fitzroy, Mr. Speaker, 20
Fletcher, Eric, 66
Follick, M., 14*n*., 60, 141, 165
Fraser, T., 182 ff.

Gaitskell, Hugh, 113
Government and private Members' bills, 86 ff., 111
  Voting in divisions, 96 ff., 187

Grace, J., 110
Graham, William, 52, 112, 114
Greenwood, Arthur, 117, 129
Grenfell, David, 71
Grimston, J., 69
Guinness, Walter, 92

Hacking, Douglas, 92
Hale, C. Leslie, 64
Harrison, Colonel J., 142
Heald, Sir Lionel, 31, 62
Henderson, Arthur, 114
Heneage, Lt.-Col. A. P., 92
Herbert, Sir Alan P., 3 f., 23, 108, 110, 120, 146, 155*n*.
Hewart, Lord, 167
Hewitson, Captain M., 176
Hill, Mrs. E., 63
Hollis, Christopher, 167
Home Rule questions, 29, 70, 128
House of Lords:
  Amendments to bills, 16, 57*n*., 65
  Bills introduced in, 17, 141
  Private Members' bills in, 41 f., 106 f., 131, 147
  Reform of, 157
Hudson, (Sir) Austin, 66, 129
Hutchinson, Geoffrey, 158
Hutchison, Colonel J. R. H., 63
Hypnotism, 65

Inskip, Sir Thomas (Viscount Caldecote), 98
Irvine, A. J., 186
Isaacs, G. A., 60

Jennings, Sir W. Ivor, 38*n*., 173
Johnston, Tom, 113 f.
Jowitt, Lord, 107
Joynson-Hicks, Sir William (Lord Brentford), 96

Keeling, Sir Edward, 157
Keeton, Professor G. W., 167
Kennedy, Thomas, 114
Kinley, J., 25, 62
Kirkwood, D. (Lord), 50, 89

INDEX

Lansbury, George, 113
Laski, Harold, 4, 162n.
Legal reforms, 145
Lennox-Boyd, A., 184
Lever, Harold, 3, 22, 64, 146
Libel, law of, 3, 22, 37, 41, 63 f., 146, 155n.
Lloyd-George, Major G., 70
Lobbying, 119
Long, Walter (Lord), 87
Lotteries, 73
Lougher, (Sir) Lewis, 142
Lucas-Tooth, Sir Hugh, 87

McCallum, Major D., 63
Macdonald, Gordon, 122
MacDonald, J. Ramsay, 40, 113 f.
Macmillan, Harold, 115
Manning, Mrs. Leah, 61
Marples, A. E., 62
Metric system, 141
Money bills and money clauses, 15, 25, 32, 104
Monslow, W., 62
Moore, Sir Thomas, 58, 186
Morrison, Herbert, 18, 51, 97, 155, 157, 169
Morrison, Robert, 163
Motions, private Members', 10 ff., 161 ff.
Muir, Professor Ramsay, 43

Nabarro, Gerald, 70, 72, 131 f.

Obstruction on private Members' days, 27, 30, 37
Opposition bills, 24, 49 ff., 126
Opposition leaders and private Members' bills, 112 ff.

Paget, R. T., 156
Paling, William, 68
Pargiter, G. A., 130
Parker, John, 136
Parliamentary Counsel, 26
Parties and private Members' bills, 59, 81 ff., 115, 157 (see also under *Whips*)

Percy, Lord (Eustace), 98, 145
Petitions, 154
Pickthorn, Kenneth, 5
Piratin, Philip, 60
Pitman, I. J., 59
Powell, J. Enoch, 142
Pownall, Sir Assheton, 143
Procedure, 13, 24, 43, 104, 173
Professions, regulation of, 147

Quorum, 27, 65, 69, 81
in Standing Committee, 36

Rathbone, Eleanor, 145
Redlich, Josef, 10
Reed, Sir Stanley, 146
Religious questions, 97
Report stage, 40
Royal Commissions, etc., 39, 123 f., 136, 146
Rural amenities, 118, 129
Russell, R. S., 59, 62

Samuel, Viscount, 35, 135n.
Scottish bills, committee stage, 34
Scottish Home Rule, 29, 128
Scurr, W., 24n.
Select Committees, 149
Shawcross, Sir Hartley, 104
Short, E. W., 71
Silverman, Sidney, 115, 147
Sinclair, Sir Archibald, 163
Smiles, Sir Walter, 23
Snowden, Philip (Lord), 95
Sparks, J. A., 181 ff.
Speaker, rulings of, 20, 28 f., 34, 44
Spelling reform, 110
Standing Committees, 16, 25, 33-7, 55, 105, 109
Steele, T., 31
Stewart, Michael, 51
Stuart, James, 163
Summer time, 97, 99, 140
Summerskill, Dr. Edith, 31, 112
Sunday observance questions, 66, 133 ff., 153
Supply, Committee of, 15

INDEX

Teeling, William, 30
Ten Minutes Rule, 17 ff., 154–61
Thomas, J. H., 112
Time, distribution of, 22, 42 ff., 68
Tomlinson, George, 59
Trade Unions, 122, 130
Turner-Samuels, M., 185*n*.

Unballoted bills, 17 ff., 150 ff.
Ungoed-Thomas, Sir Lynn, 64, 71
Unopposed bills, 18

War, private Members' time in, 11
Ward, Irene, 122
Wedgwood, Josiah (Lord), 87, 113
West, D. G., 30
Wheatley, J., 31, 97
Whips:
  Influence on voting, etc., 35, 104 ff., 135, 157, 187
  In relation to possible reforms of private Members' time, 42

Whips (*continued*):
  Suggesting bills, etc., to Members, 24, 107, 163
White, Mrs. Eirene, 39, 62, 109, 124
Whiteley, William, 89
Whitley, Mr. Speaker, 28 f.
Wilkinson, Ellen, 47
Williams, Charles, 184*n*.
Williams, G., 172*n*.
Williams, Sir Herbert, 25, 158
Williams, Tom, 188
Wills, regulation of, 30, 104, 145
Winterton, Earl, 129
Withers, Sir John, 110
Women, status of, 162
Wood, E. F. (Earl of Halifax), 99
Workmen's compensation, 130

Yate, Colonel C. E., 87
Young, Sir Hilton, 129
Young, Sir Robert, 163
Younger, Kenneth, 58, 182

For Product Safety Concerns and Information please contact our EU
representative GPSR@taylorandfrancis.com
Taylor & Francis Verlag GmbH, Kaufingerstraße 24, 80331 München, Germany

www.ingramcontent.com/pod-product-compliance
Lightning Source LLC
Chambersburg PA
CBHW061443300426
44114CB00014B/1806